REPORTING:
An Inside View

Also by Lou Cannon

Ronnie and Jesse: A Political Odyssey
The McCloskey Challenge

REPORTING:
An Inside View

Lou Cannon

Library of Congress Catalog Card Number: 77-796-91
1 2 3 4 5 6 7 8 9 0

Acknowledgements and Sources

Many persons made this book possible, but the credit for its idea must go to Douglass Cater, the former director of the Aspen Program on Communications and Society. Cater, whose own writing in *The Reporter* magazine and especially in *The Fourth Branch of Government*, influenced a generation of Washington reporters, proposed early in 1975 that I take a leave from the *Washington Post* and come to Aspen, Colorado, to write a book about reporting. I am grateful to the Aspen Institute and its president Joseph Slater, as well as to Doug Cater, for making this book possible. And I am especially appreciative for the cooperation and encouragement of my editors — Benjamin Bradlee, Howard Simons, Richard Harwood and Harry Rosenfeld. They gave me time to do this book and also provided valuable interviews, as did Katherine Graham, publisher of the *Washington Post*.

Thomas Hoeber, the publisher of *California Journal* and of this book, gave wise and needed counsel. I thank him for the faith he showed in *Reporting*. Ed Salzman, the *Journal* editor, helped tighten and improve the book.

Reporters are highly dependent upon other people for all but the simplest news story. My dependence on my colleagues was magnified many times over in the course of the reporting, research and writing of this book. I am thankful to Haynes Johnson of the *Washington Post*, John Herbers of the *New York Times* and Leroy Aarons for their kindness in reading the manuscript and making suggestions. And I am especially grateful to William Lee Miller of the Poynter Center at Indiana University for his counsel and for the care with which he twice reviewed the manuscript, each time making recommendations which improved this book. Bob Schmuhl, coordinator of the Citizen and the News Project at Indiana University, gave important technical advice.

My colleagues at the *Post* contributed especially. The comments of David Broder and Jules Witcover were particularly helpful for the chapters on political and public affairs coverage, as were the views of Haynes Johnson for the chapter "Beyond the Watergate Legacy." George Lardner's 1962 thesis at Marquette University, "Two Views of Objective Reporting: An Analysis," provided several of the ideas for my chapter on "The Biases of the News Business." Hobart Rowen on economics coverage, John MacKenzie on the Supreme Court and Phillip Foisie and John Goshko on foreign coverage were primary sources for the chapter on "Specialists." Interviews with Bob Woodward, William Greider and Robert Maynard yielded material that was of use in several different chapters. Other thoughtful comments came from interviews with Herbert Denton, Leonard Downie, Edwin Goodpaster, Donald Graham, Margot Hornblower, Peter Silberman, Barry Sussman, Sander Vanocur and George Wilson.

I owe a special debt to Richard Harwood, deputy managing editor of the Post for his reflections on many aspects of the news business. These are quoted frequently as are the views of freelance reporter and writer Richard Reeves. The chapter on White House reporting owes much to the observations of the late Peter Lisagor of the *Chicago Daily News* and to three television colleagues who presently or formerly covered the White House — Robert Pierpoint of CBS, Tom Brokaw of NBC and Ann Compton of ABC. The section on diplomatic coverage was greatly assisted by an interview with Leslie Gelb, formerly of the *New York Times*. In discussing what I call the "sad state of public affairs coverage" I drew upon the observations of Bill Boyarsky of the *Los Angeles Times*, who with his wife Nancy, is the author of *Backroom Politics*. My friend Martin Salditch of the *Riverside (Calif.)*

Press-Enterprise, formerly that newspaper's state capital correspondent and now its correspondent in Washington, shared his insights for this chapter on public affairs reporting as did Harrison Humphries, a longtime regional reporter in Washington for the Associated Press. Others in the news business who helped with interviews or information included Norman Cherniss, the executive editor of the *Riverside Press-Enterprise*, James Hoge, editor of the *Chicago Sun-Times* and Larry Allison, associate editor of the *Detroit Free Press*. Reporters who assisted included Bob Boyd of Knight Newspapers, William Steif of Scripps-Howard Newspapers, Martin Arnold, John Herbers, Nat Sheppard and Nancy Hicks of the *New York Times*, Adam Clymer of the *New York Times*, Mary Neiswender of the *Long Beach Independent-Press Telegram*, Hays Gorey of *Time*, Paul Healy of the *New York Daily News*, David Rohn of the *Indianapolis News* and Douglas McMillan, formerly of the *Riverside Press-Enterprise*. Three of my former colleagues at Ridder Publications — William Broom, Gil Bailey and Albert Eisele, now Vice President Mondale's press secretary — were especially helpful. Russell Baker of the *New York Times* was kind enough to forward some observations on the news business which he had made previously during a seminar at Duke University. Fred Friendly of the Ford Foundation, Jules Duscha of the Washington Journalism Center and Peter Braestrup of the Smithsonian Institution, all of whom have observed the news business from outside and within, gave useful interviews. Russell Hurst, executive director of Sigma Delta Chi, The Society of Professional Journalists, was kind enough to provide some needed back issues of *The Quill*.

Not all of the assistance came from colleagues. I am indebted also to a select group of public officials for their interviews. The views of President Gerald Ford on candor and openness, of Senator Hubert Humphrey on political coverage, of Ambassador Elliot Richardson on Richard

Nixon's downfall and on deficiencies in public affairs coverage and of former Rep. Jerome Waldie on congressional coverage all find a place in this book. Former White House Press Secretary Ron Nessen and Joseph Laitin, the former deputy defense secretary for public information, also were helpful, as were Bill Moyers, once a top aide and press secretary to President Lyndon Johnson and now with CBS; Al Abrahams, a veteran Republican campaign official and former Senate aide; and Dr. Robert Goldwin, former White House assistant.

Much of the information on state government coverage, other than the passages deriving from the author's own experience, was furnished by Larry Margolis, director of Legis 50 (formerly the Citizens Conference on State Legislatures) and Donald Quinn, director of communications for that organization. I also am appreciative of the comments on state coverage from Ed Salzman.

Many persons in the academic community provided helpful articles or observations. Dr. Robert O. Blanchard, chairman of the department of communication at American University in Washington, shared the results of a survey on congressional coverage and also was kind enough to make his library available for my research. Everette E. Dennis of the University of Minnesota school of journalism was helpful on several matters, especially in providing an evaluation of coverage of the U. S. Supreme Court. The comments on education coverage in this book owe much to the research of George Gerbner, dean of the Annenberg School of Communications at the University of Pennsylvania, as do the comments on science coverage to Percy H. Tannenbaum, a professor of the graduate school of public policy at the University of California, Berkeley. Other information was provided by William L. Rivers of Stanford, James B. Lemert of the University of Oregon, Oguz B. Nayman of Colorado State University, Richard W. Hainey of Northwestern and Galen R. Rarick of Ohio State University.

Published sources are credited as used and in the bibliography. But I would be remiss here not to mention my indebtedness to four books — *The Information Machines* by Ben Bagdikian, *Behind the Front Page* by Chris Argyris, *Reporters and Officials* by Leon V. Sigal and *History of American Journalism* by James Melvin Lee. Two journalism classics which were consulted and quoted were *Public Opinion* by Walter Lippmann and *Freedom of the Press* by George Seldes. Two magazines of journalistic criticism — *MORE* and the *Columbia Journalism Review* — were indispensable sources.

No writer is better than his research. I was fortunate enough to have assistance from several able researchers, especially Sunday Orme of the *New York Times*, Patricia Davis, formerly of the *Washington Post*, and Foxie Kirwin, the librarian of the David Mayer Library at the Aspen Institute. My son Carl Cannon, a reporter on the *Columbus (Ga.) Ledger*, also assisted capably in the research.

A number of other persons helped in various ways, among them Michael Nyhan and Pat Singer of the Aspen Program on Communications and Virginia Callinan, King Woodward, Pat Clark and Wes and Betty Millan of the Aspen Institute. Sidney Hyman contributed a reflective interview, Michael Novak was kind enough to read and comment on "The Biases of the News Business" chapter and Christopher Sterling of Temple University provided some needed statistical information. Donna Crouch, Connie Gray, Sue Challis and Nancy May, all of the *Washington Post*, transcribed a number of tape-recorded interviews. The manuscript was carefully typed by Cheryl Klein, Sally Rugaber and Suzy Sterling. And my wife Virginia Cannon, with her customary competence, served as consultant, researcher, proofreader and critic on top of a fulltime research job of her own.

It goes without saying, but I will say it anyway, that no one save the author is responsible for whatever errors of fact, logic or opinion pervade this book.

This book is dedicated to reporters everywhere and specifically to the following people in the news business who have, by instruction or example, been a help and inspiration to the author:

David Broder	Richard Harwood
William Broom	Haynes Johnson
John Burns	Peter Lisagor
Douglass Cater	Walter Ridder
Tyrus Cobb	Martin Salditch
Dale Cockerill	Peter Silberman
Albert Eisele	Jules Witcover
Harry Farrell	

Contents

About This Book

Rudyard Kipling once described a good reporter as the noblest work of God. Hildy Johnson, the hotshot reporter of *The Front Page,* held the less lofty view that a newspaperman was "a cross between a bootlegger and a whore." And press critic George Seldes, brimming with enthusiasm on his first newspaper job in 1909, was told by his editor: "A newspaper needs a lot of young fools — foolish enthusiasm and foolish ideals. We love ideals. And we love enthusiasm. At nine dollars a week."

I have been a reporter or editor for more than 20 years and can see some merit in all these descriptions. I have covered sports, police beats, city halls, county governments, California state government, Congress, the White House and politics, and I have been a general assignment reporter. I also have worked as managing editor, sports editor, assistant news editor and on the copy desk. Wherever I went or whatever job I did, I observed that many otherwise well-informed people seemed to know very little about the news business and its values and motivations. They knew little because those of us who worked in the business told them little about it beyond soapbox editorials on freedom of the press. At least we didn't tell them very much until the testing time of the 1960s when the press found itself on the list of institutions conspicuously distrusted by many Americans.

The political attacks made on the press during this period prompted some newspaper publishers and television station owners to begin explaining the processes of their business to readers and viewers, and encouraged higher standards of self-criticism in the newsroom, where editors and reporters are being called upon to be more thoughtful, more accurate and more accountable to those who depend upon us for information. The discussions I have had in the course of preparing this book convince me that the people in the news business, both those coming into it and those who have been at it for a long time, are asking fundamental questions about the work in which we are engaged. What are our biases and our values? What are our limitations and achievements? Why do we select one story and reject another? How can I say it better in 700 words or 30 seconds? This book is an attempt, from a reporter's point of view, to answer some of these questions. It is my hope that it will do its small bit to promote continuing examination and criticism about the nature and quality of the news business.

Vienna, Va.
March 13, 1977

CHAPTER ONE

Reporters

All the reporters in the world working all the hours of the day could not witness all the happenings in the world. There are not a great many reporters.
— *Walter Lippmann in* PUBLIC OPINION

Benjamin C. Bradlee, the editor of the *Washington Post,* is fond of telling a story about the two young reporters who were hired by him on the same day. "They were both WASPs. They were both about twenty-seven years old. They had had Ivy League educations. They both had non-newspaper experience between college and their beginning in journalism. Bob Woodward had been in the Navy and this other kid had been in the Peace Corps. They both had beaten *Washington Post* reporters in their beats and their clips were comparable, that's all I can say. And we hired both of them and Woodward went on to become Woodward and this other guy left three months later because he didn't have it. I've forgotten his name."[1]

Bradlee can enumerate with ease the qualities he seeks in a reporter. He looks first for energy and says he is "depressed by the number of bright young people who don't have the desire to work the hard and long hours that I think the business requires." He looks for commitment to the news business and for people who take their work home with them. After that he looks for knowledge, ability, "people who know as much as possible about the fields they have been in," judgment and the quality of putting information in perspective. Bradlee

---

[1] From an interview with the author. The practice that otherwise will be followed in this book will be to identify quotations from published works and testimony and *not* to footnote the many quotations taken from the author's interviews.

knows what he wants, and he enjoys a buyer's market in hiring reporters. And yet, no less than an editor of an obscure weekly, Bradlee concedes that what the *Post* gets in the way of reporters is largely a matter of chance. "In the last analysis," he says, "you've got to hunch it."

This mystery about what makes a good reporter reflects the mystique of a craft which never has been able fully to explain the nature of its own business. We prize exactitude, but we are imprecise and often contradictory when it comes to defining what we do and why we do it. There is no general agreement on the nature of news. There is no agreement on whether reporting is a craft or trade, as I regard it, or a profession. There is not even agreement by those who consider newspapering a profession on what the professional requirements are or by those who consider it a trade on what would make it a profession. The requirements of reporting remain essentially as vague and mysterious as they were in 1922 when Walter Lippmann described the press as being "like the beam of a searchlight, bringing one episode and then another out of the darkness into vision."

Why are droves of people attracted to this craft with its long hours and (until recently) slender financial rewards? The number of aspiring journalists has vastly increased since Watergate, but there always have been more candidates for newspaper and broadcast jobs than there are jobs to fill. A plurality of the people whom I interviewed for this book seem to have been impelled toward the news business by some parental influence. The father of one reporter was a salesman who wanted to write and won poetry contests sponsored by the *Cleveland Plain Dealer*. The father of another reporter was a Baltimore newspaperman before taking a government job which offered better pay and more security. The mother of another reporter is a Minnesota newspaperwoman. Haynes Johnson, a Pulitzer Prize winning reporter on the *Washington Post,* is the son of a Pulitzer Prize winning reporter.

But people also become reporters because they seek to have some social impact on the world. The desire to promote change was a motivation for reporters long before modern "advocacy journalism." I remember an editor nearly twenty years ago defending the excesses of a young reporter with the phrase, "Scratch a reporter and you'll find a reformer." This is one reason that the "crusading" reporter of the past and the "investigative" reporter of the present always have been treated warily by those who favor things as they are. "Reporters are frustrated reformers as television people are frustrated actors," says Jules Duscha. "They look upon themselves almost with reverence, like they are protecting the world against the forces of evil." Duscha, the son of a St. Paul salesman, became a reporter and worked in Minnesota, Illinois and Washington. His boyhood heroes were William Allen White, editor of the *Emporia Gazette,* and George Seldes, the press critic. He is now director of the Washington Journalism Center and has a son who is a reporter for the *Sacramento Bee.*

The reforming impulse often combines with what Duscha calls "the attractions of the byline and of being in on things." Margot Hornblower, a metro (cityside) reporter on the *Washington Post* is the daughter of Edith Kermit Roosevelt, a newspaperwoman and conservative columnist. Hornblower started her career at twenty on the *Charlottesville (Va.) Daily Progress* where she wrote a story about citizen objections to the location of a country club which the publisher recently had joined. In the publisher's view the story gave too much emphasis to the opinions of the objectors. Hornblower was fired, but the publisher relented and hired her back. She has no apologies for the story which led to her temporary firing, but she looks on her break-in period at the *Daily Progress* with insight into her own motivations. Hornblower was covering Albermarle County at the time, and her chief reportorial targets were a county supervisor and a county executive who had a preference for doing public business

in private. "I think it's good to start out on a small paper
because as an aggressive young kid you get all the bile
out of you. You work off all your prejudices," she says in
retrospect. "Now, I wouldn't be as wound up in what I
was reporting. Then, it got to be a personal crusade with
me. It's a fine line. You should report things without
getting emotionally involved. I think I felt myself to be in
opposition to the supervisor and county executive who
wanted to close everything. They felt I was on a ven-
detta." Hornblower's desire to reform the governing practices of Albermarle County combined with a reporter's
customary delight at being able to see her work in print.
She is married to an attorney and has observed that he
must wait years to see the results of his own work. "On a
newspaper there's the instant fix — your byline," she
says. "You have the daily satisfaction of seeing something with your name on it. It's one of the reasons I'm a
newspaper reporter rather than a book or magazine writer."

Curiosity also is an impelling motivation for reporters.
Perhaps it is the most important one. Bob Woodward of
the *Washington Post* grew up in Wheaton, Illinois, where
his father is a judge. "I was raised in a very small town
and I think I learned there that everybody always has a
secret," Woodward recalls. "The secrets would either
come out in gossip or conversation or some cataclysmic
event. I always found the secret life much more interesting than the public life people had and that's what I
thought of investigative reporting as being. What are
people's secrets? It was challenging to find out that there
was much more conflict and turmoil than what was on
the surface. I was attracted to that." Woodward
graduated from Yale in 1965 with the avowed intention
of going to law school. But he joined the Naval Reserve
Training Corps, and his service was extended because of
the Vietnam War. "I used to call it an eighteen-month
Gulf of Tonkin resolution on me," says Woodward. "And I
was very unhappy, restless, felt my brain might dry up

and roll out my ear almost. It's a very stultified existence. I got out of the Navy in August of 1970 and planned on going to Harvard Law School that fall. But I'd always wanted to be a newspaper reporter, or at least try it. It seemed that all of the stereotypes were exciting. You make momentary entries into people's lives when they're interesting, and then you get out of their lives when they're not interesting, so you're doing interesting things. And I liked the upward mobility. It was easy to get to the top, or easier than the law. If you became a lawyer, you almost had to go through a period of indentured servitude."

Woodward had college classmates who were clerking for the Supreme Court or doing other important work, and he wanted to catch up with them. His attraction to reporting, was heightened by the My Lai stories of Seymour Hersh, who then was operating as a free-lancer. "I thought, 'here's nobody and he can go in and do these stories,' " says Woodward. "It showed you could do something very rapidly and psychologically I felt terribly behind because I'd spent five years not doing anything." Woodward had completed his naval duty at the Pentagon, and he decided to apply for a job at the nearby *Washington Post*. As Woodward recalls it, he knocked on the door of Harry Rosenfeld, then the metro editor, and said he wanted to work at the *Post*. Rosenfeld asked him how much experience he had, and Woodward said he didn't have any. "You've got to be kidding, this is the *Washington Post*," was Rosenfeld's first response. But something about Woodward's manner or persistence impressed the editor. He decided to give Woodward a tryout, which he flunked. None of the fifteen stories which Woodward laboriously wrote in two weeks of day-and-night work made the paper. "I felt crushed, really crushed," says Woodward. "But there was something about the newsroom, something about working there, about being in the flow of things. I liked it." The *Post* editors helped Woodward find a job at the *Montgomery County Sentinel*, a

nearby Maryland suburban paper. He worked there for a
year and scooped the *Post* on a number of local government stories. He also was sued for libel.[2] In September
1971 Woodward was hired by the *Washington Post*,
where he made a big impression on editors from the beginning. "He was aggressive, skeptical and basically
fair-minded, which is what I look for in a reporter," recalls Barry Sussman, then the city editor. "If a reporter
doesn't have all these attributes, he isn't any good. I also
would like a person who can write if he has all these
other qualities, but writing isn't high on my list. Woodward never could write and can't today. We managed to
make his stuff read well enough so that its presentation
didn't affect what was being told." When the burglars
broke into Democratic headquarters on June 17, 1972,
and launched the story that was to end with the fall of a
President, Woodward already had several local investigative stories to his credit. He was the natural person to
assign to the Watergate story.

Reporting also satisfies a need in some people of explaining things to their fellow human beings. Fred W.
Friendly, the accomplished former producer and news division director at CBS, compares this need with the need
of comedians to make people laugh. "Journalists are not
great scholars, most of them," he says. "Some are very
bright but they don't have scholarly brightness. What
they have is some kind of drive to explain. And maybe it
comes out of the frustration of not being able to communicate as a young person." Sometimes, it can also
arise from a literary frustration. David Rohn is a young

---

[2]A Maryland school principal won a $281,000 libel judgment against the
Montgomery County Sentinel in November 1973 and a token judgment
against Woodward after a 1971 article by reporters Woodward and William
Bancroft called him "unsuited" for his job. In defending their story from an
allegation that it was written with malice the reporters said that "experts"
had studied the school system and reached the same conclusion. The reporters declined to name the experts, saying they were confidential sources protected from disclosure by the Maryland shield law. The case was reversed on
appeal.

admirer of Ernie Pyle who says he wanted in college to be "the great American novelist." Like most of us, he isn't. But Rohn liked writing and a summer intern program gave him a chance to continue it at a newspaper. He now writes politics and legislative news and does a column for the *Indianapolis News.*

Howard Simons, the most intellectual of the *Post* editors, believes that there are recognizable types of people attracted to all professions and crafts, including reporting. "Begin with the premise that lots of people who come into the newspaper business are somewhat hyperactive, somewhat creative and somewhat causists. I don't mean that in the contemporary sense of the word. I mean they have some sense, rooted in their stomach, of injustice which the newspaper gives them an instrument to correct. They also have a high capacity for psychic income — the byline, the being out with the big hitters, the being able to do things that are big for them as opposed to their roots. Lots of people at the *Post* come from the small towns in America. And reporters also have a high capacity for neuroticism, they have a high capacity for skepticism, they have all these things in different measure but they are similar things which bring them into the newspaper industry. I would guess that many of them are inherently pro-underdog, pro-citizen participation and anti-big business. Which leads me to the conclusion that when people talk about objectivity, I don't know what that means because there is no way I can squeeze out of any single editor or reporter at the *Washington Post* the inculcations of twenty to thirty years."

The attraction of journalism for people from small towns cited by Simons is an important one. Journalism in America always has been a pathway to the top for talented people who lacked money or the right connections. Unlike their colleagues in Great Britain, journalists in America are not automatically accorded second-class status. Journalism in the United States is an inter-class calling, and reporters are equally at home in the slum,

the drawing room or the Oval Office. At least it looks that
way to many young people growing up in the small towns
of the South, the Middle West and the West.

In 1947 Richard L. Harwood was twenty-two years old
and a Marine veteran of some of the bloodiest fighting in
the South Pacific. He was attending night courses at
Peabody College in Nashville, Tennessee, when a reporter from the *Tennesseean* spoke to the class. Reporting
struck Harwood as "a helluva life." He applied for a job
on the *Tennesseean* and became a general assignment
reporter at $27.50 a week. Harwood went to school at the
same time and acquired a degree from Vanderbilt. "The
Tennesseean was a very interesting Southern paper at
the time," he recalls. "It was a very liberal paper by the
standards of the South. It also was an extremely partisan, unfair political paper. Our function in life was to
elect to office the people that the publisher wanted
elected. His great enemy was Boss Crump of Memphis,
and we supported Estes Kefauver in his first campaign
and Albert Gore and various candidates for governor that
the publisher was interested in. This partisanship and
this propaganda function that we served extended all the
way down to city council races. At one point I was covering a candidate for the state legislature and I'd write a
story about him and I'd write his speech and then I'd
write an editorial about his speech. By the time I
graduate from Vanderbilt in 1950, I was feeling very
uncomfortable about that, and I didn't like the partisanship."

Harwood went job hunting and wound up in 1952 at
the *Louisville Times* and quickly became an investigative reporter and the newspaper's top political reporter.
"I absolutely loved the paper," he remembers. "It was
fair, it was not partisan. We had a sense of integrity
working for it. I loved Kentucky, and I loved Southern
politics. I liked the oratory and the characters who came
along." Harwood went to Washington for the Louisville
paper and then to the *Washington Post,* where he became

an award-winning reporter, ombudsman and three times the national editor. His early disgust with newspaper partisanship never left him, and he became known at the *Post* for his determination to keep ideology, personal causes and stereotyped labels out of the news columns.

Some reporters seem attracted to journalism — or journalism to them — as by a magnet despite any preparation or display of conscious interest toward a journalistic career. The *Oakland Tribune* once decided to hire a reporter from among the construction workers who were building the forward span of the Golden Gate Bridge, under the theory that someone similarly bold and daring was needed on the staff. The theory produced a crackerjack reporter. Other reporters are found in even more unlikely places. Richard Reeves' preparation for a journalistic career, by his own account, was mostly negative. "I suppose I became a reporter because I always wanted to be a reporter but I didn't know I wanted to be a reporter," says Reeves. "I was an engineer and a lousy engineer." Reeves grew up in Jersey City and graduated from the Stevens Institute of Technology in Hoboken. "I didn't know you could write for a living; nobody ever told me that," remembers Reeves. "I grew up in a poor neighborhood. My father was a starving lawyer and there were no guidance counselors in the high school. I literally did not know you could go to college and read books, because that's what I would have wanted to do. I thought you had to go to college and learn how to do something like be a doctor or a lawyer."

Reeves had a friend whose uncle wanted to start a newspaper in Phillipsburg, New Jersey. He found the man in a deserted movie theater which the friend's uncle had just bought for $4,000 and they sat there in the empty theater talking about making it into the plant for a weekly paper. Reeves had not been successful as a designer of pumps, and the Ingersoll-Rand company had given him a battery of psychological tests and put him to work in the company's advertising department. For

four-and-one-half years Reeves worked days in the advertising department and nights on the newspaper he
was helping to create.

The friend's uncle sold the ads. The paper was called
the *Phillipsburg Free Press,* and Reeves learned about
the newspaper business the hard way, the old way. He
liked to do investigative stories that told about the town.
One story he did was about a slumlord who owned a
section of town with open gas heat and wooden plumbing.
The slumlord turned out to be the Reeves family physi-
cian, and the Reeves had to find another doctor. In
another case Reeves went after a local politician who
owned the garage which did work on the Reeves car.
"They wouldn't work on my car any more after that,"
says Reeves. "Their kids wouldn't talk to my kids." This
kind of journalism impressed other newspapers in New
Jersey. The *Newark News* offered him a job in its Morris-
town bureau for $90 a week, a huge cut from his salary as
an engineer. Reeves took the job and quit Ingersoll-Rand.
He went from the *Newark News* to the *New York
Herald-Tribune* and made a reputation as a political reporter. On April 23, 1966, the day the *Herald-Tribune*
folded, Reeves was hired by the *New York Times.*

Reeves believes that many good reporters are introverts who are attracted to journalism because it gives
them an institutional base to fulfill personal needs.
"Most of us are terribly curious introverts and we need
the institutional cloak," says Reeves. "I could go to a
party and never say a word to anyone — I don't know how
to begin a conversation. But if I say, 'Excuse me, I'm Dick
Reeves of the *Times,*' that breaks the ice for me and I can
deal with the situation. I've often wondered if that isn't a
lot of what we're about."

Newspapers once were the beacon for the shy, curious
small-town kid who wanted to make a name for himself.
Now, television performs that function. In Harwood's
generation of the 1940s a young man saw newspapers as
the path to an exciting and productive life. In Tom

Brokaw's generation of the 1960s newspapers seemed a pale alternative to broadcasting. Brokaw grew up in Yankton, South Dakota, a town with 12,000 people and two radio stations. One of the stations was small and poor and it hired Brokaw when he was a 15-year-old high-school student. Brokaw played records and read the news. The radio station was in competition with a local newspaper and Brokaw liked the immediacy of radio in comparison with the paper, which carried the news the following afternoon. "More importantly," he remembers, "I didn't have any good newspaper models when I was growing up. The newspapers back there are mediocre to bad, whereas I could sit at home at night and watch Edward R. Murrow, Cronkite, Huntley-Brinkley. And they provided very good models for me. You'd pick up the newspaper and it was full of pretty pedestrian writing."

By the time Brokaw reached college he had accumulated enough experience to get a summer job at a commercial television station in Sioux City, Iowa, writing the news and doing booth announcing and commercials. It financed his last two years of college and gave him exposure to television. Brokaw recalls being greatly helped by David E. Schoumacher, now the resourceful anchorman for WMAL in Washington, who came from Northwestern with "new ideas and a kind of broader vision of what the news could be." After obtaining a degree in political science at the University of South Dakota, Brokaw went to Omaha as the morning news editor with KMTV. He went from there to WSV in Atlanta where he became the night news editor and covered civil rights stories for NBC on a holding basis until the network could get a correspondent to the scene. NBC hired him fulltime in 1966 and sent him to Los Angeles, where Brokaw became known as a bright and well-prepared interviewer, particularly on political subjects. He went on to the White House and the Today show.

Television's record at providing job opportunities for women, and for various minorities, is better than that of most newspapers. Ann Compton, now an ABC White House correspondent, was a drama major who became interested in television as a college senior and interned for WDBJ in Roanoke, Virginia. "It was helpful to be a girl," she recalls. "I was riding the crest of the women's wave. It's not going to last, but I've made the most out of it. I had a voice that was all right, willingness to work, energy. And there weren't that many women around. Still, the whole business of getting into television was haphazard and becoming a political correspondent was more haphazard still. I lived closest to the airport and I was the junior member of the staff, so overtime costs for me were least. There was a candidate for governor that year (Democrat Bill Battle) who had a penchant for holding morning press conferences at the airport. They sent me. Then, to balance it, they sent me to (Republican candidate) Lin Holton's press conferences, too. The whole haphazard business was typical of too much of television reporting. We learned on the job. Eric Sevareid said we learned at the expense of the audience."

And so have we all, whether we are reporters for newspapers or reporters for radio and television stations. The reasons we became reporters are many and diverse, although I would agree with Howard Simons that the news business is populated with certain recognizable personality types. Perhaps what we all share in common is the characteristic identified by my friend and colleague at the *Washington Post*, David S. Broder, who has developed a stock response when young people ask him why he became a reporter. "It is a somewhat facetious answer, but only somewhat," Broder says. "We like to watch, and we like to watch close-up and see what people are doing. I think the essential lure is that we're voyeurs."

CHAPTER TWO

What's News and What Isn't

". . . We mortals hear only the news and know nothing at all."
— *Homer*, THE ILIAD.

The classic definition of news known to all beginning reporters is credited to John Bogart, a long-ago editor of the *New York Sun*. It is not really a definition at all but an illustration. "When a dog bites a man, that's not news because it happens so often," said Bogart to a young reporter. "But if a man bites dog, that is news." This aphorism has remained alive because it dramatically states the enduring value of novelty to the news business. But it is not much help, except in the most superficial way. Most of the pronouncements, decisions and "official news" which fill up our newspapers are less rare than a dog-biting man. Even putting these stories aside, it is likely that one man's novelty in a diverse and highly technical society is apt to be another man's normalcy. A murder is front-page news in a small community where murder is a rarity. It has to be a novel murder or have a novel murderer or victim to be considered news in Washington or New York. In any place, however, novelty is apt to be related to calamity. Reporters assume with other people that houses will not burn down, that cars will stay on the road, that bridges will not collapse. I remember an old cartoon — some today might regard its message as male chauvinist — in which a car has run off the road and collided with a telephone pole and the woman driver is explaining, "Look at all those telephone poles I didn't hit." Under the man-bites-dog formula this accident would not be much of a story unless the telephone pole wandered onto the road and hit the car. But it would have been no story at all if the driver had reached her destination without accident. Meg Greenfield of the *Washington Post*, in a delightful parody of the news as Spiro Agnew might have written it, once composed a headline: "BACK WHEELS STAY ON '59 FORDS."

A more modern definition of news than Bogart's is offered by Turner Catledge, former managing editor of the *New York Times*: "News is anything you find out today that you didn't know before." This definition stresses the importance of timeliness, long a pre-eminent value of reporting. While it is a step forward from the man-bites-dog description of news, it also is far from complete. At the *Washington Post* and many other metropolitan dailies the editors each day receive a list of held-over stories that have been set in type. On the *Post* this is known simply as the "in-type list." Some of the stories on this list may remain unused in the newspaper for days or even weeks. One common reason is that a story is so long that a place cannot be found for it in the paper without substantial cutting. The editor saves this in-type story for Sunday, when there usually is a lot of space, only to find that an airplane has crashed or a brushfire war has broken out on Saturday. So the story is saved for another Sunday, and perhaps another Sunday after that. Sometimes a story which an editor regards as high quality winds up on the in-type list because the news editor is unexcited by it or because other departments have better stories. The editor then decides to hold it on the in-type list for a day or two in the hope of getting it on page one on a dull news day — that is, a day when there is a shortage of calamity-novelty stories. When the story finally comes off the in-type list onto page one, as it frequently does, it usually is indistinguishable from other stories which have been written the day before. In short it is "news" just like all the other stories even though the information contained in the in-type story has been known to the newspaper for several days. As Edward Jay Epstein has pointed out, this practice is even more com-

monplace in television.[1] Network television — and this is
as good a place as any to say that my use of the word
"press" embraces newspapers, magazines, television,
radio and various specialty publications — instructs its
correspondents to get "timeless" film which may be
edited and used days or weeks later to illustrate a thematic story presented to the viewers as "news." At the *San
Jose Mercury*, where heavy advertising on Wednesday
and Thursday created a news space ("newshole") too
large to be filled on the day of publication, editors were
assigned to prepare as many as thirty or forty columns of
stories marked "SOS" — the abbreviation for "same old
shit" — and sent out weeks in advance. Wire service
features were ideal for this purpose, but it was always a
discovery to me how many news stories intended for
next-day use could be tailored to the requirements of SOS
with some discreet removal of the time element. Usually,
the system was a marvel of economic effectiveness although it certainly had very little to do with telling
people anything that was new. But I do not recall that
any reader ever complained that the paper was three
months late in reporting the details of the Kurdish rebellion.

Even the *New York Times*, the most complete newspaper in the United States, would have some difficulty living by the Catledge definition. The *Times* has its in-types
too, and along with other newspapers also prints stories
which are old enough to be safely recycled as new material. I remember an editor in California who accepted a
reporter's story with the comment that it was so old that
it was new. This formula would apply to certain stories
which have been published in both the *Times* and the
Post. On May 25, 1975, for instance, the *Times* published
a two-column story at the top of page one headlined
"Submarines of U. S. Stage Spy Missions Inside Soviet
Waters." It was written by Seymour M. Hersh, the great

---

[1] See Edward Jay Epstein's *News From Nowhere* (New York, 1973), pp.
144-49 and pp. 166-67.

Times reporter who deserved the Pulitzer Prize for his stories on domestic spying by the Central Intelligence Agency. But there was nothing prize-winning about this particular "news." Under a Washington dateline Hersh's story began:

"For nearly fifteen years, the Navy has been using specially equipped electronic submarines to spy at times outside the three-mile limit of the Soviet Union and other nations.

"The highly classified missions, code-named Holystone, have been credited by supporters with supplying vital information on the configuration, capabilities, noise patterns and missile-firing abilities of the Soviet submarine fleet."

The story was an interesting one. It also was more than sixteen months old. On January 4, 1974, a story written by Laurence Stern appeared in the *Washington Post*. The headline was nearly identical: "U. S. Subs Spying in Soviet Waters." The main facts of the story were nearly identical, too. It began this way:

"The United States maintains a fleet of electronic eavesdropping submarines operating close to the Soviet coastline to monitor Russian submarine activity and secret military communications.

"These submarines, described as 'underwater U-2s,' roam within Soviet territorial waters, according to intelligence sources with access to documents describing the spying operations."

A subsequent paragraph gave the code name of the program and described it as "probably the most hush-hush of all U. S. electronic intelligence operations which are also conducted by spy satellites and aircraft. The subs are equipped to gather a wide variety of electronic, communications and radar intelligence. One of their chief missions is to monitor Soviet nuclear submarine activities . . ."

This recycling is not peculiar to the *Times*. In 1974 some *Newsday* staffers were incensed with a front-page story in the *Washington Post* by Ronald Kessler describing purported banking and stock activities of Nixon intimate C. G. (Bebe) Rebozo. Much of the material had appeared in *Newsday* months earlier, and none of it was credited in the *Post*. However, Kessler added some details and an allegation which led Rebozo to sue the *Post* for libel, a lawsuit that is still unresolved.

Sometimes stories are recycled simply because reporters and editors fail to read their own newspapers as carefully as they should. I remember with embarrassment a story of my own which attributed to a White House source the information that a particular Nixon administration holdover was going to be retained by President Ford. This information appeared as the second paragraph of a story which announced the name of a new Ford appointee. Unfortunately, the news of the holdover appointment had appeared near the bottom of another *Post* story a few days before when it had been announced at the White House. Neither I nor any of the editors who read my story recalled the earlier announcement. The source's breathless prediction of an appointment that already had been announced ran through all editions of the *Post*.

These few illustrations ought to be sufficient to demonstrate the inadequacy of "newness" as a definition of news. But do not be misled by them. Newspapers value the *appearance* of newness almost above everything else and this value is doubled or trebled if the story appears to contain exclusive newness. The surest way to get a story on page one at most papers is to come up with information that appears not to have been written before. White House appointments, the example cited above aside, are a good example of how this value operates at the *Post*. Many stories of less important appointments have appeared on page one or page two on the basis that they were obtained before they were announced. In many cases the stories would not have qualified for this treatment if they had come from an official announcement.

This high value placed by newspapers on exclusivity
and on the appearance of newness is neither reasoned nor
capricious. Rather, it is the understandable product of a
pre-broadcast tradition in which newspapers competed
for readers, prestige and advertising dollars on the basis
of their ability to bring original, bulletin-style information to their subscribers. Most of today's editors and reporters have been trained in that tradition. They believe
that being first is being best even though most Americans, and the number is increasing every year, now get
their first news from television and from radio. Traditions die hard. A story beginning "Additional details
have been learned about the American submarines spying in Soviet waters" might have had a hard time making the paper, much less page one. Most wire service
stories, still the overwhelming source of national and
foreign news for American newspaper readers, operate
on the premise of bulletin journalism which brought
them into being. "Conditioned by its own past, journalism often acts as if its main task was still to report the
exceptional and dramatically different against a background of what everybody knows," wrote Max Ways in
Fortune in 1969. This is not as true now as when Ways
wrote it and it did not apply even then to the *Wall Street
Journal*. But most newspapers still operate on the premises of novelty and apparent newness. It is a deeply em-
bedded and deeply limiting tradition.

In the above passages we have considered the limitations of two popular definitions of "news" without offer-
ing any alternative definition. Indeed, I know of no comprehensive alternative, although it is easy enough to
conclude that some items of information — an assassination, the outbreak of a war, the burning down of a city —
qualify readily under either the Bogart or Catledge
definitions, not to mention a third broad definition by
Charles Dana that "news is what people talk about." It
also is rather easy to see that many of the everyday activities of human beings — the eating of breakfast, say,

or the arrival after a safe automobile journey — do not constitute news under any definition. But what if there is no breakfast to eat or if gasoline costs so much money that the journey cannot be undertaken? Modern newspapers and television networks would consider these conditions news, but only if they affected a sigificant number of people and could be reported on in a thematic way. The *New York Times* on June 6, 1975, the day Nguyen Van Thieu resigned as president of South Vietnam, found space on page one for two thematic stories. One, by Grace Lichtenstein, recounted the legacy of "hatred, violence and fear" on the Pine Ridge Oglala Sioux Reservation. The other, by Nicholas Gage, told how Latin America had become the major source of hard drugs entering the United States. The Lichtenstein story had a premonitory quality. Less than two months later, two FBI agents were murdered on the same reservation and largely as a result of the conditions she had described.

Such thematic stories obviously have an easier path getting into a newspaper when "nothing is happening," the favorite lament of weekend editors who are looking for something current for page one. On Monday mornings throughout the United States all sorts of secondary stories lead newspapers as editors take the most novel or dramatic event of the previous day and put a big headline on it. The Monday, July 14, 1975 *Washington Post* led the paper with one of a series of raids which Israeli bombers had staged on targets in Lebanon. Its front page had one other story, the Soviet rejection of a second joint space flight with the United States, which was news that had been discovered the day before. The other five stories — accounts on the shortage of investment capital, on changes in the Black Muslim movement, on reduced access to the judiciary, on series installments on commuter problems and on the end of democracy in India — could have appeared a week earlier or a month later for all their timely content. Did that make them any less interesting or important to the reader?

It is a paradox observable to reporters and readers alike that newspapers which stress timeliness often have a highly repetitive quality. There are simply not enough dramatic catastrophes or presidential impeachments in this world to make one day's newspaper that much different from the next day's. News has a sameness even more repetitive than life. A reporter who goes away on vacation beyond the reach of a newspaper or television often finds that the newspapers which greet him on his return seem much the same as the newspapers he was reading when he left. One of the reasons for this sameness is that newspapers and wire services are able to cover only a limited number of newspoints, or "beats," and that the news from these usually official sources of information flows in recognizable and repetitive forms. Often, these forms are barriers to the recognition of real news which does not fit into a familiar pattern. It took dramatic protests and the burning down of great sections of major cities to make many newspapers realize the significance of the long-building black rebellion of the sixties. Nor did most newspapers discover the world food shortage or the energy crisis until these problems were well-advanced in their impact upon the American people. These and myriad other issues were certainly newsworthy long before they were written about, but they did not become "news" until they were discovered by the press. Leon V. Sigal,[3] in a valuable study, observes that there is "not much relationship between (what) newsmen say news is and what the news media transmit." Newsmen's definitions of news, Sigal says, fail the crucial test of describing what the press actually does in practice, a contention which can be supported by a week's examination of any daily newspaper.

---

[2]Leon V. Sigal, *Reporters and Officials: The Organization and Politics of Newsmaking*, (Lexington, Mass., 1974), pp. 1-2. Sigal's book is a study of the decisions which affect the processes of national and foreign news coverage at the *New York Times* and the *Washington Post*. It also examines how news channels are used by officials in government.

One of the reasons why these definitions flunk an empirical test is that they are not really definitions at all but descriptions of what might be called "exceptional news." It is obvious, even with the newsprint shortage, that insufficient "man-bites-dog" items exist to fill the ravenous news requirements of a modern metropolitan daily. It is less obvious but equally true that "anything you find out today that you didn't know before" fails to describe many of the news stories which actually appear in any paper. Not even the Dana definition of news being what people talk about suffices to describe the content of a newspaper, with the exception, perhaps, of a few gossipy weeklies. Much "news" is so trivial, or transitory, that it is not even talked about by very many people. Thoreau's famous complaint, in *Walden,* was that he had "never read any memorable news in a newspaper. If we read of one man robbed, or murdered, or killed by accident, or one house burned, or one vessel wrecked, or one steamboat blown up, or one cow run over on the Western railroad, or one mad dog killed, or one lot of grasshoppers in the winter — we never need read of another. One is enough. If you are acquainted with the principle, what do you care for a myriad instances and applications?"

Others have reached the same conclusion. Novelist (and former reporter) Mark Harris, deploring the preoccupation of the news business with the "second-rate drama" of Watergate, calls upon people to trust their own powers of observation rather than the observations of the press. ". . . The unspeakable problems of society remain, not merely ignored but effectively obscured by thousands of reporters roaming the world with a marvelous opportunity for revealing the urgent news of the world if only they were encouraged to do so," writes Harris. "True news comes to us very slowly, if at all, though we boast of our incredible advances toward instantaneous communication." To Harris, as to Thoreau before him, "true news" is buried beneath the trivia which forms the warp-and-woof of the modern newspaper.

And yet, this trivia is more important than it seems. Modern newspapers which have tried to de-emphasize crime news, or accidents, or even the statistical accumulations of births, marriages and deaths which clog provincial newspapers, often find there is a demand from their readers for precisely such "unmemorable" information. Partly this may be because ordinary human beings can stand only so much uplift. Partly it is because the "trivial" accumulation of calamities reminds people of their own mortality, or of their temporal good fortune, and in doing so gives them a sense of inter-relatedness to others. The importance of the trivia of news can best be appreciated through the glass darkly of societies where there is no news as we know it but only an official rendering of reality. Inevitably, this official reality stresses the significant events of life, as viewed by The State, and consciously eliminates the myriad re-occurances of everyday life. These re-occurances tell us more than we realize about the condition of our lives. Their omission from newspapers in the majority of societies that do not enjoy an uncontrolled press invariably is noticed by Americans abroad, of whatever philosophy. "Out of the variety of news and opinion in the Western press one can sift even the most unpopular truths," I.F. Stone wrote after a visit to the Soviet Union two decades ago. "To read the Soviet press one has to become expert in decoding a peculiar kind of party language, developed to hide the facts rather than to make them public." Stone, no foe of socialism, found the Russian press "matchless for turgidity and obscurity." Hungering for news from abroad, he concluded: "It is impossible to imagine unless you have been there what it means to live in a country in which you do not know what is going on outside."

But it is not only Westerners who have a craving for the news. In the People's Republic of China there is an official newspaper, distributed to all who can read it, and a private newspaper circulated only to a few million senior cadres. This private newspaper is off limits to

Westerners in China. Those who have seen it, however, remark that it contains precisely those "trivial" stories of happenstance and gossipy comment which are omitted from the official *People's Daily*. Though the Chinese rulers lay claim to a philosophy which they believe explains world events, it is this private newspaper that is the guide for the cadres. The ordinary citizen in China must make do with rumor and surmise.

It should come as no surprise to us then that rumors circulate with especial efficiency in closed or semi-closed societies. (This is largely true in the closed or semi-closed institutions of the West, also, with the Army the outstanding example.) In Yugoslavia scores of underground radio stations flourish on low power and forbidden frequencies. They specialize in rock music and the local news events and gossip which are omitted from the official newspapers. Some of these stations are believed to be discreetly tolerated by the authorities, who recognize that they perform a useful function. And so they do. Human beings have a need for conversations about the happenings of our common life, a need rooted in the social nature of man. For most of us, it is "the news" which serves this common need. It is impossible to conceive of a free society without it.

CHAPTER THREE

Values

I want to tell you what a newspaper means. It's a serious sacred business. The least smell of corruption, fear or favoritism must not creep into its news columns . . . Avoid even the appearance of evil. Never again do anyone a favor which might compromise the newspaper you are connected with. To get the news you may kill, steal, burn, cheat, lie; but never sell out your paper in thought or deed. A newspaper doesn't belong to the men who run it or to those who own the plant. The press belongs to the public, to the people.

–Editor Josiah M. Ward to Gene Fowler[1]

Most newspapermen would not go as far as Joe Ward, an early 20th century editor of the *Denver Republican,* in their zeal to get the news. In fact, Ward himself would not have gone that far. He was making a point to Fowler, who became one of the nation's top reporters, after Fowler had committed a minor indiscretion in the paper's name to impress a girl he loved. The *Republican,* it should be noted, did not last very long. It was taken over by a rich businessman with no interest in newspapering and sold to another rich businessman who merged it with the *Rocky Mountain News.* Before the merger Ward was fired. Fowler's most important story, an account obtained by eavesdropping, of how Colorado big businessmen had browbeaten the governor into sending the National Guard to break a miner's strike, was suppressed. The *Republican* turned out to belong to the man who owned it, not to the people.

---

[1]Gene Fowler, *A Solo in Tom-Toms,* (New York, 1946), pp. 317-318.

Nevertheless, it is doubtful if an editor ever better stated the basic values of the newspaperman's trade than Ward did in this little speech in his office. Newspapermen really believe that a newspaper is a sacred proposition with an importance that transcends the business purpose of its owner. For this reason they are likely to mourn the passing of any newspaper, even a bad one. And they tend to be exalted by a newspaper's triumphs and diminished by its defeats.

As Ward perceived, reporters also carry around in their heads a high blown notion of what a newspaper's ethic ought to be. They are quick to suspect their own newspaper of selling out, either to an advertiser or to a prominent official, and they are scornful of a publisher's "sacred cows," even when compelled to respect them in their copy. The cynicism which many persons find in reporters is a corruption of this rather naive expectation that newspapers will respond, as a few of them do, to a higher ethic than the profit motive. This expectation is not easily extinguished in the best reporters and editors, who are invariably disillusioned when a publisher operates by the same code as the shoe merchant. Broadcast journalists are somewhat more realistic on this score since their own medium never has made any secret of its sentiments when profits are opposed to news values. Even in television, however, there is an expectation among the correspondents that favoritism and pressure will be resisted in the name of news. When Fred Friendly quit as head of the CBS news division in 1966 because it refused to interrupt commercially profitable morning re-runs with publicly important Senate hearings on Vietnam, he quoted the words of his late partner, Edward R. Murrow: "Upon occasion, economics and editorial judgment are in conflict. And there is no law which says that dollars will be defeated by duty."[2]

---

[2]Fred W. Friendly, *Due To Circumstances Beyond Our Control*, (New York, 1967), p. 252.

The other value reflected in Ward's speech is the most
enduring one for reporters — and the most troublesome.
It is the value which says, "Get the story at all costs."
Ward defines it in terms of "the news" but to a reporter it
almost always is "the story," which means the story he is
working on and the story he wants to get first. We have
seen how this impulse can lead a great newspaper to
overplay a story it might well have not run at all. The
greater problem, however, is that the overriding importance of Getting The Story can distort a reporter's normal
ethical sense so that he violates either the law or his own
best instincts in the name of his purpose. Few reporters
would do what the late Harry Romanoff, the so-called
"Heifetz of the telephone," did for various Chicago newspapers and impersonate public officials, including the
governor, to get a story. But many reporters, including
this one, have benefited because people they were dealing
with did not know they were reporters and were not told.
Nor is the conversation which *Washington Post* reporters
Carl Bernstein and Bob Woodward held with the grand
jurors in the Watergate case as rare as it seems. The
rarity is that the two reporters told about it in their book,
All the President's Men, and admitted their wrongdoing.
Writing about themselves in the third person, Woodward
and Bernstein said; "They felt lousy. They had not broken the law when they visited the grand jurors, that
much seemed certain. But they had sailed around it and
exposed others to danger. They had chosen expediency
over principle and, caught in the act, their role had been
covered up. They had dodged, evaded, misrepresented,
suggested and intimated, even if they had not lied outright."[3]

What is instructional about the Woodward-Bernstein
episode is not that reporters skirted the law but that the
Post confronted the issue of seeking out the grand jurors

[3]Carl Bernstein and Bob Woodward, *All The President's Men,* (New York,
1974); p. 224.

at its highest editorial echelons and decided to go ahead with the enterprise even though its Number Two editor, Howard Simons, was opposed on ethical grounds. Some of the other editors voiced opposition, too, although it is Woodward's recollection that they were concerned more with the problem of getting caught than with the issue of whether the law would be broken. And while the story of Watergate was unique, this kind of discussion is not. Reporters on investigative stories frequently are given glimpses of closed records or see copies of testimony that has been sworn to secrecy. Sometimes we print supposedly secret material even while the newspaper itself is editorializing against it, as was true during the investigation of Vice President Spiro Agnew. It is immaterial that the accusations which were printed were for the most part true, and then some. As David S. Broder has observed in a column, "the great lesson we supposedly learned from the McCarthy era was that responsible journalism requires that accusations against individuals not be delivered naked to the reader but be presented with due regard to the motives and credibility of the accuser." I was involved in the Agnew investigation at the *Post* and was vastly more concerned with Getting The Story than with the consideration of whether Agnew's accusers were motivated by self-interest. So, it seems to me, were my colleagues on the *Post* and on the *New York Times* and the *Washington Star,* all of which contributed important stories to the Agnew investigation. All three of these newspapers editorialized against the leaks coming out of the Agnew investigation, leading Broder to comment: "There hasn't been such a suspiciously conspicuous display of civic virtue since a San Francisco madam led her string of girls to a Red Cross blood bank during World War II." The editorialists did not blame their own newspapers for printing the leaks. Rather, they avoided the question of journalistic propriety by associating themselves with Agnew's statement that "the blame must rest with those who give this information to the press." This strikes me as a cop-out, on the order of the tired defense, "We only print the facts." What was operating in the Agnew case, as it does in every important story and some that are not so important, was the desire to get the story and to get it first. It is the most deeply imbedded value of American journalism.

I would not favor suppression of the type of material we printed in the Agnew case. Instead, I think newspapers have an obligation to state their own interests and, whenever possible, the interests of their sources rather than rationalize that the leaks are the fault of the leakers. If a story said that information about the pending allegations came from a source which had an interest in seeing Agnew indicted and convicted (or, in the usual dodge, from someone "close" to such a source), its impact would be different than the impact of a story which gives the impression that the source is a disinterested party. But it seems to me that we would have been wrong in withholding the Agnew stories until an official action was taken. Agnew was Vice President of the United States. He could have become President in a twinkling. It would have been wrong for a newspaper to have withheld from the public the fact that there were serious criminal allegations pending against a man who might become President. In a society where governance is premised on the notion of an informed citizenry, Getting The Story is a worthwhile value, for all its abuses. The other two values of journalism which Ward celebrates — serving the public and remaining free from corruption — are meaningless unless a newspaper conceives it as a duty to pass on to the public what it knows.

Subsidiary values flow from the three primary ones. The transcendent value of Getting The Story attaches a high premium on candor and openness by public officials, which helps in getting stories. The belief in the importance of incorruptibility nourishes the reformist interest in scandal and corruption. The related value of regarding the newspaper as a public trust rather than the personal property of the owner fosters a healthy intolerance for people in public life who do not hold a similarly lofty view of their own offices. This belief that newspapers have a public responsibility also tends to make editors and reporters more attentive than they might otherwise be to the claims of individuals or groups which they consider to be ignored, repressed or discriminated against. I know a number of reporters and editors who will take the time even under deadline pressure to attempt to explain to a naive or hostile critic the reasons for something their newspaper has done.

Some harmful attitudes also derive from the basic journalistic values. The reporter's view that he is performing a sacred calling can cloak him with an annoying self-righteousness about his mission which ordinary Americans find disturbing. Out of this attitude of mission sometimes arises an insensitivity and a mistaken belief that a reporter is entitled to ask anyone anything at any time. Invasions of privacy were once presumed to be synonymous with the news business, and their impact, like the impact of anything else, can be magnified by television. A few years ago in Washington a television newscaster sought the emotional reaction of the survivor of a mass murder who had just seen his children slain. He asked the survivor whether anything like what he had just experienced had happened to him before.

Speed is another high value of the news business, both because of the concern with exclusivity or its appearance and because of the difficult technological requirements of getting out a daily newspaper or preparing a broadcast. It is a value which competes with the value of accuracy, and in competitive situations it is difficult for accuracy to gain the upper hand. We put half-baked stories that need further checking on the air or into the newspaper when the stories certainly could wait another day. We value most, as we should, those reporters who can perform high-quality work and do so in a hurry. But within news organizations we sometimes are more scornful of those

reporters who can't meet deadlines than of those whose
standard of accuracy bears only a remote relationship to
the facts. Perhaps this over-emphasis on speediness once
was necessary for newspapers. Perhaps it is still a necessary emphasis for the wire services and the broadcast
media. But in an age when many people expect their
newspapers to provide a context for the information they
already have received on radio and on television, speed
should be less of a value than it used to be. Jack Nelson,
the Washington bureau chief of the *Los Angeles Times,*
once paid tribute to his former national editor, Ed
Guthman, by recalling an incident where Nelson was
pressing to get a story into the paper when there still was
reporting to be done. "We would like to have the first
story, if that's possible," Guthman said in urging Nelson
to wait another day. "What's more important is that your
story be the best story, as I know it will." The rest of us
would do well to emulate this high standard.

CHAPTER FOUR

The Biases
of the News Business

*We shall endeavor to record facts on every
public and proper subject, stripped of verbiage
and coloring . . .*
   *– James Gordon Bennett describing
the mission of the* NEW YORK HERALD
on May 6, 1835.

No newspaper presents a complete picture of the world,
nor could it. News, as Paul Weaver has observed, is "a
genre, a distinctive mode of writing and depicting experience." What is acceptable in that mode depends upon a
myriad of commercial, professional and philosophical
considerations. These considerations are influenced by
the training, perception and biases of the men and
women who make them and by the pressures and constraints of the bureaucracies in which they operate. "Every newspaper when it reaches the reader is the result of
a whole series of selections as to what items shall be
printed, how much space each shall occupy, what emphasis each shall have," Walter Lippmann wrote in 1922.
"There are no objective standards here. There are conventions."[1]

Any editor or reporter can immediately recognize the
validity of Lippmann's statement. In their own daily
dealings these editors and reporters understand that the
determination of "news" is a subjective one based upon
an amalgam of traditional forms of coverage, personal
judgment and the availability of space. Newspaper con-

[1]Walter Lippmann, *Public Opinion,* (New York, 1922), p. 223.

ventions provide a framework for decisions. Within this
framework there is subjectivity. Any reporter, for instance, knows that different editors on the same newspaper favor different types of stories. One editor, for instance, may be extraordinarily receptive to lifestyle
stories. Another may prefer analytical pieces which
examine a process or the workings of an institution. Still
another editor may consider the analytical story "a lot of
talk" and prefer a hard, factual lead which never de-
viates from the day's most immediate events. One editor
may like a lot of supporting quotes; another editor may
tend to regard most quotations as rhetoric and excise
them from the story. Some editors will welcome a colorful
or humorous sidelight; others consider levity of any sort
in a news story as a threat to the readers comparable to
the bubonic plague. These attitudes and biases play an
important role in shaping the news of the day. So do the
attitudes and biases of the reporters on the beat. So do
the moods, tiredness, intelligence, imagination and conceptual abilities of both reporters and editors. At every
step of the process subjective elements, operating within
the framework of journalistic conventions, help define
the news.

"I think the real question that we have to ask ourselves
in journalism is whether the picture of the world we
select and produce every day is a truly representative
picture," says Richard Harwood, former editor of the
Trenton Times. "The related question is whether it
should be truly representative. Obviously, we have limited space, even in the large newspapers. We have limited resources. We have great biases built into all of our
newspapers in favor of certain kinds of news. We decide
every day on our paper, and I think on every paper in
America, that the sports department will have X columns of space, whether it's the World Series that's going
on or whether there's nothing going on but Little League
baseball. And that space we devote to sports every day is
a helluva lot more space than we devote to national news

as a category, to foreign news as a category, probably to metropolitan news as a category. In Trenton we devoted two pages a day to the comics, Ann Landers and that kind of thing. This is a commercial function. We know that we've got to do this to hold the interest of our readers. So we make decisions that aren't rational in a philosophical sense. So when you ask, do we every day produce a representative picture of the world we live in, the answer is no. Could we do a more representative picture? Yes. There are biases in the newsroom. There is a bias toward the coverage of public bodies. There is a bias toward the coverage and pronouncements of politicians. There is a bias toward the coverage of the bizarre, the random event, the car crash that killed twelve people, the tornado, the murder. There is a bias toward the establishment, if you will. A statement by the President of the United States on almost any subject will get more space in American newspapers than a statement from a scientist or from a university faculty member who may have something a helluva lot more important to say on that day. We do not cover, we do not give a picture. We're biased in terms of class. The poor, the blacks, the people in trouble, we don't tell our readers much about the world they live in. Now if they go out rioting or if all of a sudden you've got ten percent unemployment we'll start writing about these things, but we don't deal with the lives of blue-collar workers except in some Archie Bunker way. We don't deal with the lives of the black people who are struggling to earn a living, whereas we will write world-without-end statistical stories about welfare."

This emphasis on "world-without-end statistical stories" and many of the other biases Harwood described have their roots in the traditions of American journalism. When editors and reporters make their practical decisions in the newsroom, they do so within the context of a long tradition which had determined that some kinds of happenings and stories constitute news while others do not. In explaining the workings of their craft to others,

people in the news business often accept this tradition
without much reflection and behave as if the news was a
finite body of information ready to be set into type or
related to the television viewer. "Our reporters do not
cover stories from their point of view," said Richard Salant of CBS News. "They are presenting them from nobody's point of view."[2] Associated Press has proudly advertised that it "*never* estimates, *never* guesses, *never*
predicts." And editor Herbert Brucker, one of the modern
authorities on objective journalism, sees the traditional
form he celebrates as a hope of the world. If objective
reporting were adopted worldwide, wrote Brucker: "Inevitably the ensuing world-wide access to identical facts
and views would make the various nations see their
common crises in all their colors, as they are, rather than
through the monochrome lenses of national prejudice."[3]
Brucker's avowed goal is "completely opinionless news
columns." He believes that the tradition of objective reporting "keeps the vast majority of American news reports free from bias and leads editors and publishers to
segregate their opinions about the news in clearly iden-
tifiable editorials, columns, cartoons and special articles."[4]

Such a deeply-rooted belief in the efficacy of an opinionless journalism does not spring fullblown like Athena
from the brow of Zeus. It flows from the wellsprings of
early journalism where the press in England was subject
to licensing or censorship before publication ("prior restraint") for more than the first two centuries of its existence. American journalistic histories tend to focus on
the exciting pamphleteering newspapers of the Revolutionary War period when newspapers became the organs
of the developing nation. But the American newspaper

[2]This quotation, from a Salant article in *TV Guide*, became the title quotation for Edward Jay Epstein's *News From Nowhere*, a valuable account of
how bureaucratic considerations influence the selection of television news.
[3]Herbert Brucker, *Freedom of Information*, (New York, 1949), p. 206.
[4]The same, p. 267.

also is the offspring of a longer colonial tradition when newspapers were the subservient organs of the crown. The first intended newspaper in the colonies, in 1690, was killed by prior restraint because of the candid reporting proposed by its creator, Benjamin Harris.[5] It was not until 1721 and the advent of James Franklin's *New-England Courant* that any colonial newspaper was issued in defiance of authority. The acquittal of John Peter Zenger, printer of the *New-York Weekly Journal,* is justly celebrated as the greatest single advance for press freedom in this country because of attorney Alexander Hamilton's success in establishing truth as a defense to libel. But it was decades before this principle became generally accepted in the colonies.[6] "The fact must not be lost sight of that during the early history of the country newspaper censors were ever present who, clothed by the law with authority, never hesitated to annoy the poor printer whenever he put anything interesting in his paper," wrote journalism historian James Melvin Lee. "A jail sentence rather than a libel suit was the sword of Damocles which hung in every newspaper office should something be printed which reflected in any way upon the government."

What happened in the revolutionary period was not that American newspapers became anti-authority. In-

---

[5]The proposed newspaper was called *Publick Occurences, Both Foreign and Domestick.* It contained frank accounts of military losses in battle with the Indians, which may have been a reason for its suppression, as well as casualties of a smallpox epidemic "which has been raging in Boston." It was a small, four page sheet, 7½ by 11½ inches with two columns to the page except for the fourth, which was free of printing. A copy was discovered in the London Public Record Office in 1845. Harris returned to England a few years after this venture and became editor of the *London Post* in 1695.

[6]In law schools the Zenger case has greater fame for the jury's decision that it was the judge of the facts in the case. As Melville E. Stone describes it: "First, the jury took the bit in their teeth and asserted their right to be sole judges of the law and the facts. Second, they decided that the oldtime rule that 'the greater the truth the greater the libel was an unwise one.' Zenger was acquitted. And so it came about that there was a famous revolution in the colonial law."

stead, they transferred their loyalty to the emerging authority of the coming revolution which wielded power for
years before the war. The passage of the Stamp Act in
1765 was so unpopular in America that it would have
taken far more editorial courage to support it than to
come out in opposition. A few newspapers suspended publication but most of them ignored the act or appeared
with such heads as "no stamped paper to be had." After
the first few weeks of the law newspapers using such
subterfuges adopted their old titles. "A most diligent and
careful search," wrote Lee, "has not revealed among the
thirteen original colonies a single newspaper which appeared on stamped paper."[7]

Newspapers, some of them little more than pamphlets,
became outright patriot organs during the Revolutionary
War. Afterwards, they provided a frail link among the
newly liberated colonies in the absence of a strong central government. These newspapers were anything but
objective. As James B. Lemert puts it, "Objectively reported news was certainly not essential to the
rationalist-utilitarian thought underlying the First
Amendment, which generally assumed a highly partisan
press."[8] It is no accident that Alexander Hamilton, John
Jay and James Madison chose a newspaper, the *Independent Journal* of New York, in which to publish articles
favoring a new Constitution. The articles, signed "Pub-
lius," were addressed to the voters of New York and appeared under the standing head of "The Federalist." But
once the Constitution was established, the new central
government found many of the newspapers a nuisance or
worse. The Alien and Sedition Acts of 1798, under which

---

[7]This quotation (p. 83-84) and the one in the previous paragraph (p. 28) are
from *History of American Journalism* by James Melvin Lee, (Garden City,
New York, 1917). Much of the discussion of James Gordon Bennett in this
chapter also is based on Lee's valuable account.

[8]James B. Lemert, "Craft Attitudes, the Craft of Journalism and Spiro
Agnew," a paper by the director of the division of communications research
at the University of Oregon, 1970.

editors were jailed, were largely an attempt to suppress journals critical of the Federalists and of George Washington. By this time newspapers already had evolved from their roles as revolutionary organs into instruments of the unforeseen political parties which had arisen in the nation. Hamilton, in particular, was mindful of the use of newspapers as party organs. He helped finance *The Gazette of the United States* in 1789 and moved it to Philadelphia when the government moved there a year later. Thomas Jefferson backed a rival paper, *The National Gazette,* which was established in Philadelphia in 1791. The editors of both newspapers were in the pay of the government. John Fenno, editor of the *Gazette of the United States,* was named printer to the Treasury Department at a then-munificent salary of $2,500 a year and Philip Freneau, editor of *The National Gazette,* held a "clerkship for languages" in the State Department at $250 a year.

These newspapers printed what their sponsors gave them to print, contributing mostly their own invective. For the next generation, and more, the newspapers of the early Republic fairly glowed with invectives like "obscene vagabond," "venemous reptile," "foreign imposter," "habitual liar" and "polluted wretch." This also was the period when editors came into their own. The colonial editor usually had called himself "a printer" and had made most or all of his living from this trade. The most controversial opinions often were expressed by contributors, many of whom during the wartime period preferred the form of pamphlets. The early republic absorbed the pamphlet into the newspaper, and the editor became the dominant force of American journalism.

This early press had many readers but few subscribers. Newspapers cost six cents a copy, and it was a badge of status to subscribe to one. What changed the press was what changed the nation. The victory of Andrew Jackson in the presidential election of 1828 signaled the ascension of the expansionist democratic West over the East-

ern mercantile establishment. "A vast tide of migration
to the Midwest produced not only the social and political
influence of the frontier, but new markets for a slowly
industrializing East," wrote Edwin Emery. "This was the
start of the American Industrial Revolution in which the
factory system supplanted hand-craft production. It was
marked by the rise of a working class interested in labor
organizations, a spreading of general education and intellectual progress, and great advances in mechanical
and transportation facilities."[9] Among the advances was
the development of the steam-driven press and cheaper,
better-quality newsprint. Postal routes were extended,
the Erie Canal completed and the first great railroads
built. Newspapers of mass circulation became a possibility.

The notion of a popular press grew in the minds of
editors with the advent of these technological and social
changes. Abortive efforts were made in 1830 to create
low-price newspapers both in Boston and in Philadelphia. A two-cent paper came out in New York in 1833.[10]
That same year Benjamin Henry Day, a printer, brought
out a penny paper, *The Sun,* and hired a reporter, George
W. Wisner, for four dollars a week. Wisner was instructed to concentrate on court news. While the older
established papers focused on the fight between President Jackson and the United States Bank, *The Sun* became an instant success with daily reports of assault-
and-battery cases. *The Sun's* achievement encouraged a
flood of imitators, of which James Gordon Bennett's *New
York Herald* was by far the best.

---

[9]Edwin Emery, *The Story of America as Reported by Its Newspapers,
1690-1965,* (New York, 1965), p. 35.

[10]The Boston newspaper, which appeared the first two days of the week,
was the *Daily Evening Transcript,* which sold not for a penny but for the low
rate of four dollars a year. The Philadelphia paper, probably the first one
which actually sold for a penny, was *The Cent,* which died a quick death. The
New York two-cent paper was *The Morning Post,* begun on January 1, 1833,
with Dr. Horatio Shepard, Horace Greeley and Francis W. Story as its printers and publisher.

Bennett is the father of modern objective journalism even though he was one of the most personal journalists ever to draw breath. Quoting Ophelia, the first *Herald* on May 6, 1835, disclaimed "all steel traps, all principle, as it is called — all party — all politics. Our only guide shall be good, sound practical common sense, applicable to the business and bosoms of men engaged in everyday life." These principles meant long news stories on the murders then commonplace in New York and emphasis on crime stories involving women. It also meant coverage, much to their annoyance, of the various religious organizations. And it meant publishing items of foreign news as soon as Bennett could lay hands on them. The publisher never lost sight of his "common sense" principles, by which he meant reporting that was "light and spicy" and which focused on the daily turbulence of events. If Bennett was assaulted on the streets by citizens who objected to this frank approach, he gave an account of it in the *Herald* next morning under a standing heading, "Bennett Thrashed Again." His success inspired other penny newspapers, notably the *Baltimore Sun* and the *Philadelphia Ledger*. All of these penny newspapers excelled in police reporting, in timely accounts of local events, in coverage of the frontier and of the Mexican-American war. "The penny papers," wrote James Lee, "went on the principle of what the Lord let happen ought to be printed in their sheets." Stories were vigorously written, often embellished by the opinion of the reporter. The word "objectivity," not yet in common use, meant an account devoid of partisanship, not of color.

What transformed vivid reporting into the objective-neutral prose of modern wire services was the telegraph and the commercial combinations it made possible. The telegraph came along in 1844, on the heels of widespread adoption of the steam-driven press. Baltimore and Washington were linked by telegraph that year, and the Baltimore newspapers soon began to print items headed "By Morse's Magnetic Telegraph." When the telegraph line reached the Jersey coast opposite New York, the proceedings of Congress were sent from Washington and published under similar headings in New York newspapers. Horace Greeley, at first a skeptic about the telegraph, was given a private demonstration by its inventor, Samuel Morse, and said to him, "You are going to turn the newspaper office upside down with your invention." Greeley proved a better prophet than a performer in this instance. He allowed James Gordon Bennett to steal a march on him, and the *New York Herald* soon specialized in dispatches which came by telegraph rather than by mail. By the outbreak of the Civil War, the *Herald* had 75,000 subscribers — more than any other paper in the world.

The telegraph gave the mass-circulation newspapers a vast edge over their competitors. And it also spurred the development of press associations, which first were formed in the mid-1840s to share the marine news. Before the telegraph — and afterward for a period of time, especially during the Civil War — newspapers emphasized the reporting of their own correspondents, who often wrote in a regional or personal style they deemed suitable for the readers of the newspapers which employed them. The early costs of the telegraph prompted an emphasis on terseness and timeliness rather than on style. Reporters developed a taut, coded method of filing which aimed at conveying the maximum number of facts in the minimum number of words. These telegraphic dispatches were the forerunners of modern wire service stories, from which they do not greatly differ. At the same time the sharing of news by the press associations encouraged a neutrality of language so that dispatches would be of equal value in every region of the country and in every type of newspaper. As often happens in the newspaper business, a technique became a value. By 1860 a Washington correspondent of the Associated Press could write: "My business is to communicate facts; my instructions do not allow me to make any comment upon the facts which I communicate. My dispatches are sent to papers of all manner of politics, and the editors say they are able to make their own comments upon the facts which are sent them. I therefore confine myself to what I consider legitimate news. I do not act as a politician belonging to any school, but try to be truthful and impartial. My dispatches are merely dry matters of fact and detail."[11]

This emphasis on "dry fact and detail," communicated at the greatest possible speed, became a basic value of the news business. Reporters were instructed to be impartial, to give "both sides" of a controversy by direct quotation and to refrain from expressing their own opinions in stories. In most cases particularities of style which heightened or colored stories also were discouraged. The Federalist papers had been published in what would now be called the news columns of a paper, but the emphasis on objective reporting diverted expressions of opinion to pages of their own inside the newspaper. This process tended to trivialize opinion, which reporters were taught to think of as having a lesser value than news. But newspaper readers never fully accepted the myth of the editorial page, believing with some reason that the opinions of publishers could find other avenues into their papers. Then and now, critics of a particular newspaper often view the selection of facts in a news story as mirroring the editorial views of the newspaper — whether or not the stories are actually influenced by the editorial opinion. However, the division between news and opinion did encourage a new standard of professionalism among reporters, who were taught that comment upon the facts they transmitted was a cardinal sin. The cardinal principles of Objective Reporting as they become codified and developed have been summarized by George E. Lardner, Jr.:

---

[11]Quoted in Oliver Gramling, *AP, The Story of News,* (New York, 1940), p. 39. The AP correspondent was Lawrence A. Gobright.

1. The reporter may relate, on his own authority, only the observable facts of an overt event, that is, what he can see and verify — immediate sense knowledge.

2. The reporter should relate what is controversial by stating the views of the parties controverting one another. This usually represents an attempt to give the "why" of an event while restricting the reporter to a narration of what is, for him, simply more sense knowledge, that is, what he heard the parties say about the controversy.

3. The reporter must be impartial in the gathering and the writing of both the observable facts and the opposing viewpoints. He must not let his own beliefs, principles, inclinations or even his own knowledge color the raw, overt material or the statements controlling it.[12]

These principles became the controlling elements of a reportorial tradition which today governs the operations of the most basic source of newspaper news, the wire services. And even on newspapers like the *New York Times* and the *Washington Post,* an overwhelming number of news stories still conform closely to these principles, which have nurtured a bias that the truth can be ascertained from the observable facts and the balancing of opposing viewpoints. It is a bias so ingrained that many reporters are no more aware of it than they are aware of their own breathing. Objective reporters accept on faith the importance of the overt event — of something that can be seen, heard, smelled or felt. They believe, in Brucker's term, that there are "agreed facts" of such an event from which the truth can be derived. Objective reporting does not admit that the selection of facts, even by a trained reporter, is a subjective process. More importantly, it provides no mechanism for dealing with that which is conditional, speculative or a state of mind. Under the assumptions of objective reporting the

---

[12]George E. Lardner, Jr., "Two Views of Objective Reporting: An Analysis," pp. 9-10, a master's thesis at Marquette University, May 1962. Lardner is a colleague on the national staff of the *Washington Post.*

circumstances which led to the Watts riots, the war in Vietnam, the development of a system of medical care for the aged or the energy crisis could not be covered until "something happened" in the form of an overt event. News became, as Lippmann called it, a signalizer of events rather than an analysis of a situation or an explanation of a human condition. But it was not always this way. For all their partisanship and invective, the newspapers of the pre-telegraphic age often published what we would now call thematic stories and discoursed on the conditions of the age and how they could be changed. They did not require an overt event as the excuse for their account. The values of timeliness, of conflict and of Getting The Story which we now see as inherent in the news are the values not of eternal truth but of 140 years of writing and depicting human experience in a particular way. The values of the objective reporting method are apparent when an event occurs where the agreed facts can be readily ascertained and where timeliness is of the greatest consequence. But these same values do not prompt examination of the daily frustrations of masses of citizens, not, at least, unless these masses conduct some reportable overt event such as destroying the cities in which they live. Nor do these values encourage analysis of the state of mind and conditions which lead a nation into a war it does not want. Objective Reporting discriminates against analysis in favor of narrative, against insight in favor of exposition and against truth in favor of the facts. It is a method which perpetuates the most damaging bias of American journalism — namely, that bias can be excluded from news accounts written by human beings.

Objective reporting always has been peculiarly open to manipulation by public officials who understood its limitations. These officials usually know, for starters, that their statements will be considered "news" no matter how outrageous they are and sometimes will be more newsworthy if they are particularly outrageous. The of-

ficials also know that the reporter can do little more than
report what they say and attempt to balance the remarks
with statements made by somebody else. This has been a
recurring phenomenon in public affairs reporting, but it
remained for Senator Joseph McCarthy of Wisconsin to
demonstrate just how much harm can be done when objective reporting is manipulated by a man who understands how it works. Writing while McCarthy was on his
rampages, Douglass Cater analyzed in painful detail the
"frozen patterns" of press coverage which accompanied
McCarthy's accusations of disloyalty against many
Americans. "Faced with a phenomenon as complex as
McCarthyism, the 'straight' reporter has become a sort of
strait-jacketed reporter," Cater wrote in *The Reporter* of
June 6, 1950. "His initiative is hogtied so that he cannot
fulfill his first duty, which is to bring clearer understanding to his reader. It results in a distortion of reality."
Cater then proceeds to give several examples of what
"straight" reporters did not point out in their copy,
among them the fact that a reporter for the *Chicago
Tribune* fed McCarthy most of the material for his original Wheeling, West Virginia, speech. "Straight reporters
did not investigate the sources of the abundant financial
aid which McCarthy is receiving or the expert assistance
provided by men like Kent Hunter of the Hearst newspapers," Cater wrote. "On the other hand it could and did
publicize the fact that (Senator Millard) Tyding's committee got twenty-five thousand dollars for operating ex-
penses. It thus gave the impression, deliberately created
by McCarthy, that he is a lonely crusader fighting
against powerful odds." As McCarthy well knew, objective reporting gives the accuser a powerful advantage
over the accused. This is because the accusation usually
becomes the lead and the lead becomes the headline. The
denial might be carried in a subhead in newspapers that
used them; otherwise the reader had to plow through the
story to find the denial even though all newspaper editors
are aware that many readers do not get beyond the first

few paragraphs. Sometimes, if the accused is unreach-
able — Owen Lattimore was in Afghanistan when
McCarthy leveled his charges against him — the answer
may lag several days behind the charge. In these cases,
the reply never succeeds in catching up with the accusation.

Many reporters would contend that the McCarthy
example is no longer relevant. They point to the hysteria
of the time, and they would say that the press today is far
more careful of unsubstantiated charges. Perhaps we are,
but recent history gives pause. When retired Air Force
Colonel L. Fletcher Prouty telephoned Daniel Schorr of
CBS News in July 1975 to tell him that Alexander Butterfield had been a CIA spy in the White House, Schorr
put Prouty on the CBS morning news with the accusation. So did Fred Rowan on NBC News. On both networks
Prouty stopped short of calling Butterfield a CIA spy,
much as Senator McCarthy had pulled his punches when
talking about specific individuals in the early stages of
his Communist-hunting escapades. On the CBS program
Prouty said that Butterfield's function was "to open doors
for CIA operations." On NBC he agreed with a description of Butterfield as "a man with CIA connections."
There was no rebuttal from Butterfield, who was on the
West Coast looking for work, between the time the
charges were aired on Friday morning, July 11, 1975,
and the following Tuesday evening when Butterfield accepted the invitation of Mike Wallace to appear on the
CBS program "60 Minutes." At that time Butterfield
categorically denied all of Prouty's statements, including
the meaningless charge that Butterfield had been the
man the Central Intelligence Agency called when a CIA
official wanted to see someone in the White House.

Butterfield, like some of the Army officers who were
McCarthy's targets, claimed a distinguished Air Force
career and a record in the White House which had been
unstained by the scandals which surrounded him. He
was widely celebrated for his honesty in making known

the existence of the Nixon tapes. Many in Washington think that the linking evidence which pried Nixon from office never would have been accumulated without this revelation. But Butterfield's record of integrity did not save his job as Federal Aviation Agency Administrator in the Ford administration, and it did not save him from the press when Prouty made his accusations. Newspapers throughout the country played the story heavily, although no reporter had succeeded in finding Butterfield and obtaining a comment from him. The stories the day after Prouty's allegations did contain a denial of their accuracy from the Central Intelligence Agency. Considering the disrepute of the CIA at the time, this was roughly the same as getting a denial from a left-wing organization that so-and-so was not a member would have been in the McCarthy days. And, as in the McCarthy period, the accusation was bigger news than the subsequent discovery that the accusation was false. The *Washington Post* is perhaps typical. It played the original Butterfield accusation as its lead story on July 12. When Senator Frank Church, head of the Senate Intelligence Committee investigating the CIA, determined a week later that Butterfield was not a CIA spy the story was given a one-column headline below the fold on page one. In any case, denials are no more a match for accusations than they were twenty-five years ago. Butterfield was looking for a job when Prouty made his accusation, and he believes that his prospects for employment were damaged. "And it is a fact of life," as Charles Seib wrote in the *Washington Post,* "that undoubtedly there will be some who will say years from now when his name comes up; 'Oh yes. He's the guy who scuttled Nixon for the CIA.' "

The Prouty story was in many ways more inexcusable than the early McCarthy stories. McCarthy was, at least, a senator with no immediately discernible ax to grind. Prouty's ax was transparently apparent. In 1973 he had written a book, *The Secret Team: The CIA and Its Allies*

In Control of The World, which charged that the spy agency had put its own people into high places in American government and in business and academic communities. The entire tone of the book is ultra-conspiratorial. By way of introduction to what he calls "the real power structure" in America, Prouty writes: "At the heart of the Team, of course, are a handful of top executives of the CIA and of the National Security Council (NSC), most notably the chief White House adviser to the President on foreign policy affairs. Around them revolves a sort of inner ring of Presidential officials, civilians, and military men from the Pentagon, and career officials in the intelligence community. It is often quite difficult to tell exactly who many of these men really are, because some may wear a uniform and the rank of general and really be with the CIA and others may be as inconspicuous as the executive assistant to some Cabinet officer's chief deputy." Prouty's unproven accusations in this book were more than two years old but in the anti-CIA atmosphere which existed in Washington in 1975 he became the sort of "expert witness" that McCarthy and others had made of various ex-Communists a generation before. Schorr, without any consideration of Butterfield's own track record, said in his own defense that Prouty had furnished accurate information once before. *Time* quoted Schorr two weeks after the event as saying: "I still think my only alternative was to go. We're in a strange business here in TV news. You can't check on the validity of everything . . . I can't be in a position of suppressing Prouty. What if he's right? I can't play God." Schorr, making a better case against *Time* than he does for himself, told me that the words deleted by the ellipsis in this quotation were "while conducting a live interview." This softens the quote without changing the point. Of course, one cannot check on facts during a live interview, but the interview could well have been delayed at least until Butterfield was able to appear simultaneously. When I suggested this possibility to Schorr, he stressed the com-

petitiveness of his network with NBC and said he would
do the same thing again in the same circumstances.
The statement that a newsman "can't play God" is one
of the most familiar defenses of Objective Reporting. It is
now the defense of television, the primary source of news
today, as it was the defense of the wire services when
they were the main source of news a generation ago. It is
a defense which teaches reporters to rely on "the facts,"
which can mean nearly anyone's non-factual accusation
against somebody else, and which forbids them from trying to ascertain the truth. When the "facts" turn out to be
false, it is the fault of the accuser and not of the reporter
who transmitted them.
Objective reporting as a form always has been too constraining for some journalists. It is weakest in wartime
when the heightened level of human emotions produces a
demand for personal journalism. But even in peacetime
the conventions are too binding for some reporters. A few
abandon the news business to write fiction; many more
give up reporting to take sides. Gene Fowler, in *A Solo In
Tom-Toms*, tells the story of a turn-of-the-century reporter named Don McGregor of the *Denver Express* who obtained evidence that "a number of gunmen strike break-
ers" had put on the uniforms of National Guardsmen in
their attempt to break a miners' strike. When Fowler
tried to get this news past military censorship the general in charge flew into a rage and called him a "damna-
ble socialist." Fowler was recalled on the general's demand but McGregor stayed on as a reporter. After the
Ludlow massacre in which women and children were
machine-gunned by the troops McGregor joined the
strikers, carried a saber in a subsequent battle and was
later reported to have died at Pancho Villa's side in
Mexico. Other reporters meet less romantic-tragic-heroic
ends, but make the same choice to leave the news business.
On the surface the last decade of the nineteenth century and the first years of the twentieth seem in retro-

spect to have been a setback for objective journalism. Examination of any *large sampling* of newspapers in this period will indicate this was not the case. These were the years when the feuding, autonomous press associations combined, resulting in the triumph of the Associated Press in 1900. The AP and many of the provincial newspapers in the country stressed a literal, objective journalism. That it does not seem that way in retrospect is a tribute to the force of the "yellow journalists," so called after a character, The Yellow Kid, in a comic strip in Joseph Pulitzer's *New York World* and later in William Randolph Hearst's *New York Journal.* The chief exponents of the vigorous journalism were Pulitzer's *St. Louis Post-Dispatch* and *New York World* and William Randolph Hearst's *San Francisco Examiner* and *New York Journal.* In this early and most productive period of his career Hearst was an ally of the working man and vied with Pulitzer for the title of "people's champion." Both Hearst and Pulitzer attracted top-quality reporters who engaged in noisy but valuable crusades which had little to do with objectivity. But despite the celebrated achievements of the *World* and the early Hearst papers, newspapers which permitted the reporter to abandon objective guidelines remained very much in the minority. Much of the best work of the muckrakers, those rebels-with-a-cause against the cult of objectivity, did not appear in the newspapers but in such crusading magazines as *Collier's, McClure's* and the *American.*

Objective reporting, which had done little to prepare American newspaper readers for the coming of World War I, was weakened by that war. First there was the war reporting, with its emotional, personal, partisan and anti-German perspectives. Then there were the post-war tabloids, three of them in New York City alone, which appealed to the sordid, the sensational, the graphic. Then there was *Time,* the weekly newsmagazine, the brainchild of the fertile imaginations of Briton Hadden and Henry Luce. *Time* owns the distinction of being the first publication of importance to recognize that interpretation is equal to fact. Its creators carried this perception beyond its logical conclusion and dispensed with the editorial page. Individual journalists also began to express their doubts, as Vincent Sheean did, about the worthwhileness of the reporter's role as "perpetual spectator." Sheean, who had caused a sensation at the University of Chicago by inadvertently pledging a Jewish fraternity, went to Palestine on behalf of a Zionist organization. He soon sent the money back and wrote an account of Palestinian strife which showed sympathy to the Arabs as well as to non-Zionist Jews. Sheean wound up believing that reporters had a duty to discover the inner logic which underlies the chaos of immediate events. He became concerned with "mood, temper, states of minds," and with a "long view" of mankind which required analysis and the expression of opinion. He also concluded, after three feverish days of filing on-the-spot accounts during the middle of Arab-Jewish fighting, that he no longer wanted to write for newspapers at all.[13]

The non-objective reporter had his own biases to answer for in the decades between the wars. Reporters are carried along on the currents of the times. When they are no longer moored to impartiality by the forms of their craft, which is one of the historic arguments in behalf of objective reporting, they are apt to be swept out to sea by passionate opinion. The currents of the age carried journalists, with a few honorable exceptions who pulled themselves onto dry land, toward the Soviet Union. Today it is embarrassing to read Sheean and George Seldes on the Soviet Union and worse than embarrassing to read the then-celebrated Walter Duranty, who rationalized for most of what he saw in Soviet Russia, including Stalin's show trials.

However, objective journalism with its reliance on official sources fared no better in evaluating the Soviet

---

[13]Vincent Sheean describes these incidents in the chapter "Holy Land" in his autobiography, *Personal History,* (New York, 1934).

government than did the sympathetic reporters. Americans who have depended on their newspapers for information about the Soviet Union were surprised by the Stalin purges, by the Hitler-Stalin pact, by Stalingrad, by the Russian break with China and by Sputnik, to mention just a few events. With conspicuous exceptions neither personal journalism nor objective reporting has kept American newspaper readers up to snuff about the Soviets.

The New Journalists of the present era represent another reaction to the constraints of objective reporting. Their term, "New Journalism," is an old one and was first applied in the 1880s to the newspapers of Pulitzer, a penniless immigrant from Hungary who made it big in the new world. Pulitzer founded the *St. Louis Post-Dispatch* in 1878 and purchased the *New York World* in 1883. He promised in his first edition of the *World* that the newspaper would "expose all fraud and sham, fight all public evils and abuse (and) serve and battle for the people with earnest sincerity." Most of Pultizer's efforts were devoted to the editorial page and he recognized a distinction between news columns and editorials which some of today's New Journalists would not accept. Tom Wolfe spoke for many of them in calling for both a new style and a new content in reporting. ". . . One discovered that the basic reporting unit is no longer the datum, the piece of information, but the scene, since most of the sophisticated strategies of prose depend upon scenes," Wolfe wrote. "Therefore, your main problem as a reporter is, simply, managing to stay with whomever you are writing about long enough for the scenes to take place before your eyes."[14] These New Journalists also differed from their predecessors in their fondness for making themselves the heroes of their stories and for a transient approach to journalism. "What they had in common," wrote Wolfe, "was that they all regarded the newspaper as a motel you

---

[14]Tom Wolfe, "Why They Aren't Writing the Great American Novel Anymore," *Esquire,* December 1972.

checked into overnight on the road to the final triumph. The idea was to get a job on a newspaper, keep body and soul together, pay the rent, get to know 'the world,' accumulate 'experience,' perhaps work some of the fat off your style — then, at some point, quit cold, say goodbye to journalism, move into a shack somewhere, work day and night for six months, and light up the sky with the final triumph. The final triumph was known as The Novel."[15] From Norman Mailer on down, the New Journalists have sharply challenged the conventions of objective journalism. *Rolling Stone,* the best of the breed, is read in newsrooms throughout the country. So are a variety of local journalism reviews and *MORE*, which has vigorously pressed for a journalism that goes far beyond objective reporting.

I have suggested in this chapter that the greatest bias of journalism is the objective form itself. But newspapers and newspaper reporters also have a goodly share of cultural, economic, ideological and personal biases. The success of the mass-circulation newspapers coincided with the rise of capitalism. Often the most successful newspaper publishers — such as James Gordon Bennett, who had started with five hundred dollars, two wooden chairs and an old dry-goods box — were themselves new capitalists who had triumphed over the old aristocrats. For nearly three quarters of a century, at least outside the South, every technological and political development seemed to favor both the rising capitalism and these newspapers, many of whom became its spokesmen. The securing of the Union, mass transportation, popular education, the growth of population and its concentration in large cities, the Atlantic cable and the transcontinental railroad, the discovery and use of electricity and, above all, the development of brand-name advertising as a stimulus to mass sales were all tremendous benefits to newspaper publishers. Many of these publishers became

[15]Tom Wolfe, "The Birth of 'The New Journalism,' " *New York,* February 14, 1972.

the enthusiastic advocates of the developing society, and were well rewarded for their advocacy. Civil War taxes on newspaper advertisements were repealed during the Reconstruction period, never to return. Publishers succeeded in obtaining favorable postal regulations and, for a long period, low postal rates. Through business combinations newspapers steadily reduced the cost of newsprint, which sold for fifteen cents a pound in New York in 1867 and dropped steadily in price nearly every year after that for three decades. At the turn of the century the large newspapers were buying newsprint in rolls for one and six-tenths cents per pound.

Newspapers which enjoyed such commercial advantages were apt to think well of the system which provided them. Advertisers, particularly in the medium-sized and smaller cities, were suspected of holding great power over publishers and often did, particularly in suppressing stories unfavorable to their businesses. As Carey McWilliams once put it, "Nothing ever happens in a department store." When George Seldes wrote *Freedom of the Press* he could condemn the seven (!) competing papers of his Pittsburgh years as all corrupt, all subservient to the big Mellon banks or to the Pennsylvania Railroad or to U.S. Steel. Even newspapers which resisted any outright favoritism to advertisers often identified with them on issues because the publishers were big businessmen themselves. More often than not, they also identified with the party which seemed big business' reliable spokesman. "It would seem," said a politician, "that the overwhelming majority of the press is just against (my party). And is against (my party), so far as I can see, not after a sober and considered view of the alternatives, but automatically, as dogs are against cats. As soon as a newspaper . . . sees a candidate of (my party) it is filled with an unconquerable yen to chase him up an alley."[16]

---

[16] I am indebted for this example and for many other useful ideas to a piece by Stephen Hess, "Is The Press Fair?" in the Summer-Fall 1974 issue of *The Brookings Bulletin.* Hess' article is especially valuable for its examination of

The speaker was not then-Vice President Spiro Agnew in 1970 but Democratic presidential candidate Adlai Stevenson in 1952.

Stevenson, of course, was talking about newspaper publishers. Reporters, until recently, never were well paid enough to be Republicans. Throughout my own career I have known dozens of reporters who quit the news business to go into corporate public relations or into government at two or three times the salaries they were making. Reporters who stayed on were conscious of their personal financial sacrifice, particularly if they had a family. They were apt to be unsympathetic to the giants of industry, including their own industry. This was an inclination fostered by reportorial temperament, encouraged by observation and nourished by poverty. Traditionally, the low pay scales of the craft tended to reinforce both the idealism and the class consciousness of reporters. All but the most cynical were appalled when a story was killed or softened to placate an advertiser or twisted to help a political candidate favored by the publisher. On the whole, reporters tended to sympathize with labor unions in a contest with management and with an underdog in a contest with anybody. Few reporters of my acquaintance have been on the side of the big battalions.

However, the economic conditions which persisted when those of us who now are middle-aged reporters came into the business have changed remarkably, and they are likely to change more. A twenty-five year-old reporter on the *Washington Post* in 1976 earned a minimum of $25,000 a year with four years of experience. This is roughly twice the annual average family income. Higher-status reporters earn far more, and television celebrities and columnists often are in six-bracket figures. Of course, there still are plenty of underpaid reporters in the country, but the number is decreasing every year thanks to The Newspaper Guild and a few

---

the dangers of a reporter becoming too close to his sources.

reasonably enlightened managements. As reporters climb up the income scale, their social values also change. Reporters who a few years ago were preoccupied by the basic economic issues of life are now more likely to be aroused by energy or environmental issues or, for a long decade, by the Vietnam War. This is deliberately painting with a broad brush. In all periods there have been plenty of reporters who were interested in war or issues of human freedom, and there are reporters today who are concerned about gut economic issues. Nevertheless, the gulf is growing between reporters and working-class Americans. Michael Novak points out that this is particularly likely to be true on the big national newspapers and television networks where reporters, correspondents and editors are apt to be in the upper ten per cent of national income levels. "The fact is that reporters are by no means any kind of a cross-section," says David S. Broder, national political correspondent for the *Washington Post.* "We are over-educated, we are overpaid in terms of the median and we have a higher socio-economic stratification than the people for whom we are writing. And there is clearly a danger of elitism creeping in." Broder recalls the 1972 presidential campaign when Senator George McGovern was under fire in the California primary over his $1,000 "Demogrant" proposal, which would have refunded tax money to persons in lower-income brackets. "They flew some wizard out from the Brookings Institution to explain it to us," recalls Broder "and he came in with his charts showing how it would affect people at different income levels. I looked around that room at my colleagues, and among all of those guys there was a sudden terrible realization that this was going to cost them some money. Anybody who thought there was a great liberal press biased toward McGovern should just have seen the faces in the room at the time."

This new status of the top level of the press was not lost on the propagandists of the Nixon administration. Pat-

rick J. Buchanan, who wrote the early Spiro Agnew
speeches attacking the press, called the network news
correspondents and executives "ranking members of the
privileged class, the most prestigious, powerful, wealthy,
influential journalists in all history."[17] The Buchanan
speeches (as I always think of them, for Agnew was
merely the mouthpiece) shrewdly capitalized on the distrust felt by many working people for the networks and
for the big newspapers as remote, powerful institutions
with no understanding of the lives of ordinary Americans. In 1972 Barbara Bowman of National Public Radio
interviewed Ed Sadlowski, a thirty-six-year-old high
school dropout who had challenged the leadership of the
United Steelworkers Union and been elected director of
the union's mammoth Chicago-Gary district. Sadlowski,
who has since tried and failed to win the union presidency, talked about how the children of steelworkers automatically were channeled into industrial arts courses
and told to learn a trade:

> It was instilled in you — get a trade. Man, you can
> never go wrong if you get a trade. Nobody ever said, you
> know, "Learn to play the violin." They never said that,
> and that's kind of tragic. That's kind of where it was all
> at. That guy (Sadlowski's South Chicago working-class
> friend) is still getting screwed, you know. He's getting it
> sixteen different ways. Politicians are nailing him and
> corporations are nailing him and, God, he's being hound-
> dogged to death. Then society in general says he's a red-
> neck and he's a slob, Archie Bunker. That's bullshit. I
> haven't met no Archie Bunkers in my life.
>   The press does a lot of that. They like to categorize, you
> know. All the young black kids are Superfly, and all
> young middle-class white kids smoke pot and wear
> leather jackets, and all construction workers got flag de-

---

[17]Patrick J. Buchanan, *The New Majority,* (Philadelphia, 1973), p. 19.
Buchanan's book remains the best account of the Nixon strategy vs. the press
by a member of the administration. It also provides an excellent overview of
Nixon's political strategy, sans Watergate, for the 1972 campaign.

cals on their hats and beat long-hair kids over the head,
and all steel workers leave the mill there and go home in
a T-shirt and open up a can of beer and watch quiz programs and Westerns. That BS.

Sadlowski hits us where it hurts. There is nothing in
the forms of journalism or in our higher-income brackets
which compels a reporter to deal in stereotypes.
"Nevertheless," as Richard Harwood wrote in 1971, "the
mass media are still full of stereotypes, labels, cliches
and code words that confuse or mislead more than they
inform . . . We still talk about 'suburbia' and 'ghettos' as
if the geographical concepts had assembly-line characteristics. We still discourse on the 'middle class,' the
'military-industrial complex,' 'the poor' and the 'Eastern
Establishment' as if, like bottles of milk, they are
homogenous entities. We still hang on our politicians
empty labels such as 'liberal,' 'conservative,' 'hawk' and
'dove' as if we — and the audience out there — had some
clear idea of what these labels are intended to convey."[18]

Some of the most dangerous code words are non-
neutral words which are used as if they had a neutral
meaning. James Q. Wilson has taken deadly aim at misuses of the word, "reform," in an article which reminded
this reporter of his own sloppy use of the word on various
occasions. "To reform," as Wilson reminds us, "means to
improve by alteration, to abolish abuse or malpractice, to
make a change for the better. We all understand and
follow this usage when we speak of the reformed drunk,"
writes Wilson. ". . . Journalists and politicians understand none of this, however. To them, any change that is
broadly liberal or participatory in intent, and some
changes that are libertarian in intent, are 'reforms.' Now
such presumption is understandable in politicians, whose

[18]This quotation is from an article by Harwood for the *Washington Post* on
March 18, 1971, "Putting People Into Pigeonholes" that was reprinted in *Of
the Press, By the Press, For the Press (And Others Too)* by the Washington
Post Writers Group in 1974. The other Harwood quotations used in this
chapter are from an interview with the author.

vocation requires them to be propagandists, but is unfor-
givable in journalists, whose craft enjoins them to be
fair."[19] Wilson then gives several prevalent examples of
the misuse of the word, of which the most telling is "campaign reform." He also reminds us that many present
objects of "reform" — including prisons, the Interstate
Commerce Commission and the FBI — were themselves
"reforms" when proposed. I think that the drumfire in
behalf of "campaign spending reform" had a negative effect in 1974, when various Republican congressmen were
trying to disassociate themselves from the Nixon scandals by changing the campaign laws. More than one GOP
congressman of my acquaintance went along with
some of the most dubious provisions of the Federal campaign spending legislation to show that he truly believed
in "reform." Politicians of both parties are now trying in
the courts to reform this reform. Reporters, concludes
Wilson, should write "campaign spending laws" instead
of "campaign reform" and "party rules changes" instead
of "party reform" and "opposition candidates" instead of
"reform candidates." I hope that we all take his advice.

Some of the other biases relating to language are deeply ingrained. Stephen Hess, after absolving the press of
partisan bias, writes in the *Brookings Bulletin:* "The
Washington press corps over the years has exhibited a
stylistic bias. Reporters are most attracted to a political
style that might be characterized as elegant, urbane and
cosmopolitan. Ideology aside, they prefer a John Kennedy or a John Gardner to a Lyndon Johnson or a
Richard Nixon. Thus it is possible for a 'liberal' press to
be anti-McGovern and pro-Buckley." In my experience
the inelegant or non-urbane politician rarely understands this and is likely to attribute his "bad press" to the
ideology of the reporters who cover him.

All of the biases which have been discussed in this

---

[19]James Q. Wilson, "Abolish 'Reform'," *The Alternative: An American
Spectator,* (May 1975). This article was reprinted in the *Wasington Post.*

chapter, with the possible exception of the stylistic one, are open to correction. I do not take the view that we are so trapped by our traditions and our origins that we can do nothing about our prejudices. Instead, I think we have to be willing to proclaim our biases as a pre-condition for dealing with them. An editor, for instance, certainly can eliminate code words and stereotyped labels from stories which cross his desk. More positively, he can do what Harwood did in Trenton and send out reporters to write about the community. One result in the *Trenton Sunday Times* was a twenty-four page section on Chambersburg, the largely Italian-American section of the city. The section is an understanding and comprehensive document on the lives, customs, religion, politics, myths, history and values of the people and it deserves to be emulated on a regular basis by other newspapers. Orde Coombs' warm and searing accounts of a black middle class family fall in the same category. They were written as newsletters on an Alicia Patterson fellowship but would grace the pages of any newspaper.

I think that newspapers also can deal with the deficiencies of Objective Reporting without encouraging a nation of advocacy journalists and pamphleteers. One way is to insist on "fairness" as the guideline of sufficiency rather than on "objectivity." Objective Reporting, as we have seen, is a form which excuses its own deficiencies by an appeal to an undefined body of outside information known as "the facts." Its greatest bias is that it proclaims no bias at all. Fairness in its full meaning requires the reporter to be alert for biases, including his own. It requires the reporter to say, in the words of the late Peter Lisagor of the *Chicago Daily News,* "Hell, we're not created out of some kind of a cookie cutter that robs us of our biases and prejudices. We're talking about an unreal world if we believe we could produce a group of journalists who have no biases, prejudices, attitudes and outlooks." But Lisagor added: "There is a degree of professionalism we bring to our job and if there isn't, we

oughtn't to be here. Our papers oughtn't to have us here.
And we have no business in journalism." I believe that
most Americans readily will accept this notion of professionalism and of a standard of fair play which many of
them share. What they are unlikely to accept is some sort
of God-given neutral omnipotence which claims to see
the facts as they are without coloring or shading.
A true standard of fairness requires newspapers to
trust their reporters far more than many of them do.
Objectivity teaches reporters and editors alike to play it
safe. One 1964 study of advanced journalism students
showed that they tended to bend over backwards against
their prejudices when writing news stories. More damagingly, they also tended to "wash out" the highly colored
and opinionated material they had collected and replace
it with neutral content.[20] Reporters do this all the time in
their efforts to present a supposedly balanced story. A
"fairness" standard requires more of reporters in understanding and analysis while relieving them from a
mechanistic standard of balancing each quotation on one
side with a quotation on the other. This standard also is
more useful in dealing with a Joseph McCarthy or an L.
Fletcher Prouty, both of whom prompted stories that
were objective but unfair. Fairness permits a newspaper
or a network to withhold a story about unsubstantiated
charges or, alternatively, to frankly label stories as unsubstantiated in the opening sentence. A fairness standard also can help encourage reporters to make the daily
examination of underlying conditions which they now
are apt to reserve for a major "takeout" in the Sunday
section. And fairness would go a long way toward giving
newspaper readers a more representative picture of their
frequently unfair world.

---

[20]Jean S. Kerrick, Thomas E. Anderson and Luita B. Swales, "Balance and
the Writer's Attitude in News Stories and Editorials," *Journalism Quarterly,*
(1964).

CHAPTER FIVE

Limitations

"The press is a child – it is essentially an immature institution. It's a lovable little thing, distracted by bits of color and light, eager and irresponsible, honest in its simple way. And, it has trouble concentrating on more than one thing at a time.
– Richard Reeves in A FORD NOT A LINCOLN.

In the early years of television, and to some degree even now, television reporting seemed a joke to those of us whom the commentators call "the print media." We laughed at the hygienic smiles and the maroon (or blue, or yellow) jackets of the television correspondents and at their vacuous questions which betrayed a thirty-second acquaintanceship with the subject matter. Most of us did not consider them reporters at all. A friend of mine who mysteriously made the transition from print to television reporting in the early 1960s was driven to distraction by the conversation of his colleagues at a small California station. "Christ," he said, "they don't talk about the news at all. They talk about their hair pomade." John Lindsay of *Newsweek*, a fine all-purpose reporter who is known to political writers as "the *real* John Lindsay," has regaled planeloads of campaign correspondents with his portrayals of the mythological local television team of Larry Largelungs, who last reported a story for the AP fifteen years ago, and Terry Splendid (or Sterling Stunning), who is all teeth. Terry, full of ignorance and self-importance, usually asks presidential candidates tough questions like, "Senator, when did you first become a great man?"

This is not to say that we felt this way about everyone in television. Most of us were fans of Edward R. Murrow, for instance, and some of us mistakenly supposed he had been a newspaper reporter. But Murrow came from radio, and newspaper reporters of my age grew up with that medium. We may have made fun of Walter Winchell's broadcasts and Drew Pearson's predictions that proved 110 per cent accurate, but we listened seriously to Murrow, Elmer Davis, Edward P. Morgan and Charles Collingwood. They were part of our lives. Television we did not take seriously as a news medium, even though we theoretically were aware that it could transmit a picture of the world which went far beyond the printed page in vividness and immediacy. Perhaps there was a touch of envy in this, but I think it was mostly that we failed to appreciate the potential impact of television news once the techniques of the medium were mastered. We comforted ourselves with the supposed ignorance of the television correspondents and the belief that reporting meant writing for a newspaper. And we did not notice when television reporting began to change.

These remarks are the prelude to a heresy. The heresy is that television reporting, for all the things wrong with it, probably is doing a better job of bringing Americans the daily "bulletin" news than newspapers ever did. Television has the large vice of its own great virtue, which is that it is a visual medium and poorly suited to the transmission of ideas. But television does what newspapers almost never do by presenting news as a structured whole in which the events of the day are related to other events. Network news, in particular, is inevitably thematic. This is a development derived largely from necessity. Every broadcast journalist operates within what Fred Friendly calls "the time prison" of his medium. Sixty seconds is a long time on television. Within that time the television reporter must make an opening statement, present "both sides" of a controversial issue and summarize with a synthesizing statement. Ideally, this narrative melds with the accompanying visual images to form a dramatic whole. Most television

stories have a beginning, a middle and an end. By definition, the story is presented in a context, often a familiar
one to which the viewer can easily relate. Various critics
have pointed out that the contextual formulas acceptable
for television stories are limited and rely heavily on
stereotypes.[1] However worthwhile that criticism may be,
television at least starts with a context which is al-
together absent from most printed news stories.

A printed story, in the tradition of objective journalism, begins with a fact or with a lot of facts. Its form is
the "inverted pyramid" order with the most important
facts presented in the first paragraph and with the other
facts arranged in descending order of importance. Skillful reporters will squeeze in a phrase of context here, a
sentence of context there. But in its pure wire-service
form a news story is mostly an array of facts relating to
the event at hand rather than to any thematic issue.
Most newspapers consider this a satisfying form, perhaps
because they have used it so long. With some notable
exceptions, newspapers continue to use it while the percentage of Americans who obtain their news from television climbs steadily.[2] But this method of presenting information flies in the face of what the social scientists are
constantly telling us about the accumulation of knowledge. It took nearly 1,750 years from the birth of Christ
to double human knowledge. Human knowledge quad-

---

[1]See especially Epstein, *News From Nowhere*, pp. 164-65. Also see Paul
Weaver's essay, "Newspaper News and Television News" in *Television as a
Social Force: New Approaches to Criticism,* (Palo Alto, California, 1975).

[2]Surveys taken by the Roper Organization for the Television Information
Office show that 65 per cent of Americans said in November 1974 that they
get "most of their news" from television compared to 47 per cent who get it
from newspapers, 21 per cent from radio and 4 per cent from magazines. (The
numbers add up to more than 100 per cent because of people who gave
multiple answers.) The trend, with an occasional dip, has been moving in
favor of television since the surveys started in 1959 when 51 per cent obtained news from television, 57 per cent from newspapers, 34 per cent from
radio and 8 per cent from magazines.

rupled in the two centuries after that at the rate of once each half century. Today we are doubling human knowledge about once every six months. This accumulation overloads the traditional forms of conveying information. News is atomized and the chunks of information which big-city newspapers dish out to their readers every day usually lack the interrelatedness necessary to give them meaning. Often, I suspect, these readers, like the Communist prisoner in Arthur Koestler's *Darkness at Noon,* must suffer from "fatigue of the synapses." Certainly, any thinking reporter knows that some of his best stories go unread even by persons who have reason to read them. There is just too much unrelated information in a daily newspaper for even interested and enlightened readers to digest.

Take this typical example. On July 27, 1975, a wire-service story appeared in the *Denver Post* about the Senate's override of a health bill which had been vetoed by President Ford. The *Post* printed thirteen paragraphs of this story. Its lead says: "President Ford Saturday vetoed a $2 billion health bill which included funds for community mental health centers, rape prevention, treatment of hypertension and nurse's training. A few hours later the Senate voted 67 to 15 to override Ford's veto." The story goes on, in succeeding paragraphs, to describe the number of vetoes Ford has made and the number of times the Democratic Congress has failed to override them. It gives the cost and the purpose of the previous bill vetoed by the President. It also includes two paragraphs of quotation from Ford critical of the costs of the bill, which he said was "not consistent with development of an integrated, flexible health services delivery system." These paragraphs are balanced by two paragraphs of criticism of the veto by a spokesman for the American Nurses Association. The spokesman says "the veto indicates that the administration places a very low priority on the country's health needs." The story then gives the amounts of money allocated by the bill for treatment of hypertension, rape prevention and control, "home health demonstration agencies," and hemophilia treatment and blood separation centers. Without providing the dollar amounts the next paragraph states that the bill also allocates funds for government agencies which provide services for the mental health of the elderly, for epilepsy and Huntington's disease. The penultimate paragraph concerns what the story calls "one of the most controversial portions of the bill," a provision providing for a fine of up to $1,000 or a year in jail or both for any government official "who coerces abortion or sterilization by setting it as a condition for benefits." The concluding paragraph says that two similar bills were pocket-vetoed by Ford last year.

This is a representative wire-service story, and a fairly good one. In order to evaluate the wisdom of the veto, or have some idea what the legislation might mean, the reader must know on his own what a home-health demonstration agency is, and he also must have some idea of what Ford meant by an "integrated, flexible health services delivery system." This vague description is balanced in the story by the rhetoric of the American Nurses Association spokesman. Both of these statements are directed at mobilizing political action in behalf of the veto and the override, respectively; the story uses them to demonstrate the attitudes of "both sides" without explaining what the President's preferred "delivery system" is or why the veto indicates a low priority for health needs. The story fails to describe what rape control measures are envisioned or the dimension of the rape problem. It tells us nothing about hypertension, either, beyond the fact that $30 million is allocated for its treatment. There is no information on the history of any of these proposals or even a clue to the kind of medical treatment which is now being provided in the categories covered by the legislation. The selection of the Nurses Association spokesman's statement as the only criticism of the President's action might suggest that the nurses training aspect of the bill is the most important, but the reader cannot be sure. No figure is given on the amount of money the legislation would provide for nurse's training, let alone any material that would demonstrate the shortage of nurses, if there is one. Nor is there any mention about the probable fate of the veto in the House. The House action will be treated as a separate "spot" event when it occurs and the story about that event will recycle many of the paragraphs of this story. The reader who is trying to form his opinion of the wisdom of Ford's veto, or of the congressional override, must look to other sources for his information. He must provide the context for this wire-service story in the *Denver Post,* for the story itself does not.[3]

No doubt it is necessary for newspapers to provide this sort of "day story," with or without context. Norman Cherniss, the thoughtful executive editor of the *Riverside (Calif.) Press-Enterprise,* contends that it would be unwise for newspapers to operate on the premise that their readers had watched the television news the night before. He has a point, even if the majority of the readers have watched television news. Apart from the people who never watch the TV news or rarely watch it, there always are viewers who were late getting home the previous evening or who were answering the telephone during the television story on Ford's veto. And there also are readers who expect to find in the newspaper the next day the story which they saw on television or heard on radio. But it seems clear that these readers would be better informed if daily newspapers insisted that their stories of

---

[3]For this examination I deliberately used the AP story as it appeared in a representative newspaper rather than the wire copy itself which might have provided more detail in subsequent paragraphs. Few newspapers run more than thirteen paragraphs on any spot story, and this story was the longest national story on any spot event which appeared in the *Denver Post* on this date. One of the persistent problems with the inverted-pyramid story form is that contextual detail often is limited to the final two or three paragraphs, which means that it never appears in most newspapers.

events met some minimum contextual standard. "What we need is a steadier diet of contextual reporting," says James Hoge, editor of the *Chicago Sun-Times*. "There's a deep gap between the day story, which often has no context at all, and the social-significance takeout, which is full of it." Hoge maintains that he has a difficult time getting thematic coverage out of his Washington bureau. "Housing is an example," he says. "We don't get the stories unless there's a bill passed or a press conference held. What I want is a story on how the logjam on housing might be broken and traditional policies changed. I read it in the *Christian Science Monitor,* so I know it can be done."

However, there are many barriers of time and tradition to getting it done. Wire service reporters, for competitive reasons, have to write their stories immediately after the event or while it is still going on. The premium values of their trade are speed and factual accuracy, not research or thought. And daily newspaper reporters are mindful that the surefire way to page one often is to write a story as "hard" as possible, which means the old-fashioned, inverted pyramid approach with reams of facts listed in descending order of importance. In some cases, even at the *Washington Post,* reporters are encouraged to furnish a hard factual lead rather than one that is more explanatory, more evocative, more contextual. Usually, however, reporters don't have to be told that the "soft lead" is perilous. They know from experience the kinds of stories their editors want.

"What the editors want" is the product of a press tradition in which readers were valued only in the aggregate, as circulation. The creators of the penny press chose to derive their revenue from advertising and to sell their product to readers for less than it was worth. Newspapers accordingly developed a primary regard for advertisers, who paid the bill, and a secondary regard for readers, whose value was primarily as a means to more advertising. On the news side this limited opinion of readers was

incorporated into the maxims of reporting and handed
down from generation to generation of editors and reporters. One of the first instructions I received on a daily
newspaper was from an oldtimer who said that stories
should be written for the "dimestore girl." A Hearst
editor once instructed a chorus girl hired as a reporter in
San Francisco to write *her* stories for the gripman on the
Powell Street Cable car, adding, "Don't write a single
line he can't understand and wouldn't read."[4] And even
on the *New York Times,* writes Robert Darnton, "reporters used to believe that their editors expected them to
aim their stories at an imaginary twelve-year-old girl.
Some thought that she existed in *The Style Book of the
New York Times,* although she existed only in our
minds."[5] While several newspapers, especially the *New
York Times,* now write with a far more informed audience in mind, the tradition of reporting remains an-
chored to the audience of the lowest common denominator. The epitome of this approach in our time is
the *San Francisco Chronicle,* where a former editor was
quoted as comparing part of the paper to a circus barker
in front of a tent saying, "Hurry, hurry, hurry, the girls
are just about to take off their clothes." At the *Chronicle,*
presumably, it is a precocious twelve-year-old whom the
reporter keeps in mind.

Newspaper readers undervalue even more than they
are undervalued. Long before it became a staple in the
19th century saloons of America, the newspaper reader
had come to expect a free lunch. The reader's expectation
was based upon an assumption which lies deep within
the wellsprings of democracy that "the truth" is a discernible commodity which can and must be made available to a self-governing citizenry. It is recognized that
the ways in which the citizens presume to act upon this
truth will produce divisions. But the ready availability of

---

[4]Ishbel Ross, *Ladies of the Press,* (New York, 1936), pp. 61-62.
[5]Robert Darnton, "Writing News and Telling Stories," *Daedalus,* Spring
1975.

truthful information upon which the citizens can act usually is assumed into evidence. "This insistent and ancient belief that truth is not earned, but inspired, revealed, supplied gratis, comes out very plainly in our economic prejudices as readers of newspapers," Walter Lippmann wrote in *Public Opinion*. "We expect the newspaper to serve us with truth however unprofitable the truth may be. For this difficult and dangerous service, which we recognize as fundamental, we expected to pay until recently the smallest coin. . . . Nobody thinks for a moment that he ought to pay for his newspaper. He expects the fountains of truth to bubble, but he enters into no contract, legal or moral, involving any risk, cost or trouble to himself. He will pay a nominal price when it suits him, will stop paying whenever it suits him, will turn to another paper when that suits him. Somebody has said quite aptly that the newspaper editor has to be re-elected every day."

Lippmann went on to point out that this one-sided relationship between readers and the press leads the readers to judge a newspaper as they would a school or a church, not as a business. Newspaper readers are unwilling to pay directly for the news. They pay indirectly, through the prices paid for advertised commodities, but this payment is not thought of by the reader as a cost for his news. "The public pays for the press," concluded Lippmann, "but only when the price is concealed."

These words, written in 1922, have an additional validity in a television age. Even the penny press required readers to pay a pittance for the commodity of news. Television encourages its consumers to believe that the truth is not only cheap but free. Most people purchase television sets because they want entertainment, which has never been considered by its consumers as something that could be obtained without cost. They get the news, those of them who want it, as an added attraction at no extra cost.[6] And even more than newspapers, television

---

[6]Television news, of course, is far less revenue-producing than most televi-

maintains the illusion that truth is a discernible and definable commodity. Newspapers are shopping bags where the reader is likely to find conflicting truths. Even the "hardest" of new stories trails off into inconclusive detail which leaves some questions open and some truths unresolved. In contrast, the thematic form of television news has a beginning, a middle and an end and tends to finish even inconclusive stories with a conclusive statement. Walter Cronkite signs off every night by saying, "And that's the way it is." It is the ultimate ratification of the democratic notion that truth is revealed rather than earned.

Many consequences flow from this undervaluing of the news, one of which is the undervaluing of the journalistic craft itself. If the truth is a discernible commodity, anyone can be trusted to harvest it and dispense it to the public. Since this function was not perceived as requiring particular talent or professional training, journalists could be, and were, hired and maintained on the cheap. Most of them were neither trained nor taught to engage in intellectual enterprises that could not be related readily to the dimestore girl. Those that were trained or talented often tired of the low pay scales, if not of the repetitive processes of journalism. Modern publishers and editors often act as if this is a problem of the past, and they observe that reporters today are better paid and better educated than they ever used to be. That is true enough, and it is true, also, that the achievements of investigative journalism have made the profession profoundly attractive for young people. But the traditions of the news business die hard, and these traditions are neither intellectual nor analytical. Ben Bradlee is fond of saying that the good reporter is the one who sees the sun

---

sion entertainment, as network executives never tire of reminding their news division directors. As Fred Friendly points out in *Due To Circumstances Beyond Our Control*, some of these costs of the news are due to bookkeeping devices in which the news division is charged part of the cost for facilities the network would need even if it gave no news.

as it is rising, not as it goes down. Unfortunately, the track record of most newspapers most of the time would indicate that reporters and editors prefer watching sunsets. "Journalism follows more than it leads," writes Garry Wills. "And the competition to follow more closely is part of the fun in watching journalists or in being one."

The record of 20/20 hindsight applies to many of the great issues of our time — the black revolution, the women's movement, the Vietnam War, the flight from the cities, school busing, the development of a nuclear technology. One characteristic of all these issues is that they were neglected until they became "in" — and they were then covered widely to the exclusion of other issues. Once they became "out," they were covered by very few newspapers.

Newspapers are oriented to vogues, to what the late Stewart Alsop called "fashions in the news." Most newspapers do not have an editor whose function simply is to think — to anticipate stories or trends of consequence, to browse the scientific literature, to ponder about the political issues that might be raised after the next session of Congress or the next election. And while many newspapers internally preach the virtue of "follow-up," few newspapers have anyone who is systematically responsible for this function. How many newspapers have done significant articles on the developments which have occurred in black communities a decade after the urban riots?[7] How many newspapers have explored the changes which have occurred in that once fashionable institution, the Peace Corps? How many newspapers have evaluated the success of civic or educational programs introduced in their own communities with great fanfare? How many reporters know that the United States had an energy

---

[7]Roger Wilkins, of the *New York Times* editorial board, wrote persuasively in the July 1975 issue of *MORE* that most editors have little more grasp of the problems in minority communities than they did in 1965. "In fact," he adds, "editors may now be less capable of handling the racial story effectively because they think they've been covering it all along and there is a tendency to overestimate how much they actually know."

crisis in the 1920s? Lack of historical perspective and
follow-up creates at every turn a horizonless journalism,
which means that every new development is treated as if
it were a bolt from the blue. James Reston, writing about
the "woefully slow" response of newspapers to the energy
crisis, said: "All the facts were available to us months
and even years before the Arab oil embargo. They were
published in the official reports of the federal government, the United Nations and even the Petroleum Institute every month. With seven per cent of the world's
population in the United States, we were consuming over
thirty per cent of the world's gas and oil. We knew something about the law of supply and demand, but were insisting on selling our products to the highest bidder while
assuming that oil producers wouldn't do the same. . . .
This was a problem not for heroic editors who could confront the mobs, but for thoughtful editors who could read
and analyze the facts and trends, but we didn't really pay
much attention to the problem until the Arab embargo
forced us to line up at the corner gas station."[8]

There is no single answer to the problem of horizonless
journalism, although I think newspapers might give
serious thought to employing a "futures editor" who
would be concerned with issues near the end of the hori-
zon or over it. Haynes Johnson of the *Washington Post*
suggests that newspapers waste a good part of their limited resources by insisting on having their own people
cover routine stories when use of the wire services would
save both time and money. "It's the psychology of the
news business," he says. "We allow ourselves to be trapped by today and by the competitive desire to have our
man on a particular story, even though the fact is that
our man could be used profitably in a much different way
and the wire service could be used for the routine, headline coverage of the news. And I think it's an attitude.

---

[8]From an address in 1975 at Colby College, where Reston was honored as
the 22nd Elijah Parish Lovejoy fellow.

One of the big problems is that editors have a stake in assignment of their men to stories; it helps their careers. Reporters have a stake in being on a story, or think they do, and in being in the paper regularly when in fact it might be better to be in once a week rather than seven times a week if that once a week is really suberb and says something that makes some sense. We need to take the routine coverage and boil it down and not worry about the pride of organization. The way you really distinguish yourself is the insight you give to news and to events."

CHAPTER SIX

The Commercial Connection

*A newspaper is a private enterprise owing
nothing whatsoever to the public, which grants
it no franchise. It is therefore affected with no
public interest. It is emphatically the property of
the owner, who is selling a manufactured product at his own risk. . . .*
                              – William P. Hamilton of the
                                 WALL STREET JOURNAL

Many years ago William Allen White of the *Emporia
Gazette* wrote that journalism used to be "a noble calling;
now it is an eight per cent investment and an industry."
Newspapers, in the argot of the men and women who buy
and sell them, are "properties" — and very valuable
properties at that. Newspaper advertising, which has
been rising steadily since World War II at a rate exceeding inflation, now brings in $8 billion a year. The typical
newspaper, depending on what figures are used, realizes
annual profits ranging from twelve per cent to twenty-
three per cent.[2] What has changed in the forty years

---

[1]Quoted in Theodore Peterson, "The Social Responsibility of the Press,"
Four Theories of the Press, (Urbana, Illinois, 1963), p. 73.

[2]Profit margins for twenty publicly owned U.S. and Canadian newspapers
in fiscal 1975 averaged 8.7 per cent, nearly twice the 4.7 per cent average
estimated by the Federal Trade Commission for U.S. manufacturing as a
whole. But the averages do not tell the full story. Such organizations as the
Thomson Newspapers lived up to their owner's description as "cash boxes"
with a 17.6 per cent profit margin to lead the industry. Near the other end of
this profit spectrum were the *New York Times,* with a 3.1 per cent profit
margin, and the Washington Post Co., with 3.9 per cent. Many family-owned
newspapers of moderate size are believed to return profits in the range of the
Thomson Newspapers margin or higher, but the data to support this belief is
spotty. Most newspaper publishers do not include a report on their profits
within the definition of the information that their readers have "a right to
know."

since White issued his indictment of newspaper commercialism is that newspapers have become vastly more profitable, largely because of a trend toward chain ownership and one-newspaper towns. Less than three per cent of American cities now have competing daily newspapers, and in half of these competing cities the papers are published under a joint printing arrangement with joint advertising rates that encourage or force advertisers to buy space in both papers. The printing presses in many of these non-competitive cities might as well be printing money as newspapers.

In considering the commercial context of reporting it is well to remember that the *New York Times* and the *Washington Post* are not the norms of American newspapers. Neither are the competitive Chicago newspapers, the *New York Daily News,* the *Los Angeles Times,* the *Baltimore Sun,* the *Boston Globe,* the *St. Petersburg Times* or the *Louisville Courier-Journal.* Nor are such excellent small newspapers as the *Riverside (Calif.) Press-Enterprise,* the *Pine Bluff (Ark.) Commercial* or the *Mountain Eagle* of Whitesburg, Kentucky. What these newspapers, all of which perform different functions in different ways, have in common is a devotion to the untypical notion that a private newspaper is a public trust. Except for the *Mountain Eagle,* these newspapers are able to combine this devotion with money making, sometimes even at the expense of countinghouse newspapers. "The source of the profits is obvious," Ben Bagdikian has written. "The country is rich, it is reading and it is interested in public affairs. The source of underlying trouble with newspapers is almost as obvious: most of them are riding this easy tide, complacent in their monopoly status, without making basic reforms that they and the readers deserve."[3] These words were written nearly a decade ago, and they are even more true today. Hundreds of American newspapers fill up the spaces around their

[3]Ben H. Bagdikian, *The Effete Conspiracy and Other Crimes by the Press,* (New York, 1972), p. 7.

advertisements with wire copy or cheaply purchased
syndicate material, secure in the knowledge that readers
have no recourse other than to watch the nightly news.
(The economics of television news are another scandal
but beyond the scope of this book. The reader is referred
to *Due to Circumstances Beyond Our Control* by Fred
Friendly or *News From Nowhere* by Edward Jay Epstein.) Newspaper readers do, of course, watch the
nightly news but they are dependent upon their newspapers for local news, sports, comics, menus, weather reports, tide tables and advertisements. Nothing can force
a monopoly countinghouse newspaper to adopt a standard of excellence except a publisher who has such a
standard himself.

Monopoly newspapers are not an unmitigated evil. In
some instances the profits they provide have encouraged
publishers to spend more on the news side of the business
and to hire better reporters and editors. The security of a
monopoly position also has prompted a few publishers to
take advanced positions on issues without the necessity
of appealing to the lowest common denominator of their
readership. Dick Harwood, who is more sanguine than I
am about the constructive character of monopolies, believes that corporate-owned newspapers often show "a
greater sense of responsibility and of public accountability" than the family newspapers they have replaced. Bill
Moyers, a director of the Texas-based group of Harte-
Hanks newspapers, thinks that publicly held corpora-
tions are less subject to the whims of individual publishers and thus tend to be more fair-minded. But the
trend toward one-newspaper communities has all but
eliminated the basic option of the reader, which was to
buy a competing paper if he didn't like what he read. It
undoubtedly is true that many of the monopoly papers
are more responsible than many of the competitive
newspapers they absorbed, ruined or replaced. But this is
a misleading argument, since most newspaper readers of
the past did not rely upon a single paper for their infor-

mation. According to a survey cited by Walter Lippmann, sixty-seven per cent of Chicagoans used to read two or three newspapers and another eighteen per cent read from four to eight newspapers. Only fourteen per cent read a single newspaper.[4] This survey was taken in 1916, when daily newspapers reached a peak of 2,461. The number has been declining ever since, with the greatest periods of decline coming during the Depression and the two world wars. At the end of 1974 there were only 1,768 daily newspapers in the United States, slightly above the all-time low.[5] But the decline in newspaper readership is greater than this statistic shows. In the past two decades, while television has become the chief source of news, the per capita circulation of newspapers has been plummeting. According to census data, newspaper circulation in 1950 was 1.24 papers per household. It dropped to 1.12 papers by 1960 and to 0.99 papers by 1970 and is still dropping. Most Americans who read newspapers today read no more than one newspaper, and a number do not read any paper at all.

The trend to monopoly has left its mark upon the craft of reporting. Traditionally, newspaper reporters were poorly paid, highly independent and nomadic. A reporter with professional competence could move easily from one metropolitan paper to another, and there were plenty of papers to move to. Reporters are better paid today, but they are likely to have fewer job options within the news business. A reporter who works for a satellite or suburban daily often can advance to the nearest metropolitan daily or find a job on a metropolitan daily in another region. But a mid-career reporter who has made it to a metropolitan daily and finds it to be a countinghouse newspaper is apt to have limited alternatives. He can

---

[4]Quoted by Walter Lippmann in *Public Opinion,* p. 37. It is taken from a survey by W.D. Scott in *The Psychology of Advertising,* (1916), pp. 226-248.

[5]According to figures in *Editor & Publisher,* December 1974. There were 1,449 evening newspapers with a total circulation of 35,732,231 and a total of 340 morning newspapers with total circulation of 26,114,966.

reconcile himself to the mediocrity of his newspaper (which he is more apt to do if he is mediocre journalist); he can leave the business (which he is more apt to do if he is talented, or money-motivated, or both); or he can find a spot on the dozen or so exceptional newspapers in the country (which he is more apt to do if he is lucky). All of the really good newspapers in this country, and even some which aren't so good, are deluged by applications from disillusioned reporters who want to use their talents to better purposes. The prospects of most of them are not good. There are many more applications at the good papers than there are jobs, and the job turnover is likely to be quite low. The *Washington Post,* for instance, in 1976 had 162 reporters and 129 editors employed in its news operation. The *Post* has more than 2,500 applications a year for these jobs. And only 18 reporters and editors were hired in 1976, less than the number of job applications on many days.

When George Seldes wrote *Freedom of the Press* in 1935 he documented the efforts of newspaper publishers, individually and in combination, to block legislation requiring truth in drug and patent-medicine advertising. He also showed how American newspapers had withheld stories about scientific reports which even then demonstrated the dangers of smoking cigarettes. And he recalled the "contract of silence" first disclosed by William Allen White which patent-medicine advertisers had inserted in their contracts with newspapers: "It is mutually agreed that this contract is void if any law is enacted by your state restricting or prohibiting the manufacture or sale of propietary medicines." If the reader is tempted to think of this as a voice of the past, let him ask himself some questions about his own daily newspaper. When is the last time he has seen a story comparing prices of products sold at different stores in his community? Or an analysis of the practices and policies of local automobile dealers? Or a story about the pricing and marketing policies of grocery store chains, which often charge higher prices for certain items in the poorest sections of the community they serve? When the then-irregularly published *San Francisco Bay Guardian* a few years ago cracked the secret dating code used by supermarkets in the San Francisco Bay area, it was performing a service which most dailies would never attempt. But the *Bay Guardian* had no grocery advertising, one of the mainstays of the daily newspaper. Ben Bagdikian maintains that "corporate policy making in newspapers has shaped news policy" and that newspapers have not looked critically at business practices in the cities where they are published. "Newspapers for decades have concentrated on 'welfare cheaters' and burglars, while ignoring commercial enterprises that killed people with unsafe medicines and unsafe automobiles, or cheated consumers of billions of dollars with price fixing and manipulation of regulatory agencies," wrote Bagdikian. "The racial caste system and poverty have existed in an affluent society dedicated to equality and equal justice partly because newspapers and broadcasters have had built-in biases over what is news and what is important. For years newspapers have rejected staff members who wanted to report on such severe social pathologies. Race and poverty become news only when they become violent."[6] Or as Morton Mintz, my colleague at the *Washington Post* has put it in a codification he calls Mintz's Mass Media Proposition: *If it's really important, it doesn't get the attention it deserves, or gets it late, or gets it only because some oddball pushes it.* The early successes of Ralph Nader were almost entirely made of issues which the newspapers had it in their power to investigate but which they largely ignored. Nader's achievements are a constant rebuke to the lack of vigilance, courage and independence which distinguishes most American newspapers.

If the foregoing seems to have an "anti-business" tone to it, it is not because I think that business is more

---

[6]Bagdikian, *The Effete Conspiracy*, p. xiii.

worthy of investigation than any other institution. What
I do think is that most newspaper publishers have failed
to apply the same critical tests to the people who pay
their bills that they do to others even though many publishers are principled enough to stand up to direct pressure from advertisers. One of the most pro-business publishers I know literally hurled an advertiser out of his
office when he tried to use his considerable business with
the newspaper as a lever to influence the publisher to
oppose a school bond issue which would raise commercial
property taxes. However, publishers are generally big
businessmen who tend to share the views and the
blindspots of their class. They eat and drink with other
executives, belong to the same clubs and send their children to the same schools. The simplest and most probable
cause of the pro-business bias of most newspapers is that
publishers are businessmen themselves.

While newspapers usually eschew critical coverage of
the business community, they can rise to action in behalf
of issues which serve their own business. The most
notorious example is the so-called Newspaper Preservation Act, which is, as Peter Barnes has written, "like a
license to create an unregulated monopoly." Though the
testimony on this legislation failed to demonstrate that
the act would preserve any newspapers, it was voted
through after a vigorous lobbying effort by newspaper
publishers in 1970. The law originally allowed forty-four
newspapers in twenty-two cities to pool profits and fix
prices without any worry about prosecution under the
anti-trust laws.[7] I was covering Congress at the time and
remember at least three Congressmen who told me off
the record that the bill was a "turkey" but that they
would vote for it because of publisher pressure. One in-

---

[7]The Justice Department in 1975 allowed the two daily newspapers in
Anchorage, Alaska to merge, thus extending the law to twenty-three cities
and forty-six papers. A major court challenge to the law was averted in San
Francisco on May 23, 1975 when the morning *Chronicle* and afternoon
Examiner settled a lawsuit for $1.35 million rather than risk a court test. Of
this amount, $500,000 went to the *Bay Guardian*, which launched the suit.

fluential Democratic congressman with a liberal reputation, Phillip Burton of San Francisco, told me that he was going to vote against the bill, then walked on the floor and voted for it. Many of the congressmen who went the other way did so in defiance of extreme lobbyist pressure. A California congressman named John Rousselot was by coincidence talking to me at a press reception in one of the House office buildings when the bells rang signifying the final House vote on the Newspaper Preservation Act. Rousselot was under pressure from the publisher of his newspaper in Pasadena to vote for the bill. He also knew that the measure would pass, a situation in which many congressmen "vote their district" by rationalizing that their own vote will not make any difference to the outcome. However, Rousselot is a dedicated conservative (and a lifelong member of the John Birch Society, which has its national headquarters in his district) who takes seriously his beliefs that government should not interfere in business affairs, either for better or for worse. He voted against the bill, which carried by a 292-87 vote. Many of the eighty-seven votes were cast by principled congressmen of the Left (men like Ab Mikva of Illinois, Don Edwards of California, Don Fraser of Minnesota) or by principled congressmen of the Right (Rousselot, John Schmitz of California, John Ashbrook of Ohio). With a few distinguished exceptions the less-quixotic politicians of the Center stuck with their publishers, who in this battle demonstrated a greater devotion to their profits than to the First Amendment.

It is unlikely that an industry which wants anti-trust exemptions for itself is going to press very hard for enforcement of anti-trust laws against others, and most newspapers have not so pressed. But it is in their own communities, rather than in the national legislative arena, that the business bias of newspapers has proved most damaging. The old slogan of General Electric — "progress is our most important product" — might well have been the slogan for many community newspapers in

the post-World War II decades, particularly in the fast
growing regions of the West and South. "Progress" invariably meant more people, more homes, more stores, more
roads, more schools — and more circulation, more advertising and higher advertising rates. I lived in California
throughout this growth period, about half the time in
burgeoning suburban communities. One of these communities was San Jose, which lies in the center of a valley that was once so beautiful that it used to be called
"the Valley of Heart's Delight." No one calls it that anymore. With the enthusiastic boosterism of the *San Jose
Mercury-News* this Santa Clara Valley was turned into a
nightmare of urban sprawl and uncontrolled development that has become sort of a model for planners on how
not to build a city. The *Mercury-News,* interested in profits and in circulation, formed a tight political alliance
with the city government and especially with a public
relations man turned city manager who was uncritically
devoted to growth at any cost. The newspaper supported
every annexation, every replacement of an orchard with
a shopping center or a gas station. Some of the public
officials in Santa Clara County became worried about the
rate of growth and the way it was being accomplished,
but their voices were rarely heard in the *Mercury-News.*
Opponents of pending annexations had an even more
difficult time getting their views published in the paper.
Annexations were seen by the city and by the newspaper
as an unmitigated good which expanded both municipal
revenues and newspaper circulation. No truly ambitious
reporter would touch the city hall beat with a ten-foot
pole if he could help it, knowing that this was the most
policy-oriented and least free assignment on a newspaper
which on most other beats did not impose policy
guidelines upon reporters. One of the city's favorite annexation tactics was to lure faraway landowners to become part of San Jose on the promise of extending sewer
service and giving them a favorable rezoning. These
sewer lines were run out to the annexing property

alongside miles of intervening orchards. When the far-away land became annexed to the city and was rezoned, the intervening land often was reassessed at such a high rate of taxation that it ultimately became uneconomic to use it for farming purposes. This land, too, yielded to homes and gas stations, usually in strips and patches of uneven development. San Jose's population increased from 95,280 in 1950 to 204,196 in 1960 and to 446,537 in 1970. Santa Clara County's population had by 1970 exceeded a million. Most of the orchards were gone, the wineries were moving away and a pall of smog frequently hung over the valley. While it would be unfair to blame the newspaper for the population growth that was characteristic of California in the two post-war decades, it is fair to say that the *Mercury* was until the mid-1960s almost totally oblivious to the effects of the unregulated growth it was encouraging. In the spirit of countinghouse newspapers everywhere the eyes of its owner were fixed firmly on the dollar signs of increased advertising and circulation growth. While the Valley of Heart's Delight was turned into a Northern California replica of Los Angeles, the morning *Mercury* and its companion evening paper, the *News*, became two of the richest papers in the country.

Though the *Mercury-News* was unreservedly for development, it took a different tack in the late 1960s when the meatpacking firm of Swift and Co. tried to locate one of its plants in an industrially zoned area near the modern fountain-decorated newspaper plant. Believing that the Swift plant would have an adverse effect on his own property, *Mercury-News* publisher Joseph B. Ridder vowed to stop Swift. Immediately, a newspaper campaign reminiscent of the old Hearst days in San Francisco was organized. Reporters were sent to the Midwest to inspect other Swift plants and to grind out horror stories about what happened to communities in which packing plants were located. The "packing plants," as *Mercury-News* stories usually had referred to such facilities, were never called packing plants again. Editors and reporters were instructed to use the less euphemistic word of "slaughterhouse" in stories about the Swift plant. And there were reams of stories, all of them unfavorable to Swift. But the *Mercury-News* did not stop at an editorial crusade. The newspaper's political editor, Harry Farrell, was sent out to revive a moribund homeowner's association which launched a "popular protest" against the Swift plant. At no time did the newspaper inform its readers of its own interest in stopping the Swift plant, let alone that it was behind the supposed popular uprising of the homeowners. One editor suggested that the newspaper would be on better ground if it frankly admitted its own stake in the battle, but the publisher did not accept the suggestion. Instead, he and the executive editor pressed reporters on a variety of unrelated beats for sidebar stories critical of Swift in particular and of slaughterhouses in general. One of these assignments came to me in Sacramento, where I was the state capitol correspondent and normally unbothered by any editor. I was told to send in a story about the impact of a small slaughterhouse on the even smaller, rundown town of Broderick across the Sacramento River. What I filed was an attempt at whimsy which began, "You can follow your nose to the XYZ Packing Plant at Broderick. . . ." As best I remember, the story included a random sample of local quotes, most of them disinterested in the slaughterhouse or mildly favorable to its presence in Broderick, which had little else. One citizen, asked her opinion of the slaughterhouse, said, "It depends on the way the wind is blowing." Another replied, "What slaughterhouse?" This story never appeared in the *Mercury-News*, being considered too lighthearted for the anti-Swift crusade.

Joe Ridder won his battle against Swift, and I am glad that he did. This story has been related not as an example of the great wrongs done to meatpackers but as a demonstration of what a community newspaper can do when it is aroused in its own self-interest. What was immediately at stake in the Swift fight was the environment of the area around the *Mercury-News*. However, conservationists who didn't give a hoot for Ridder also opposed the Swift plant, fearing that its sewage runoff would cause further damage to the fragile environment of the narrow southern end of San Francisco Bay. The *Mercury-News* gave these conservationists a forum which they rarely had enjoyed before and which they used to good advantage.

On issues affecting Bay development, the Swift campaign probably made the *Mercury-News* a more community-oriented newspaper than it had been before. The paper gave full coverage and good play to the many stories I wrote from Sacramento on legislation aimed at giving the people of the Bay region some long-needed control over shoreline development. The *Mercury-News* ran more stories than any Bay area newspaper on this bill and eventually supported it editorially. After many delays and strong opposition from some industries the legislation was passed and signed into law by Ronald Reagan. The *Mercury-News* also supported the legislation of a San Jose congressman, Don Edwards, which established a wildlife a refuge at the south end of the Bay. This, too, passed after various delays. And the newspaper ran a series of articles on the Bay by environmental writer Gil Bailey and other articles by his successor, Tom Harris, which rank among the finest pieces of their kind published by California newspapers in recent years.

But one wonders what the Santa Clara Valley would be like today if the *Mercury-News* had shown some of this same environmental consciousness during the years when the orchards were being torn down to make way for the crazy-quilt development and the urban sprawl. As a former resident of San Jose and a former employee of the *Mercury*, I can't help but feel that both the community and the newspaper would be better off if the annexations and the related issues had been considered as debatable

propositions worthy of full and fair coverage rather than
as business interests in need of uncritical promotion. It
seems clear that many of the amenities which attracted
people to San Jose in the first place could have been preserved if the newspaper had cared as much about the
public's environment as it did its own.

Unfortunately, the San Jose story is not unique.
Newspapers in any developing community are tempted
for economic reasons to identify with "progress" for its
own sake and for theirs. Newspaper readers need some
greater reliance than an occasional outburst of enlightened self-interest from publications which are businesses first and newspapers second. This reliance is unlikely to be found in any newspaper code of ethics, no
matter how nobly inspired. "(A journalist's) code of ethics
are all right so long as they do not menace newspaper
profits; the moment they do, the business manager, now
quiescent, will begin to grow again." Those words were
written by H.L. Mencken in 1927.[8] They are still true.
Even less can reliance be found in government regula-
tion. I would hope that the courts would continue to hold
that laws requiring newspapers to give access are a violation of the First Amendment. The "cure" of government
intervention to this end seems to me to be far worse than
any of the existing diseases. The press council is another
remedy frequently suggested as a means of bringing citizen pressure to bear on a supine, delinquent or unfair
newspaper. However, there seems to be a tendency to
form local press councils in communities, such as
Minneapolis-St. Paul and Riverside, California, where
the newspapers already are responsive to the public
rather than in the communities of greatest need. Working on much the same principle, the National News
Council has restricted itself to evaluating complaints

---

[8]H.L. Mencken, *Prejudices: Sixth Series,* (New York, 1927). Mencken's
essay on "Journalism in America," from which this quotation is taken, was
reprinted in *Prejudices: A Selection,* (New York, 1955), made by James T.
Farrell.

against the networks, the wires and a handful of national newspapers. It is likely to be a long time, if ever, before press councils are put to the formidable test of dealing with the problems created by countinghouse newspapers.

The only sensible alternative which our system has been able to devise is that bedrock reliance of capitalism, competition. I would agree with Bruce Brugmann, the publisher of the San Francisco *Bay Guardian* that "in the long haul only an influential competing newspaper can keep another newspaper honest — not a television station, not a magazine, not a review board." The trouble with Brugmann's Law of Journalism, as he immodestly refers to it, is that the high costs of starting a newspaper and the newspaper industry's success in getting government to ratify its own monopolies makes such competition less likely than ever before. Maybe what we need are more Brugmanns, who began the *Bay Guardian* with raised capital of $50,000 and the old newspaper passion for printing the news and raising hell. As Brugmann puts it: "The defense of journalism as more than a business and as more than a monopoly — though a business it is and a monopoly it has become — is properly the journalists' duty. It is they who must understand that many (but certainly not all) of the basic problems are attributable to the exigencies of business monopoly as applied to the gathering of information and as applied to the dissemination of information, which once was considered so important that it was granted constitutional privilege and protection. The journalist has both a professional and a public obligation to look after his inheritance."

CHAPTER SEVEN

Frustrations

The lead of a story should be a one-sentence paragraph. The second and third paragraphs should be two sentences each and the fourth paragraph should be one or three sentences to make variety. Then back to the paragraphs of two sentences.

The verb of the lead must be transitive and in the active voice.

The lead must never start with a participial phrase, which slows up the tempo.

And remember, you are writing international politics so it can be understood by the Kansas City Milkman. If the Kansas City Milkman can't understand it, the dispatch is badly written.

–From THE KANSAS CITY MILKMAN
by Reynolds Packard[1]

A friend of mine, with several children, has a sign up on the door of his house which says: BALLOONING IS MY SECOND FAVORITE PARTICIPATORY SPORT. I suppose this is a fair summation of the way I feel about the news business. A reporter's life is a good one, and for people who can write quickly and be reasonably careful with the facts, the news business provides great fun and a satisfying challenge. Most people I know in the business share a feeling that they are participating in a worthwhile enterprise. Probably, most of them love their work. But many reporters and editors, particularly those who are older, become acutely conscious that they do not have very much to show for what they've done. Until recently, most of these reporters and editors also felt underpaid,

[1] Reynolds Packard, *The Kansas City Milkman*, (New York, 1950), pp. 15-16.

and a number of them still do. They worry about deadline pressures, about their stories and about their families, not necessarily in that order. Here is Dick Harwood, an accomplished journalist who has functioned as reporter, editor and press critic, talking about the frustrations of the news business:

> The newspaper business, until recent years, didn't pay that well. When I was younger, I was bothered that I didn't make enough money. I have been bothered, at times, by the fact that the job is so demanding you have no time for your family. I've been bothered, again in the rush of life and of professional life, that there isn't time to do the reading you'd like to do, there isn't time to do a lot of things you'd like to do. I guess I've been frustrated at times that I haven't written books. I've been frustrated, at times, by the feeling of the impermanence of your work which, quite literally, the next day somebody has wrapped a fish in. I think those have been my main concerns. I have not had those great gnawing professional worries in the last fifteen or twenty years that I'm not allowed to do the great story I'd like to do, or that editors are insensitive and dumb — that kind of thing. In a professional sense I've really had no great complaints. Time is tough and producing stories on deadlines and covering a campaign is a crazy way to work, but I don't know of a better way to do it. Overall, I would say it's a very satisfying life. And what makes it especially satisfying to me is that papers are getting better all the time, and the people we work with are getting better all the time. I can really see the quality.

Newspapering is especially satisfying on those papers which encourage reporters to reach out and add an extra dimension to their stories. That, and the pervading sense of professional freedom, is what I like best about the *Washington Post.* The other side of the coin, however, is that great newspapers also create great pressures on professionals to do a better job every day. On the *Post,* for instance, the keen competition to get into the paper creates a driving, harried atmosphere which produces good professional results but is tough on the people who produce them. "It's scary to see," says Margot Hornblower, one of the top young reporters at the *Post*. "One minute a person is a fairly important sub-editor, the next he's in Prince George's County. You can never really relax. When you do a good story, there's kind of a joke that an editor says to you, 'What have you got for us tomorrow?' He's kidding, but he means it, too. You can't rest on your laurels." Hornblower, who started as a metro reporter and is now on the Post's national staff, believes that this atmosphere keeps reporters alert and hard working but takes its toll on personalities and is at least partly responsible for the high divorce rate. "There's a danger of becoming one-dimensional, of not taking enough time for your husband or your family," she says. "You don't feel you can take time off."

These pressures also are felt by the managers and the editors at the *Post*, perhaps in even greater measure. "Sometimes I'm in a Miss Lonelyhearts position where people with their marital problems or their heads not screwed on straight or career problems all come in and want some help," says managing editor Howard Simons. "And I give them help the best I can." One reason that Simons gets these calls is that he and editor Ben Bradlee maintain an open-door policy at the *Post* where anyone from copy aide to publisher can talk to them at nearly any time. Bradlee is well aware in his own life that the news business exacts a heavy personal price. "Just as we are blessed with families, we are cursed with families," he says. "Many reporters feel, and properly, that they've got to get home, that they've visited on their families really heavy, heavy burdens. You know what I'm talking about. Always late, never predicting that you can be anywhere at any given time because some sonofabitch of an editor is going to make you do this or ask you to rewrite that or send you the hell out of town. And I think that reporters get their ears bent by their wives, who say, 'Goddamn it you're never home, you don't even know

your children.' And I don't think it's any accident that
Woodward and Bernstein were both divorced. I just don't
think it's an accident at all."

On big newspapers the natural pressures of the business are compounded by bureaucratic organization.
Bureaucracies at newspapers behave much like other
bureaucracies, reinforcing institutional values and
blocking or diverting those who appear to pose a threat to
the system. Many reporters are sensitive to these characteristics of bureaucracy when they write about the government or about trade unions. But no newspaper of
which I am aware has subjected itself to rigorous
analysis from this perspective and then acknowledged
that its decisions are often bureaucratic ones based on
institutional needs. One person who tried to make this
analysis was a sociologist, Chris Argyris, who conducted
an extensive study of the bureaucracy at a major metropolitan newspaper and the pressures it produced upon
the editors and reporters. The newspaper was the *New
York Times,* but Argyris operated under an agreement to
keep the paper's name anonymous. His book about the
study, *Behind the Front Page,* called the newspaper the
Daily Planet. Because of its sociological jargon, *Behind
the Front Page* is an unnecessarily difficult book to read.
It also is a most worthwhile book, for it reveals the attitudes of fear, hostility and resistance to change which
permeate the newsroom. Under an agreement with the
newspaper's management Argyris held a series of seminars intended to change these attitudes. The seminars
eventually were discontinued, apparently because of the
objections of key *Times* executives, but not before Argyris had recorded on tape the hopes and fears of the men
and women caught up in the bureaucratic system. I am
not qualified to judge whether Argyris' methods of talking out the problems in a structured way would produce
better newspapers or happier newspaper people. What I
do know is that the anonymous comments of editors and
reporters which he brings us in *Behind the Front Page*

would seem familiar to anyone who has ever worked on a metropolitan daily. As Jim Hoge, editor of the *Chicago Sun-Times* puts it: "Newsrooms look like such communal places, but they really aren't. What Argyris described rang true for any newspaper shop I've ever seen." The reporters at the *Daily Planet* are competitive, distrustful of one another, self-centered, pessimistic about changing the system and totally committed to satisfying their own goals. Here are some of the things that the twenty reporters whom Argryis interviewed said into his tape recorder:

"If your name appears in the paper a lot then your ego is massaged a lot. If it doesn't appear very much you get jittery."

"If you have a good story, you've got to be very careful someone doesn't steal it from you."

"There is no teamwork in this business. The name of the game is competition."

(Reporters are) "at the edge of influencing events . . . it is always a problem to make sure you don't go over the edge."

"We want to be observers or analysts and not participants. We have this godlike role where we can function professionally as a god. And we make our own psychological deal to cop out when it affects us personally. Maybe this is all bullshit."

"There's really a fine sense of satisfaction when we really find out something that even embarrasses people."

"I had a story two days ago that embarrassed the hell out of N. I wrote it with relish. I knew that he would be embarrassed and he *was* embarrassed. I just hope I haven't lost a news source."

Argyris divides the reporters he interviewed into three categories: The Traditional Reporter, whose first commandment is "to be objective and to get the facts;" the Reporter-Researcher, who wants "to dig beneath the surface of events to find the critical but half-hidden forces that were shaping events;" and the Reporter-Activist, who wishes "to use journalism to change or shake up the world." The first three quotations above are from traditional reporters but are shared by reporters in all three groups. The second two quotations are by reporter-researchers and the final three quotations by reporter-activists. I have no quarrel with Argyris' classifications, although on most newspapers there is a greater exchange between these roles than one would realize from the *Times-Planet* study. Most traditional reporters of my acquaintance have upon occasion written a story to shake someone up; almost every "reporter-activist" writes some stories which are locked within the boundaries of newspaper objectivism.

If anything, the editors at the *Times-Planet* seem even more distrustful, pessimistic and harried than the reporters. They also are manipulative, fearful and worried about maintaining control. Here is what they say:

(About colleagues) "They're competitive as the devil. They're competitive for a sandwich, they're jealous of each other."

"You should know it by now, newspaper people are a combination of competitiveness and paranoia. They'll fight for visibility and they'll scream that a plot is being perpetrated against them if they don't get the best assignment continually."

"I have a horror of confrontation except under the direst of circumstances. I think others have the same horror of confrontation. So if you have this feeling, it seems to me what you do, as I do, is idle around the thing and only go to confrontation when it is the last desperate resort."

"There's no such thing as a demotion. We ease out the person and put him on the shelf."

"This is a management by secrecy and conspiracies."

"After awhile, you wonder if all this is worth it. What the hell is life all about? Is this what I should be doing? Maybe I should go back to my typewriter."

The "human atmosphere" at the *Planet,* as these comments show, tends to magnify conflict and fear. "Since it is difficult to express tension, frustration and dissatisfaction," writes Argyris, "these feelings may be suppressed or sublimated. To the extent they are suppressed, persons will spend much energy building up and maintaining personal defenses against blowing up. To the extent that they are sublimated, persons may become 'carriers' of low morale and seek to infect others; they may work very hard and take out their aggresson in the kinds of stories they write . . . or they may work long, hard hours . . . in' order to prove their loyalty. This last alternative is especially troublesome for the individual because it forces him to admit not only that he is unable to leave but also that he cannot even express his anger openly."[2]

But it is difficult for the newspaper to change. Events are magnified far beyond their importance and the management, "given the norm against open confrontation . . . may find itself increasingly reacting to assure people that the newspaper, as an organization is kindly and humane." If organizational performance in some section of the newspaper is defective, management selects aggressive executives to correct it who are charged with "cleaning up the mess" while being warned to "go easy lest there be union difficulties or someone hurt." It is no wonder that the *Planet* executive in this situation feels under pressure. "He is asked to make changes which are intrinsically upsetting, in a system that magnifies the upset, without upsetting anyone!" writes Argyris. "There is also the implied threat that if he does upset the system he will not be supported."[3]

This account will not come as a surprise to those who have read Gay Talese's book, *The Power and The Glory,* which is by far the best book I have ever read about a newspaper. But reporters and editors at other papers, as

---

[2]Chris Argyris, *Behind the Front Page,* (San Francisco, 1974), p. 40.

[3]The same, p. 40.

Hoge points out, also will recognize that the processes and comments cited by Argyris are not peculiar to the *Times*. What is different is that the *New York Times* has a more highly developed bureaucracy and a more encrusted tradition. These magnify the conflicts, while also making it more difficult for any given reporter or editor to reach the top. But working for the *Times* also has its special compensations. "The good thing about the *Times* and its system," says former Timesman Dick Reeves, "is that its top people are very, very good. The other strength is just massive numbers. When the *New York Times* decides to hit a story hard, particularly things within traveling distance, they can put twenty guys on it, they can cover all the ratholes. Another great strength is to have the tradition of working for a great paper. It makes people do better and more serious work. And the *Times* will generally back up its own people in public (a point also made by Argyris), even if they know the reporter is wrong. This is a great strength for the reporter. The greatest weaknesses that I saw were that the *Times* paid very well and was secure because of the union setup. Half of the reporters no longer had the personal incentive to go out and bust their balls. They were professional enough to do their jobs, but they often gave the absolute minimum. It was a professional minimum, but it was the minimum. And the unkind way to say it was that they were deadwood."

There are many similarities between the *Washington Post* and the *New York Times,* and more than a few differences. The most basic respect in which they are alike is that both newspapers have publishers who are interested in the quality of the product and alive to their public responsibilities. Though these publishers want and get a high return on their investment, they desire a top-quality product and are willing to invest some of their profits to get it. Salaries and status are high at both newspapers. Reporters and editors are conscious of belonging to organizations which have exceptional goals and high professional reputations. But the *Washington Post,* more recently arrived, has a smaller staff than the *New York Times* and fewer bureaucratic layers. Some newspaper people believe that the *Times'* tighter discipline and more rigid organization produces papers which are better edited and more even in quality than the *Post*; others think this same system is responsible for unnecessary dullness. I will leave that for others to judge. What is clearly true, whatever one may think about the respective newspapers, is that the *Post* reporter is accustomed to a far more informal system than his counterpart at the *Times.* This can be illustrated by a point that seems small but is important to the internal process of newspapers. On the *Times,* reporters have to write a summary of their proposed story and then talk to an editor, who assigns the length of the story. On the *Post* a story often is put on the budget — the list of scheduled stories for next morning's paper — after the most casual kind of conversation between editor and reporter. On many occasions on the *Post* national staff an editor's brief question ("How much do you need on the reaction story?") will be the only conversation between the editor and the reporter before the story is actually turned in. Of course, editors and reporters have a history of working with each other and some reasonable estimate of each other's capabilities and attitudes. Even so, the system is remarkably informal. Following Bradlee's example, editors at the *Post* may drift around a bit in the afternoon and ask questions of a reporter, particularly if they think he has a story which can be sold for page one at one of the two news conferences, which are held at the *Post* at 3 P.M. and 6 P.M. Reporters also will initiate conversations with editors, either for technical reasons such as a request for more space or to inform an editor about a breaking story in which they know he is interested. As a rule, editors will point out something to a reporter which they think he ought to know and they will funnel to him any wire copy relating to a story he is doing. But it is considered unprofessional by good editors to try to get the reporter to write a story to the editor's preconception. Most of the editors I know at the *Post* more or less follow Howard Simon's prescription for management, which is that the "You will" approach doesn't work very well. "With all its hazards," says Simons, "what works best is, 'Will you?' "

Still, there are frustrations. Some reporters at the *Post* have become accustomed over the years to filing long, drawn-out stories which are rich in detail and context but which many of the editors, including Simons, think are just too long. At times there have been attempts to restrict story length arbitrarily; at other times editors have waded through stories that may run 2,500 words in length in the hope of cutting them back by one-third or one-half. These exercises invariably leave editors and reporters in a state of mutual disgust. Typically, editors who cut back one of the *Post* novellas wind up feeling that reporters are selfish people who couldn't care less about other people's stories which are kept out of the paper. Typically, a reporter who has seen his masterpiece shredded thinks that the editor just isn't interested in important detail and mentally resolves to turn in a wire service-type story the next time. Or the reporter may offer his next magnum opus to the "Outlook" section which appears every Sunday and habitually runs contextual pieces of considerable detail. But this is not satisfactory, either. While everyone is working for the same newspaper, the editors of the various staffs tend to think of the reporter in terms of their staff only and not in terms of the *Washington Post* as a whole. Most editors do not like pieces being offered to other sections of the paper unless they have originated the idea.

In the past the *Post* has suffered from internecine conflict between its national staff and the metro staff, which covers the District of Columbia and surrounding counties in Maryland and Virginia. Reporters and editors on the metro staff tended to regard national reporters as prima donnas who had forgotten how to report; some national

staffers were appalled by what they regarded as unprofessional or even irresponsible conduct on the metro staff.
Both of these attitudes were caricatures, but they added
an extra dimension of tension to a newspaper where
there already was an intense competitiveness for assignments, status and page-one play. This unnecessary
rivalry was reduced by the achievements of Woodward
and Bernstein, who helped obtain for the metro staff the
recognition it deserved and by the short-lived appointment of Harry Rosenfeld as national staff editor when
Harwood moved to the *Trenton Times*. Rosenfeld was the
metro editor during the Watergate period, and he maintained close ties with the metro staff and its editor, his
former deputy, Leonard Downie. When some vacancies
opened on the national staff, Rosenfeld improved cityside
morale by bringing metro reporters over to fill them.

Uncertainty is the greatest frustration of journalism.
No matter what paper he works for, a reporter always
writes with imperfect knowledge of events. Are the facts
straight? What do they mean? Has everyone who knows
anything been called? How much of the background material should go into the story? How reliable is the
source? What is missing? A daily newspaper deals in bits
and fragments, in what the late Philip L. Graham called
the "inescapably impossible task of providing every week
a first rough draft of a history that will never be completed about a world we can never really understand." No
matter what the reporter does, or how careful he tries to
be, inaccuracy and incompleteness are his nemesis. I consider myself a careful reporter, and yet I have made
many errors in haste or ignorance or because of a mis-
placed belief in the reliability of a source. A careful reporter is going to be misled by the same source only once,
but there are enough sources and enough stories in
Washington to make for a lot of inaccuracy. In 1975, I
reported that Melvin R. Laird, the former congressman
and defense secretary, was going to head President
Ford's campaign for a full term. I had obtained this in-

formation from two high-ranking White House sources, one of whom until then had a perfect track record for accuracy in his dealings with me. The story was partially confirmed by two other sources, one of them a congressman who also had been helpful on various occasions. However, Laird, who usually returns phone calls, was somewhere else and did not get back to me until the next day. By then it was too late. We had run the story because I wanted to get it into the paper before someone else printed it.[4] I should have waited and seen whether I had a story at all.

Newspapers live constantly with the knowledge that they may be proven wrong, a fact which may partially account for their traditional grudgingness to give corrections. "Indeed, the fear of being wrong haunted many of the star reporters" at the *Times,* according to Argyris. "Nothing would be more humiliating than to be proven wrong by succeeding events — worse yet, by a competing newspaper." Argyris quotes one of these "stars" as saying: "I have a highly developed fear of being proven wrong and being humiliated." Another reporter said: "We hate to be wrong, God, it hurts, especially in this paper with its high standards. Reporters break down when face is involved."[5]

One reporter who has developed enough confidence in his work to be able to discuss his past mistakes is freelancer Richard Reeves, who believes that it is healthy for journalists to remember the times they have been wrong.

---

[4] When Laird did call the following day, he said I had been right on a story I had written two months before recounting the personal reasons that prevented him from heading the Ford campaign. He insisted he wanted no correction of the incorrect story and left me with the impression that he might wind up heading the Ford campaign after all. I discussed this with my editors, and we decided not to run a correction on the story out of concern that we might ultimately wind up correcting the correction. In retrospect this decision, for which I take responsibility, was a mistake which compounded the original error.

[5] Argyris, *Behind the Front Page,* p. 48.

The mistake which Reeves remembers most vividly is, in his words, "one of the famous screwups in American journalism, and I sure as hell remember that." In 1968 Reeves wrote flatly in the *New York Times* that Nelson Rockefeller would announce his presidential candidacy in four days. Instead, the announcement which Rockefeller made four days later was that he would not be a candidate for President. "I remember everything about that story, everything," says Reeves, who learned about his mistake from an early-morning radio broadcast on the day of the announcement. "The story had a great effect on me and the way I worked after that. I am absolutely convinced that I was dead right when I wrote it, but four days later I was not right. I learned from that. It was really a maturing process, both professionally and personally. I should not have been writing that story and partially I was doing it because (national political writer) Johnny Apple and I were in fierce competition over that subject. I did not know enough about the subject, to begin with. That's a very simple lesson but you always learn it the hard way. I would never again write a simple declarative sentence that something is going to happen. I wouldn't write a simple declarative sentence that the sun's going to rise in the east tomorrow. I think it's just a professional error to do that. The other thing I did was that I allowed a boss to dictate to me who said he had first-hand knowledge. I originally went in with a summary saying, 'Rockefeller is expected to announce,' and it was a dope story about what had been discussed in the inner councils. Abe Rosenfeld told me he had talked to Rockefeller and Rockefeller said he's going to do it. I then checked, and people told me as far as they knew that was true and that the date and time was set — I had the time of day and everything. I would never again, I wouldn't care if it was Jesus Christ, I would never again take someone else's word, I would never take dictation from a boss, although this was really more subtle than dictation. It doesn't matter if I was right at the time I wrote it. The fact is that I embarrassed myself and I embarrassed the *Times*."

I am an admirer of Reeves because his work is suffused with the kind of integrity which distinguishes the above account. Most reporters have at some time or other allowed themselves to be nudged into hyping up a lead or in saying something flatly which they ought to qualify. These are the persistent sins of the business. An even more persistent sin is the habit of presenting a story as complete when the reporter, and frequently the editor, knows it is incomplete. One of the cliches of the news business — I used it myself many times as an editor — is to say that a story raises questions that it doesn't answer. William H. Greider of the *Washington Post* believes that any good story is likely to raise such questions, and he thinks that it would be honest of the newspaper to say so. Greider once said that stories ought to have a paragraph in them saying that Questions A, B, and C had been raised by whatever had happened and that the newspaper was unable to learn the answers to them. Such paragraphs, of course, would never survive the editor's pencil. Reeves has a related idea, which is to inform the readers of the imperfect state of the reporting that has been accomplished. In this vein he once suggested facetiously that a byline might read: "By Dick Reeves, who had a cold, hadn't been able to reach two key sources and was late to dinner."

Every day is a new day on a daily newspaper. Every day editors go through the routines of allocating space, assigning stories, budgeting stories and editing stories. Every day reporters go out on their assignments and come back to write what they have found. Though they deal with an infinite variety of events, reporters and editors are locked in a recurring series of time continuums which are dominated by the next deadline. Their lives are defined by the daily rhythm of the news. Beginning each day anew this way wonderfully equips news people to deal with events which are truly new, such as catastrophes which did not exist in the previous twenty-four hour continuum. But this short-time perspective also deprives news people of the perspectives of past and future and makes it difficult for newspapers to deal with the human equivalent of geological change. Usually the daily newspaper reporter sees neither forest nor trees but some small sliver of an event which did not exist the day before. This is the glory of journalism and also its frustration. "Editors and reporters and the press generally must understand that if they think they're telling the truth, nothing but the truth and the whole truth when they sit down at a machine, they're full of shit," says Ben Bradlee. "They're not. There are so many limits on what the truth is. There's the limit of time. There's the limit of money, if you want. If you've got a story to write by a quarter of eight at night, you've got to start writing about seven and therefore any reporting that you might do from seven till midnight or for the next four days isn't going to be in that story. You're limited by what people tell you, or what documents you see. You didn't talk to everybody. You didn't know which one of those guys was telling the truth. You only see 'X' documents, you didn't see 'X' plus a hundred. So we're not telling the truth. We're telling everything we know and what we think to be the truth at the cutoff point. One of the things I'd like to do before I die is to get this message over to the people in some way that wouldn't have them lose confidence in the press."

Uncertainty and inaccuracy are not the only frustrations. I think that all reporters, even those who love the news business most, must at times feel at least a vague dissatisfaction with the ephemeral nature of their work. The news business could be likened to a Chinese dinner which satisfies the palate and provides sufficient nourishment but leaves the diner feeling hungry soon after he has eaten. Reporters enjoy the variety and the short-time perspective, but many of them come to believe that the nature of their work is lacking in substance.

Bradlee observes that "the top reporters, the ones who work very hard, somehow no longer are satisfied with just daily journalism, and they get spread very thin. They want to write books, they want to make speeches or do magazine articles; so whereas they're working hard, they're not always working for the *Washington Post.* They're working for some kind of inner fulfillment, which takes them away."

Many reporters start out in the business believing that what they write has a substantive impact on the behavior of those they write about, or even on the behavior of the institution which they cover. This is especially true if the reporter has a defined governmental beat, such as a city council or the school board. I suspect that one reason why those of us in the news business are attuned to scandal is that stories of malfeasance or corruption provide the most tangible evidence of how a story can have an impact beyond the morning coffee. (I still have a good feeling about a story I wrote in the late 1950s for the *Merced Sun-Star* describing conditions in a county jail camp. The story helped lead to the removal of the camp director.) Most of the time, however, reporters are apt to exaggerate their influence on institutional behavior. Such exaggeration helps to dampen our frustrations about the ephemeral nature of our writing. Admitting that our stories are ephemeral and also have little impact would be too much to bear.

Leslie H. Gelb, briefly a fine diplomatic correspondent for the *New York Times,* came to the news business after a career as a Pentagon planner and four years with the Brookings Institution. He wrote contextual stories of an impressive analytical power and range. But Gelb, a careful newspaper reader when he worked for the Pentagon, found that officials in government often did not read what he wrote for the *Times.* When a general let slip the fact that a request for $818 million in grant military aid included $425 million in military aid for Cambodia after Cambodia had fallen, Gelb wrote a story about it which

appeared on page two of the *New York Times*. He viewed
Pentagon inclusion of the Cambodian aid item "once the
reason for the request had disappeared" as a significant
reflection of the way the Pentagon operates. While Gelb
had no illusion that his story was likely to change the
Pentagon's way of operating or lead to deletion of the
Cambodian aid request, he thought that the story would
prompt Congress to at least address these questions.
"They didn't," said Gelb. "No one on the Hill who worked
on the military aid bill had read the story." It is no wonder that Gelb has come to think that "writing stories is
like dropping pennies down a well."

Most journalists have had simliar experiences, particularly in Washington where the "pennies-down-a-well
feeling" is magnified for hundreds of journalists who live
in a city where their work is never seen. My friend and
former colleague Albert A. Eisele, who left Ridder Newspapers to become Vice President Mondale's press secretary, calls this "the biggest frustration of a Washington
reporter," and it is one of the reasons that many reporters
welcome an opportunity to work for one of the Washington newspapers or the *New York Times*. But even on the
Post or the *Times*, as the Gelb story demonstrates, reporters are uncertain about the impact of their work.
Robert Darnton, who had a brief career as reporter on the
Newark Star Ledger and the *New York Times* from
1959-64, has written that he "received many more responses from articles in scholarly journals with tiny
readerships than from front-page stories in the *Times*
that must have been read by half a million persons."[6]
This is one frustration which small-town journalists are
less apt to feel than their big-city colleagues. In small
towns reporters are likely to be known in the community
and receive more comments about their stories than they
either want or need.

Newspapers, in big cities or small, are basically conservative institutions. "We move very slowly, we're wed-

<hr>

[6] Darnton, "Writing News and Telling Stories."

ded to certain techniques and practices and we respond to events," says Haynes Johnson of the *Washington Post,* who points out that reporters operate pretty much as they did a century ago. Reporters have no secretaries, for example, and only a handful of newspapers have followed the useful example of *Time* and assisted reporters with trained researchers. The first and last recourse of a reporter at many newspapers is that anthology of past errors known as the newspaper clip file. Reporters, lacking any other resource material, tend to have a naive trust in the value of old newspaper clippings. However, I have worked at a few papers where reporters were saved from themselves by the eccentricities of librarians whose inspiration for their filing systems was the old radio show, "I Love a Mystery." My favorite entry was by a since-retired librarian at San Jose who filed away the stories of an ice-pick murder under "H," for "Human Pincushion." He took his cue from the headline.

The fundamental conservatism of newspapers as institutions degenerates to miserliness on some newspapers. Gil Bailey, now a Washington correspondent for Knight-Ridder Newspapers, remembers his experiences at the *Oroville Mercury-Register,* a small but profitable daily in northern California. "One ballpoint pen was issued every three months," says Bailey. "Only half sheets of copy paper were provided and they were rationed. I lasted one pen." Bailey wound up at the *Sacramento Union* in the days when it was published by the late Leonard Finder. The *Union* was *not* prosperous, and it rationed reporters rather than copy. One night the *Union* publisher spotted a big fire downtown and used the radio-telephone in his car to ask the city editor about coverage. "I've got my entire staff on it, both of them," replied the city editor. That night the Sacramento City Council meeting was covered by the copyboy.

The handicaps described by Bailey are extreme. But reporters on most newspapers are apt to be spread far too thinly because the publisher is unwilling to invest his profits in news coverage. These reporters also are apt to be frustrated by the publisher's "sacred cows" or by editorial partisanship which slops over into the news columns. On the *Merced Sun-Star*, which was in the mid-fifties a vigorous community newspaper, we were for a time prohibited from using the word "rape" because it offended the wife of the publisher. This was a handicap at a newspaper which printed a lot of crime news. In Merced, women were always "assaulted" or "attacked," leading some readers to believe that a woman who had been struck on the head was really a rape victim.

On the *Sun-Star*, at least, we were allowed and encouraged to cover political candidates without partisanship despite the strong Republican inclinations of the publisher. The same cannot be said for many California newspapers. One measure of judging how far the *Los Angeles Times*, which now gives superb coverage to state political campaigns, has come in the past two decades is to remember that as recently as the mid-fifties Democratic candidates could hardly get their names into the *Times.* The Democratic nominee for governor of California in 1954, one Richard Graves, received two paragraphs on an inside page in the *Times* when he made one of the major speeches of his campaign, a prescient address on smog control. The *San Francisco Chronicle,* which often talked Democratic and always endorsed Republican, had a policy of not identifying the partisan affiliation of state legislative candidates in political campaigns. It was an effective policy, too, in the old crossfiling days when officeholders did not have their partisan affiliations printed on the ballots. A more recent example of bias on the other side was provided by the *Sacramento Bee* in 1966. That was the year when Democratic Governor Edmund G. (Pat) Brown was running for a third term. On the Republican side a former actor named Ronald Reagan was opposing a former San Francisco mayor named George Christopher. The *Bee* was rabidly anti-Reagan, considering him a dangerous extremist who was unqualified for the governorship. This editorial opinion was reinforced by a memo sent to staffers which called for Reagan to be referred to as "the Goldwater Republican" in news stories. The *Bee's* reporters had no affection for Reagan, but they rebelled against such slanting. However, they found that if they omitted the label from their stories it usually was inserted by the desk. Martin Smith, a resourceful and fair-minded reporter, solved the problem by using the phrase in the most irrelevant paragraphs, such as "Ronald Reagan, the Goldwater Republican, got off the train at Chico." Without losing any of its animosity for Reagan the *Bee* ultimately dropped the obligatory label from its news columns.

Policy bias of this sort is enormously damaging to reporters, even more so than to the political candidates who are its obvious victims. At its best such slanting of the news tends to make reporters cynical about their own function. At worst it corrodes the reporter's sense of fairness and replaces it with the prejudices of the publisher. Most political reporters whom I know would prefer to deal from the top of the deck rather than from the bottom. When they are compelled to slant their stories, they lose a good part of the reason for being reporters in the first place.

We have been discussing frustrations of the news business which affect reporters. The frustrations of those who cannot leave the newsroom often are greater. Sometimes these are the frustrations of the man with the hoe, whose gaze is fixed solidly on the pile of unedited copy before him. In other cases it is more the frustration of the man with the shovel. Robert J. Casey, writing of his work as a rewrite man on Hearst's old *Chicago American,* tells of how he and another rewrite man ground out the entire front section of the paper nearly every day: "There were ten editions each day and there had to be a new lead on every front-page story for each of the ten editions. The theory seemed to be that people who read the *American*

read every issue of it. . . . The leads had to be rewritten
whether there was any more news or not. For the all-
edition readers apparently were just as stupid as they
were eccentric. One gathered that they agreed with the
editors that by changing the wording of a sentence you
gave it added worth and novelty. My daily average output was between fifty-five and sixty typewritten sheets of
copy a day . . . And writing was only part of the work."

Technological changes and production costs mercifully
have diminished the number of newspaper editions and
this type of deluding makework. But they have not diminished the frustrations of newspaper desk work or the
difficulties of newspaper management. It is easy, as I
know, to become something of an automaton on the copy
desk. "Copy editors tend to be a separate breed among
newspapermen," wrote Robert Darnton. "Quite intense,
perhaps more eccentric and learned than most reporters,
they are in the role of being sticklers for language . . .
Copy editors apparently think of themselves as second-
class citizens in the newsroom; every day, as they see it,
they save the reporters from dozens of errors of fact and
grammar; yet the reporters revile them." Darnton quotes
one reporter on the *Times* as saying to him: "The game is
to sneak some color or interpretation past that line of
humorless zombies."[7]

Reporters who become junior editors or who are forced
to the copy desk are aware of these attitudes. Often, a
reporter who becomes an editor feels after awhile that he
has lost touch with the news business. "Editors have to
feed their own psyche," says *Washington Post* managing
editor Howard Simons, who was a topflight science reporter before becoming No. 2 man to Ben Bradlee. "They
don't have the byline, they're not going out to Iowa to
interview somebody, they're not getting all of that aura
and romance and glory that we associate with, but is not
always true about, journalism. A creative editor will get

---

[7] The same, p. 180.

his kicks either by conceiving of a good story and then seeing it through to fruition, or by taking raw talent and molding it into really good talent, potentially great talent. It will be saving a good story from disaster, then seeing it in print the next day and knowing internally that, 'By God, that was me.' And you get your jollies that way, and it takes a peculiar person to do it." Editors who cannot adjust and "get their jollies" tend to wind up frustrating reporters as well as themselves. Herb Denton, the *Post's* District of Columbia editor, was a reporter who went on the desk for a couple of days in 1973 and stayed there. His definition of a "bad editor" is one who imposes his own value structure on a story. "At the beginning I fell into the same trap, which is a common one for reporters who got to the desk," says Denton.

Editors face a more persistent, throbbing kind of pressure than reporters, who are under the gun when they have to write on deadline but otherwise live a freer life. A reporter is out of the office a lot, and he usually has to worry only about one story at a time. Editors do not have the getting-out time or the freedom from pressure a reporter enjoys on some project-type stories. "The biggest frustration is the time frame in which you have to do your job," says Peter Silberman, the financial editor and former national editor at the *Post.* "You are constantly under the goad of the deadline. The most successful editors are those who recognize it and do not panic and work within the limits of its constraints. You simply must accept within yourself the limits of the time frame and do the best you can that day, resolving to do better the next day and the day thereafter." Silberman is one of those successful editors, both because he understands the constraints of the deadline and because he has the temperament to deal with deadline pressures. Editors who lack either the understanding or the temperament tend to transmit their anxieties to other editors and to the reporting staff with a resulting loss of efficiency.

Even with understanding there is frustration on the

copy desk, the historic dead end for newspaper reporters. One line in *The Front Page* which rarely gets any laughs from newspaper people is the one that follows Hildy Johnson's celebrated description of a newspaperman as "a cross between a bootlegger and a whore." It is the line where Hildy tells his fellow reporters in the press room of the Chicago criminal court building: "And if you want to know something, you'll end up on the copy desk — gray-headed, humpbacked slobs, dodging garnishees when you're ninety." The copy desk on metropolitan papers is more remunerative than in Hildy Johnson's day, but it has not gained any more status. If anything, its status has declined. "A first-rank problem for me at the *Washington Post,* and I have no elegant solution at all, is copy editors," says managing editor Simons. "This newspaper has changed. The copy editor used to play a significant role, and he had some measure of control over the story. With the rise of the assignment editor, who deals all day with the reporter and also edits the reporter's copy, this in effect says to the copy editor, 'You put in paragraph marks, you check for spelling, you write the headline, but goddamn it don't you touch anything because I've been over this story.' The copy editor has lost some of the exciting function he or she used to have. Moreover, there is no psychic income in copy editing. One of the things I once thought of is to put a byline at the end of the story, 'Copy-read by So-and-So.' Crazy idea and we never did it. But copy editors have no psychic income. They don't go to lunches with Barry Goldwater upstairs, or with the Vice President. They don't get a byline. And they work at night, when no one else is working, and what they have to do is sort of looked down upon as second-class work. And for a long time the copy desk was a dumping ground, and everybody knew it, which is a great way to build morale on a staff. I have not yet found a way to enhance the professional lives of these people to make them enthusiastic about what they're doing so that the paper gets to be almost error-free."

Executives on smaller papers worry about the quality of their wire editors. Says Norman Cherniss, executive editor of the *Riverside Press-Enterprise*: "I have never encountered a young journalist whose ambition was to be a wire editor." This is unfortunate, inasmuch as the wire editor, or the news editor, or someone like him — called a "gatekeeper" by the social scientists — must decide which of the many wire stories that come into a paper he will discard and which of the few stories he will use. This gatekeeper, as Ben Bagdikian has written, "in some ways . . . has more unofficial power than reporters and publishers."[8]

A Rand study of eight newspapers showed the typical gatekeeper took from one to two seconds to make a decision to discard a story. On one suburban paper which printed 110,000 words a day, the size of a typical book, the decision was made by a news editor, who discarded four stories for every one he used. On a metropolitan daily, which printed 400,000 words daily, there were three gatekeepers, two of whom also had responsibility for supervising their respective staffs.

Newspapers could do a far better job of presenting the national and foreign news by careful combination of wire stories. Almost every daily newpaper is either a member of the Associated Press or a client of United Press International. Hundreds of these dailies also have a supplemental wire service, such as the *New York Times* service, or the *Los Angeles Times-Washington Post* service. While many large dailies have both AP and UPI and various supplemental services, there is a trend among medium and small-sized dailies to take one of the regular wire services and one supplemental service in the belief that this provides a good combination of spot news and in-

[8]Ben H. Bagdikian, *The Information Machines: Their Impact on Men and the Media*, (New York, 1971), p. 89. The two succeeding examples of the Rand corporation study are from the same book, pp. 101-103. This book, which was financed and copyrighted by Rand, is the basic text explaining how both the printed news system and the broadcast news system function.

terpretive stories. However, newspapers could provide added depth and balance on almost any story by following a policy of regularly combining stories, since it is rare that one wire story is better than its rival in all respects. At the *San Jose Mercury*, where I worked for four years on the wire desk, wire editor Dale Cockerill greatly improved the quality of the paper by doing just this and by encouraging or directing his sub-editors to follow his examples. Such practices are rarer than they should be, as a glance at most newspapers will show. Partly, this is because wire copy arrives at some newspapers in the form of a perforated tape which is put directly on the typesetting machine. Any editing changes require the setting of the type by hand at slower speed and greater cost. But even where this consideration is not overruling, few newspapers provide the wire editor or the news editor with the resources he needs to provide the useful service of combining stories. A wire editor who has a second or two to decide whether a story should be used or discarded usually isn't willing or able to take some valuable additional seconds in figuring out how two imperfect stories might be combined to make a better one. The loser, as usual, is the newspaper reader.

Working for a wire service can be as frustrating as working on a wire desk. Wire-service reporters are the most skilled people in the news business at fast accurate transmission of a breaking story. They also are among the hardest working reporters, so much so that some of them think of themselves as loafing when they transfer to a newspaper where they are allowed the luxury of producing only one or two stories a day. But wire-service reporting encourages shallowness as well as speed, glibness and accuracy. Few wire-service stories are contextual. Many are recycled from previous stories with a thin new layer of information that becomes the lead. With a few distinguished exceptions (Saul Pett, the late Merriman Smith, Helen Thomas, Frank Cormier, Jules Loh and Louis Cassels come readily to mind), wire-service reporters also tend to become second-class citizens in the news business. They invariably are overworked and usually, especially on United Press International, vastly underpaid. More than most reporters, they are subject to personal restraints arising from classic notions of objective journalism. Associated Press, in particular, has strict limitations on the participation of AP reporters even on such innocuous forums as television panel discussions. Speeches or writings which might reflect social philosophy or political opinion are strictly forbidden. This requires the wire-service reporter to live his life within a narrow, "professional" range which is as unreal as the notion that news stories can convey a picture of the world by prohibiting the expression of opinion. It is no accident that the only two persons of the eighty-three I interviewed for this book who were unwilling to say anything for attribution were wire-service reporters. One of these reporters was embarrassed about imposing that condition on the interview and added, "I feel that I lack protection of the First Amendment, but that's the way it is in our organization." Both of these reporters were proud of their own work and of the opportunity given them by the wire services to witness and write about important events. But they also were disillusioned about the limits of wire-service reporting. "We are hyping up junk or fragments of a story all the time and sticking an 'urgent' on it to give the impression we are beating AP," one United Press International reporter told me candidly. An AP reporter on a public affairs beat was equally discouraged. "I used to get a kick out of knowing that my story would be read by more readers across the country than the copy filed by any of the specials (correspondents working for a single newspaper)," said this reporter. "I don't get a kick out of it anymore. We work within such narrow limits that the job has become a bore."

The formula for wire-service writing which opens this chapter is taken from a 1950 novel by Reynolds Packard, *The Kansas City Milkman*. Packard is a former wire-service reporter, and the formula actually is a parody of the one long used by UPI. His novel provides genuine insights into the grievances of wire-service reporters and the bitterness and cynicism which a career on the wires can produce. *The Kansas City Milkman* is set in Europe immediately after World War II where the thinly disguised IP (for Interworld Press Association) is trying to cover the news and re-establish clients. The hero is an old war correspondent named Clay Brewster who has become bored with wire-service formula writing and disgusted with IP's practice of constantly needling up second-rate stories to get ahead of its competition. Brewster's growing cynicism is not lost on IP executives, who think he has lost some of the "old whammo and zeppo" that once made him a great reporter. But there are plenty of young reporters waiting to take Brewster's place in the Paris bureau, where the walls are festooned with such self-celebrating slogans as "History When It's Born," and "IP Stands for Impartiality." One of these reporters is Shelby, a young well-dressed man who lacks news sense but is willing to hype up stories and present the glories of IP service to prospective clients. Brewster likes Shelby and wants to make a reporter out of him. Instead, he is told by the European manager that "good reporters are a dime a dozen in Paris. What we want are salesmen, super-salesmen who can sell the IP." Shelby proves his worth by quickly mastering the one-two formula and the notion that speed and salesmanship are the way to the top. He is sent off for some flattering interviews with Franco which enable IP to establish its wire service in Spain.

The only thing that counts other than salesmanship is beating the rival press service. The Paris bureau manager, who lives for headlines and is devoid of ideas, accomplishes this frequently, sometimes by sending an anticipated development out on the wires before it actually occurs. This tactic backfires during a close vote of confidence in the French Chamber of Deputies where

Leon Blum is deposed. Kester, the bureau manager, has already sent New York a "flash" cable message that Blum has won. But he saves the day by inventing a recount which cost Blum his premiership and gets it on the wire just before a subordinate can send a correction. "Get this straight, Syd," Kester tells the subordinate. "You don't correct a mistake. You just write new developments so they make everything all right. What you would call a correction, I call a NEWLEAD. And if you ever try to correct a story of mine again, you're fired."

Clay Brewster does not go in for such tricks. He symbolizes the honest professional, a reporter and not a salesman, who gradually sinks lower on the IP totem pole. The other honest reporter in the bureau, a woman who rebels against writing fashion articles for the wife of the Kansas City milkman, eventually quits and joins the staff of a Philadelphia newspaper. Brewster quits, too, and bums around Europe and the Middle East for a year in an unsuccessful attempt at freelancing. Down on his luck he returns to Paris where he eventually is rehired at a fraction of his former salary by Shelby, the Franco-selling cub who has made it to the top of the Paris bureau. As the novel ends, Brewster is stuck with IP for the rest of his working life.

What happens to Clay Brewster happens to many actual reporters who bump up against the constraining walls of the news business. A few expand their horizons, their ideas and their opportunities. Many more go through the motions on beats that have passed them by. Others pass into the dubious semi-retirement of the copy desk. It is a tough business and one in which there are always more people for the jobs than there are jobs for aspiring journalists. Furthermore, the good editors realize that the news business thrives on replacing old-timers with the up-and-coming youngsters. *Washington Post* editor Ben Bradlee, whose willingness to make personnel changes is one of the reasons his newspaper has flourished, provides a candid glimpse into the hard realities of the news business with his answer to a question about what would help him most in making further improvements at the Post: "I have an answer that's so revolutionary and anti-union. I'd have the power to get rid of people. And I would say it much more compassionately: the power to find other people other jobs. That's what I want. I have weeded people out, but at great anguish to me, great personal cost. If I had the power to get rid of people, I could put out a hell of a lot better newspaper."

The issue of which Bradlee speaks is very much on the mind of executives at the *Post,* and with good reason. "It is very hard to grow old gracefully in this business," says Howard Simons, "although some people do it very well. But as you grow older in the business, your family's growing older with you. It becomes a family problem in a crazy way. You want to get home at seven o'clock for dinner, not at nine or ten. And you're not as anxious to go out on the road for three or four weeks at a time any more. And so it becomes easier to stop the story a little short of where you would have stopped it five years earlier. And those young kids are nipping at your heels, and that bothers you some. Now, are there answers? I don't know. There are some insoluble problems in journalism."

From a reporter's perspective the problems of burning out too quickly are even less soluble. "Seniority brings very little comfort in journalism," says Russell Baker of the *New York Times.* "It brings a heightened sense of economic danger. It's a young man's business essentially. When men get middleaged they begin to sense very often that they are regarded as deadwood. They are tired, they are burnt out and management begins to look for places to move them aside, to get them an early retirement. That doesn't happen if you are a doctor. You could be the worst goddamn doctor in the country and if you've got the age and the seniority nobody is going to move you. They can't. That is what it means to be a professional."

Clay Brewster in *The Kansas City Milkman* is irate

when the European bureau manager values the selling of IP service more highly than the reporting of IP news. But Baker believes that reporters actually live a life which in many ways is like the life of a traveling salesman. "The print journalist has a great deal in common with Willie Loman," Baker says. "You can even look at him on the road, laden down with a typewriter in one hand and a suitcase in the other and a trench coat, trudging his way through the mob, living a rather dreary life with the reality of it romanticized with good booze, sitting up nights and telling old tales. Basically, he's a guy who is riding out there with a shoe shine and a smile, and he's easily shot down."[9]

[9]These comments were made by Baker while participating in dialogues on journalism at Duke University and are used with his permission.

CHAPTER EIGHT

Specialists

Newspapers are caught between two categorical imperatives – what readers need to know and what they're interested in. These diverge. They often are in conflict. At one extreme are dogs, Little Leagues and gardens. At the other are Tibetan stories which no one understands.
– Bob Boyd, Washington bureau chief of Knight newspapers

One of the great debates of the news business has to do with whether news organizations should employ more specialists. It is an enduring question but not an evenly balanced one, as the force of journalistic history and tradition is heavily on the side of the generalist. A typical editor considers a good reporter to be a reporter who can be sent to cover any story and do a creditable job. "The proper stance for a reporter is to be a mile wide and an inch deep," says Bill Steif an all-purpose reporter for the Scripps-Howard newspapers. Many reporters would meet this definition, and many others aspire to it.

In this chapter I propose to examine briefly the question of specialization and then to make some observations about the coverage of foreign news and the coverage of some particular specialized beats — science, business, education and the Supreme Court. If a reporter, as the old saw would have it, is a person who knows a little about everything and nothing about anything, I am qualified to write this chapter. I have covered stories abroad but never have been assigned to a foreign country. I have done some science reporting, especially about nuclear energy, and some environmental reporting but never for an extended period of time. I have covered the courts in California and taken some courses in the criminal law but have only an outside generalist's appreciation of the problems of covering the Supreme Court. While I have edited financial pages, the less said about my competence in economics the better. What follows, then, is necessarily a generalist's view of specialized reporting.

Specialization is a poor joke on most American newspapers and television stations. Less than a score of the 1,768 American daily newspapers have any foreign coverage of their own and almost none of the 7,123 commercial radio stations or 707 commercial television stations have foreign coverage beyond that provided by the networks or the wires. This is understandable, considering the cost of foreign coverage. What is less understandable is that fewer than one newspaper in every seventeen has an environmental reporter of its own, and many of the newspapers that do have such a reporter assign him to this specialized beat only part-time. According to a study that will be discussed later in this chapter, only seven news organizations have an assigned reporter who spends his full time covering the Supreme Court. The latest statistics available, and they may be overstating the case, show that only about one newspaper in four has an education specialist. In short, most newspapers are not participants in the great debate about specialists versus generalists. Readers are reminded once again that news organizations have a commercial purpose. The countinghouse newspapers are obsessed with this purpose over all others, and they are the majority of newspapers published in the United States. These countinghouse papers hire the minimum number of reporters and print the minimum amount of news. The only specialization they recognize is at the cashier's window of the local bank.

So we are not talking about most newspapers, except peripherally. Even on countinghouse papers there is apt to be a reporter or two who has a developed interest in some subject and who is allowed to explore it as the price of keeping him. Newspapers always are on the lookout

for free specialists. I have been a "legal affairs expert"
and an "environmental reporter" on various newspapers
and because I spent enough time on my own to become
superficially expert in these fields. Even on the *Washington Post,* I was once told that a good reporter can become
almost any kind of specialist on the newspaper. There is
a marvelous vitality in this idea, an enormous ratification of the democratic system, journalistic division, but it
does not say very much about the industry's devotion to
knowledge. A "specialist" on most newspapers is apt to be
a generalist from out of town.

There are, of course, several legitimate specialists at
the *Washington Post,* some of them organized into the
special unit that has been designated SMERSH, for "science, medicine, education, religion and all that shit." It is
an irreverent acronym, but it demonstrates a laudable
commitment by the editors of at least five reporters to
topics worthy of specialized coverage. The *Post* has
another asset in the specialist sweepstakes that is rare at
American newspapers. His name is Howard Simons, now
the managing editor, but a newspaperman who made his
reputation as a science writer and the editor who created
SMERSH. After attending Columbia and serving in the
Army, Simons went to work for Science Service, which
provided many of the timeless stories I used to shove into
the back pages of the *San Jose Mercury* in my copy desk
days. Simons left for a Nieman fellowship and was working again as a fulltime freelance science writer when
Alfred Friendly, then the *Post* editor, hired him as a
"hard sciences" writer to do stories about space, nuclear
energy, astronomy, physics and chemistry. This was in
1961. He stayed on the science beat until it seemed to
him "a mink-lined rut" and then became Ben Bradlee's
assistant managing editor in 1966.

Simons was a science writer during the period of the
debate in his specialty about whether it was better to
have scientists or non-scientists covering the field. Most
of the British writers at the time were scientists who

became writers; most American journalists covering science were reporters first and science writers second. The best American newspapers had been in something of a ferment about science coverage ever since the atomic bomb, and the ferment became a fetish after the Russians put Sputnik into orbit in 1957. A few papers hired scientists, sometimes with unsatisfactory results. Many newspapers assigned a generalist reporter to the science beat. Simons, an English major, paid attention to the output both of scientists and non-scientists and quickly became convinced that scientific training was not a prerequisite. "That wasn't what your readers were interested in," he says. "You were not educating them to basic biology, basic physics, and basic chemistry. You were looking for the cutting edges. More importantly, you had to translate these cutting edges into something readable for people who had less science education. Now it makes good sense to me that you get a dummy like I was who had to ask all the stupid questions of a scientist. I'm going to be better able to write a story that's understandable by the reader than if I know the jargon and the shorthand and can immediately grasp what's at hand. You can ask legitimately if there is not a role for a scientist writing for a newspaper who challenges scientists and their discoveries. But I defy you to find one who's so good across the board that he can do that. Usually, you specialize in science, and the biologist really gets lost in geology, and the geologist has no idea of what the biochemist is talking about, except for the rudiments. But you're not looking for the rudiments: you're looking for the cutting edges, the new discoveries, the new excitement. There are enough articulate, bright scientists in the United States who are willing to help. You get to know who they are and you call them up when a discovery is made and they explain it to you. You ask the questions necessary for an average reader." So, in Simons' view, modern technology which created the case for the specialist seems in a curious way to have come

down on the side of the generalist. There are too many
specialties, and no newspaper can afford technically
trained persons in all of them, even if they proved able to
write for the newspaper audience.

But there are all kinds of science writers, and not all
the generalists understood as much or wrote as well as
Simons. There is always Walter Sullivan, of course, the
renaissance man of the *New York Times,* but Sullivan
writes about science so well that he is in a class by himself. Percy H. Tannenbaum, now at the University of
California, in 1963 analyzed the communication of science information in an article in *Science,* the publication
of the American Association for the Advancement of Science. He found some remarkable things. Using an earlier
study by J.C. Nunnally, Tannenbaum pointed out that
the public's conception of one subject, mental illness, conformed much more closely to the opinions of experts than
it did to the portrayals of mental illness in the mass
media, especially on television and in magazines.[1] "The
findings were quite clear: The experts and the public
tended to agree in their conceptions of mental illness,
whereas the mass media presented a different picture.
Instead of being a true mediator between the scientists
and the public, the mass media were introducing an apparently dissonant element, featuring the more bizarre,
sordid and frivolous aspects of mental illness." Furthermore, said Tannenbaum, science writers frequently resort to "standardized, shopworn phrases" in attempting
to find substitutes for scientific terms which J. Robert
Oppenheimer once said are "almost impossible to translate" into lay language. "Typical is the use of a single,

---

[1]Professor Tannenbaum's quotations are taken from the article, "Communication of Science Information" which he wrote for Vol. 140 of *Science,*
May 10, 1963. Tannenbaum reiterated several of the same points in a conversation with the author in August 1975. The study by Nunnally which he
cites is from Nunnally's book, *Popular Conceptions of Mental Health,* (New
York, 1961).

generalized term to cover what, to the scientist, are distinctively different things," wrote Tannenbaum. "In addition, possibly to 'sell' their editors, many science writers indiscriminately use such cliches as 'major breakthrough' and 'giant step forward' in describing theory and experimentation." Tannenbaum cites the effort of science writers to translate such terms as "particle accelerator" into "atom smasher" and "nucleus" into "heart of an atom." According to Tannenbaum, studies conducted by him and Melvin Laing at the University of Wisconsin showed that "the regular science reader found most of the original scientific terms as meaningful as the lay terms."

Science writing is a specialty that is many specialties, as Simons points out. Foreign coverage is a specialty that almost by definition is also a generality, involving as it does a multiplicity of varied assignments on the same beat. Foreign assignments were once the glamour beats on a newspaper, inevitably attracting far more candidates than there were positions abroad. The bloom has now faded from that particular rose, and the "investigative reporter" has replaced the foreign correspondent as the current vogue of journalism. Nevertheless, foreign coverage continues to fascinate certain reporters, particularly reporters who especially value their independence. Tom Lippman, now a cityside reporter with the *Washington Post* and formerly a Vietnam correspondent, expressed it in 1973 in an interview with the *Post's* in-house magazine, *Shop Talk:* "Being a correspondent in Indochina is often difficult and frustrating, as well as dangerous, because of poor communications, primitive conditions, and a national tendency, encouraged by the Americans, to dissemble. But to be the Saigon correspondent for the *Post* is in some ways the best of all jobs: freedom of action, independence of judgment, a desk that avoids the second-guess and a bottomless well of interesting stories. No tie and jacket, no fixed hours, no production quota, no office politics — just you and the story."

The foreign correspondent basically is a general assignment reporter. John Goshko, one of the veteran foreign correspondents at the *Post,* calls him "a general assignment reporter with dysentery." "The thing I liked most about it was being several thousand miles away from the office," says Goshko, now at home and covering the Justice Department for the *Post.* "And though I hate the word, I'm a self-starter. If you need a pat on the back or someone to tell you what to do, you shouldn't be a foreign correspondent. The *Post* and (New York) *Times* have better communications than most overseas but you're still pretty much on your own. The foreign desk tends to take your word on what is and what is not important." Goshko spent ten years abroad, first in Latin America and then in Bonn. While in South America, the *Post* moved his bureau from Lima to Buenos Aires, one of the reasons being that Goshko was just about to be thrown out of Peru by that country's dictatorship. Goshko is proficient both in Spanish and in German, and he believes that a reporter cannot properly do his job in a foreign country unless he has mastery of the language. "Some try it, but it shows up in their work," he said.

The foreign service at the *Washington Post* was built by Philip Foisie, who came to the newspaper in 1955. While the *Post* today ranks second only to the *New York Times* in the scope of its foreign coverage, it had no correspondents at all when Foisie joined the paper except for a stringer in Rome. The paper at that time had a "world desk" which covered both national and international news and devoted less than four colums a day to foreign news, most of it from the wire services. In January 1957 the *Post* sent Murrey Marder to London as its first correspondent abroad but Marder worked half-time for WTOP, the *Post*-owned television station in Washington. The *Post* did not have any extensive foreign coverage until 1962 when it started hiring already-established correspondents abroad, a practice which Foisie often found unsatisfactory. So the *Post* turned to the practice of growing its own foreign correspondents, and Goshko, then working on the local staff, was recruited to be one of the first. At Foisie's suggestion Goshko applied for and obtained a Ford Foundation-sponsored fellowship enabling reporters to study foreign affairs at Columbia. He was the first of five *Post* reporters to win this fellowship and go abroad. One of them called it, "The Goshko Memorial Fellowship." Foisie's efforts to expand the *Post's* foreign service received a boost in 1963 with the formation of the Los Angeles Times-Washington Post News Service. Though the news service did not make a profit as quickly as anticipated, its requirement for foreign news helped create a foreign staff at the *Post* which now includes twelve fulltime correspondents abroad plus twenty stringers. The *New York Times* has thirty-seven foreign correspondents and forty-six foreign stringers. The stringers at both papers, says Foisie, run the gamut. "A stringer may be a warm body who does not speak English but gives us tips. Another stringer may be paid more than a staffer and have a status which is virtually indistinguishable."

The wire services and the big American newspapers traditionally have used a lot of stringers, both at home and abroad. Loosely defined, a stringer is anyone who files anything on a pre-arranged basis and is paid by story rate or space rate, or occasionally by a small fee each month for the protective purposes of the employer. Hundreds, perhaps thousands, of domestic American reporters, particularly on out-of-the-way papers, string for the wires or the big papers, and a few are able to substantially increase their own salaries doing this. The *Washington Post* has more than fifty stringers around the country, some of them quite good, and many other reporters who would like to string. There is no shortage of would-be stringers abroad either, but quality control is more difficult. One of the complaints of the disgruntled wire service correspondent in *The Kansas City Milkman* in that his U.S. wire service depends upon stringers who

slant the news in behalf of their governments or
nationalities. It is a valid complaint. "One of the great
scandals of journalism is how stringers are chosen," says
Foisie. "At one time a single journalist wrote all the
stories out of Burma for all the newspapers and press
services. Stringers in Cambodia were in the pay of the
government." Of course, dependence upon a foreign government of an official party line isn't limited to stringers.
The free press is a limited phenomenon on this planet,
and the journalism of Communist countries and dictator-
ships, as well as of some other nations, expressly exists to
serve the state. Even forty years ago, when propaganda
was less refined and television still on the drawing
boards, George Seldes could write accurately that correspondents could not help being affected by this "great
stream of corrupt news."[2] And they cannot. The perils of
getting more-or-less official propaganda into the paper as
news are great enough that Foisie has a standing order
that correspondents, except in unavoidable circumstances, are not to file through censorship unless both the
newspaper and the readers know that the dispatch is
censored. And the *Post* usually rotates its foreign correspondents every three years, or brings them home, a
practice which Simons says prevents reporters from "going native" or unconsciously becoming advocates for the
country or the beat they cover.

The requirements desired in a foreign correspondent
are high, perhaps unrealistically so. Ben Bradlee, who
has been a foreign correspondent, believes that assignments abroad require the reporter to have a strong family situation because he is away from home a lot, sometimes amid physical dangers. "We haven't sent a foreign
correspondent out of this country for seven years whose
wife I have not talked to at length." says Bradlee. The
potential correspondent is talked to even more by Foisie,
who in an interview in the summer of 1975, gave this

---

[2]Seldes, *Freedom of the Press*, p. 242.

picture of what he looks for on the foreign staff:

> A foreign correspondent should be a very good jour-
> nalist, a good general assignment reporter. When a corre-
> spondent goes abroad, he represents the foreign desk. He
> also represents every other department of the paper. He
> has to think in terms of the entire life of the country he's
> assigned to, not a part of it. He's the sports reporter and
> the financial reporter, too. And he has to view the whole
> of a society if he is to understand any of its parts. I look for
> a person who is mature. If a newspaper like the *Post*
> wants to be respected, the reporter abroad must be a per-
> son who earns that respect. He should be a person who
> does not succumb to anger or, easily, to frustration. He
> should be cool with a sense of humor. He should have a
> realization that what he does will reflect on his paper and
> his country. And if at all possible, he should have lan-
> guage proficiency and a knowledge of the area to which he
> is being sent. If he has all these things, that's a dream.

Foisie also regards physical health and, on many
foreign beats, physical courage as a requirement for a
correspondent. He also has a lot of negative requirements. "You must never send someone abroad who has
personal problems," says Foisie. "That will distract him.
For instance, if a reporter leaves behind a house that he
really loves and he's afraid of what the tenants will do, it
will drive him and you up the hill. Never send a person
abroad who is not confident of his relationship with the
paper. The distance creates too many barriers to send
someone out to prove himself. Never send a person
abroad who doesn't want to go abroad. Never send somebody abroad whose wife doesn't want to go. Never send a
guy abroad with a writing problem. There are some very
good reporters in this category, people who need to talk
out a story with an editor. You can't do that overseas.
Also, never send a guy abroad who thinks he's becoming
part of an elite. It tends to make him difficult to deal with
and it creates a hell of a problem on the re-entry. And in
the real world you can't send a person abroad with a very

large family because the costs just eat you up.[3] What it
boils down to is that you send people abroad you can
trust. You have to trust the correspondent on everything
— his stories, his sources, even his expense accounts." An
hour or so after Foisie had said this he sought me out in
the newsroom of the *Post* and added that his litany of
requirements, both positive and negative, assumed that
the prospective foreign correspondent had a high order of
applied intelligence. "Foreign reporting is comparative
journalism and requires intellectual analysis. It also requires an understanding by the reporter of his own country. I was impressed with a steel mill in India at a time I
hadn't seen one here. A correspondent should see his first
steel mill in America."

Foreign correspondents obviously face special barriers
of culture, language and censorship. Most of them also
are aware that their reach must inevitably exceed their
grasp. "No foreign correspondent really does the kind of a
job that a person living in that country can do," says
Tracy Wood of the *Los Angeles Times,* who worked for
United Press International in Saigon and Hong Kong. "It
takes a lifetime to know a country." But foreign correspondents outside the busy wire services also possess the
advantage that they are rarely pressed for copy as their
colleagues are back home. This is a function partly of
distance and of cable costs but even more of the relatively
limited space which most newspapers allocate to foreign
news. This absence of daily pressure to file enables a

---

[3]The *Washington Post* gives each correspondent who goes abroad a letter
signed by Foisie which provides the "understanding of the conditions" of the
assignment. The letter provides for a three-year tour of duty which the *Post*
may shorten unilaterally or extend by mutual consent. It also provides for a
cost-of-living allowance (with an understanding that it may decline if
domestic inflation increases), a devaluation allowance on a portion of the
correspondent's salary and whatever allowances have been agreed to on rent,
transportation and messenger service. The key paragraph in this letter of
understanding reads: "The controlling principle, in all financial matters, is
that you will bear all costs that you might normally bear if you were living in
Washington and the *Post* will bear all special costs that arise from the fact
that you are abroad."

foreign correspondent to function as a truly conceptual reporter, if he is otherwise capable of it. "I like to tell a foreign correspondent that if he does his job properly that at the end of his tour of duty he'll be able to take his dispatches, shuffle them and turn them over to a publisher for a book," says Foisie.

There is a presumption in the news business since the end of the Vietnam War that the American newspaper reader is less interested in foreign news and more interested in his own country. It is perhaps less a presumption than a self-fulfilling prophecy and is based on a perception of a new national inwardness or "isolationism" rather than on surveys demonstrating that people have abruptly lost interest in foreign news.[4] It seems likely to me that most Americans never were that interested in foreign news to begin with, except for the war news, and equally likely that they will become even less interested if their ration of foreign news is reduced. There also may be a commercial reason behind the recent lack of interest shown by news organizations in foreign coverage. Because of huge increases in newsprint costs most newspapers in the United States are trying to cut down on their use of newsprint. Many papers are accomplishing this by reducing their newshole, a trend which threatens to further reduce the space allocated for foreign news. Just as foreign aid has no domestic lobby in Congress beyond those who administer the program, foreign coverage has no lobby in the newsroom save the foreign desk. I have never read a letter to a newspaper, except from a foreign exile, which bemoaned lack of coverage of a foreign story, but newspapers are continually under fire for supposedly ignoring some story close to home. And local news, which

---

[4]The *New York Times* on September 19, 1975 published an article on its op-ed page by William Watts, president of Potomac Associates, contending that Americans turned toward isolationism in the decade between 1964 and 1974 but turned slightly back toward internationalism in 1975. Watts' summary figures for 1975 classify 45 per cent of the population as "internationalists," 35 per cent as "mixed" and 20 per cent as "isolationists."

has a demonstrable utility and is cheap to gather, is now in vogue. If any of the reduced emphasis on foreign news helps to improve the quality of economics coverage in American newspapers, the result might well be worth it. "Most medium-sized papers do badly and limit their so-called economics reporting to local business news," says Hobart Rowen, the *Washington Post* economics columnist. Financial reporting does not attract sufficient quality journalists in the first place, since relatively few news people are business-oriented. In the past it also has repelled many talented people because of the frequent practice of using the business news pages as a form of advertising payola. When I edited a community newspaper in California, it was a common practice for the advertising manager to funnel a certain number of ribbon-cutting and business-opening stories toward the news department, even on a newspaper where the publisher scrupulously resisted business pressure against editorial opinion. This is the sort of behavior which makes most young reporters keep a maximum distance between themselves and the financial news department. Payola practices have also reduced the impact of the business page, which in many communities is regarded as a form of unpaid advertising. In addition, there is a tendency on most newspapers, as Nicholas von Hoffman has noted, to treat economics and politics as if they were "distinct, vaguely related specialties."[5] There is substance to this accusation. "Economics" often is treated as if it were a separable subject that can be dealt with by the financial writers while "politics " is covered by the news side. And stories about the ways in which business operates usually are regarded as suitable only for the financial pages, or for the trade magazines. Few newspapers see it as their task to write about the business world on page one. I suspect

[5]Nicholas von Hoffman, "Covering Politics: the Economic Connection," *Columbia Journalism Review,* January-February, 1975.

this is a negative consequence of the traditional resistance of the news department to the business office, which fostered an attitude that business stories were in themselve unnewsworthy.

Few newspapers devote the resources to investigations of suspected corporate abuses that they devote to other investigatory stories. If knowledge of economics and an understanding of corporate practices are a requisite for this kind of journalism, few newspapers even have the resources to devote to such stories. But the deficiencies extend beyond the lack of investigative journalism. Stories which are not on the business page need to be enriched by economics analysis. One relatively homely example is Social Security, which long has been presented to readers in political terms as an "insurance policy," which it is not.[6] When the program proved for many recipients to be a bad buy, in insurance terms, and when it also, as those knowledgeable about it had long known, proved to be underfunded, it is not surprising that many persons on Social Security became alarmed. Peter Milius, who reports economics news on the national staff of the *Washington Post,* addressed these alarms in a skillful story which explained (1) how the system works; (2) what was wrong with it; and (3) why the political realities made it reasonably certain that Social Security wasn't going to "collapse." We need many more stories like this, and we also need, in Washington, more stories on the regulatory agencies by bureaus which are now content to leave this coverage to the trade press. "You can't just go after the jugular vein," says Peter Silberman, the business and financial news editor of the *Washington Post.* "It's important to cover the agencies and the economics reports on a regular basis. Most of the time the press doesn't do that."

It is probably true, or at least a number of newspaper

---

[6]The best critical account of the Social Security program appearing in a daily newspaper of which I am aware was a three-part series by Warren Shore appearing in *Chicago Today* beginning April 29, 1974.

editors think it is true, that double-digit inflation and the
recession of 1974-75 increased newspaper awareness of
economics issues. Many newspapers, responsive to the
moods of their readers, now pay more attention to
consumer-oriented stories than they did in the past. So do
many television networks and stations, where comparative stories on the price of a grocery shopping basket
have now become commonplace. *Time,* which has one of
the best business writers in John Berry, has been demonstrating for a long time that news about American
business is not necessarily synonymous with dull, uninteresting writing. In short, I think there is some evidence
for Hobart Rowen's belief that business news reporting is
getting better. Readers of newspapers where this is not
the case always can comfort themselves with the *Wall
Street Journal,* which remains the beacon for financial
journalism. As Chris Welles pointed out in an article
criticizing financial journalism in the July-August 1973
issue of *Columbia Journalism Review* "it was the *Journal*
which broke the Equity Funding fraud, the bribery and
kickback scheme at American Airlines, the conflict of
interest scandal at Kaiser Industries, the Tino De
Angelis salad oil swindle, and other exposes. Defenders
of the *Journal* point out that it obtained its almost awe-
some credibility, both inside and outside business,
through scrupulous adherence to provable facts and to
conclusions only as broad as those facts justify." As long
as the *Wall Street Journal* continues to function in this
way, there remains hope that financial reporting will be
something other than a neglected backwater of American
journalism. But even with the *Journal* to guide them, it
will not be easy for most newspapers to break the historic
mold. "There remains the problem of the institution,
which is that newspapers are reluctant to bite the hand
which feeds them," says Silberman. "The tendency is to
needle here or poke there but never cut to the bone. It
relates to the fact that newspapers themselves are among
the most secretive and the most protective about the facts

and figures of their own business. They are not likely to ask others to do what they are unwilling to do themselves."

Financial journalism, in one form or another, has been with us for a long time. The same cannot be said for another specialty, education coverage, which was launched with the advent of *Time* in 1923. Coverage of local school districts is as old as the beat system of journalism, but the *New York Times,* a newspaper pioneer in making education a specialty beat, did not have an education editor until 1941. On many papers education stories were thought of as "features" rather than as hard news. Old-time male reporters often sniffed at the education beat as "women's news" and transmitted this prejudice to newcomers to the business. George Gerbner observed in a study conducted for the U.S. Offie of Education in 1967[7] that what *Time* had described as "a boom on the school beat" was largely limited to metropolitan dailies, that only one in four daily newspapers had a fulltime reporter assigned to education news and that on papers which had such specialists the reporter or education editor "was impressed with the significance of his assignment even if still somewhat restive about his prestige in the newsroom."

I covered an education beat for a short time in 1957 and had a county school district as part of my beat two years after that. When subsequently I became editor of a community newspaper in Contra Costa County, California, it sometimes seemed as if half my time was spent dealing with issues relating to education — typically, complaints from citizens that the schools were spending too much money and forcing up the tax rate or complaints from parents that schools weren't teaching Johnny to read (it was always Johnny in those days and

---

[7]Dr. Gerbner is dean of the Annenberg School of Communications, University of Pennsylvania. His study was published in the *Journalism Quarterly,* University of Minnesota, Summer, 1967.

never Joanne) or complaints from school administrators
and teachers that the newspaper wasn't doing enough to
pass their precious bond issue or raise teacher's pay.
Those were the post-Sputnik days when American educators acted as if they were possessed by a mass inferiority
complex resulting from the achievements in the physical
sciences of the supposedly backward Russians. Those also
were the days when school districts were preoccupied by
frenzied programs of classroom building in an effort to
accomodate the school-age children of the post-war baby
boom. I can remember one assistant administrator who
was uncharacteristically obsessed with educational quality who was rudely cut short by a usually docile school
board. The board member wanted to hear from the next
speaker, the district's "facility planner," who had a proud
report on the number of portable classrooms which had
been obtained for the next semester.

I realize now that the schoolmen felt even more frustrated than the reporters. Faced with parental discon-
tent, taxpayer's revolts, media disapproval and financial
dilemmas, schoolmen naturally retreated into the jargon
of their separate world where they could talk about "the
real problems of education" which no ordinary citizen —
unless he was an advocate of a teacher's pay raise —
could possibly understand. Secrecy also was an expression of the same frustrations, and in California, of a political system which assured that a member of a school
board usually was chosen by the school establishment.
School boards and school administrations, therefore,
tended to be of the same mind in contrast to city councils
and county governing boards where a dissenter or two
usually could be counted on to blow the whistle on a
secret meeting. The result, as expressed by a reporter in
the Gerbner survey, was that school boards operated "in
ways that destroy public confidence." This reporter, who
worked for a big city daily, said of the board he covered:

Its monthly public meetings are a joke. Everything is
neatly arranged in advance. The board meets privately to

decide what it will do in public. It then goes through its paces like seals in a circus act. Its public meetings are a complete waste of time. There is never an exchange of ideas about important education issues, local or state or national. The board's budget-making procedures are equally undemocratic. It prepares a budget, decides exactly how each dollar will be spent and then, at the last minute, holds a public hearing at which all citizens are invited to speak. Then, after everyone had has his "say," the board goes ahead and adopts the budget as originally prepared, totally ignoring the recommendations of the citizenry.

This is a fair description of most of the school board meetings which I attended or which reporters under my direction covered when I was editor. It is small wonder that ordinary citizens felt left out of the educational process. Ultimately, many of these citizens expressed their frustration in voting down school bond issues or in refusing to raise school taxes.

The education reporter faces a variety of problems in dealing with the system. On no beat that I have covered, including the White House, does a reporter have to be more determined to resist co-option than he does in covering education, where there is a great tendency by schoolmen to assume that everyone shares their premises. Also, reporters are apt to be more sympathetic to a public interest than to a private one and it is always the claim of schoolmen that they are acting in the public's behalf. The education lobby both in Washington and in Sacramento is one of the most influential and well-financed, but schoolmen remain fond of the fiction that they are "not in politics." They certainly are entitled to this claim under the First Amendment, but there is no reason that any reporter with his wits about him should believe them.

Like other specialists, the education reporter also must beware of lapsing into the jargon of those he is covering. "It's the same kind of crazy problem you have with ambassadors and sometimes with foreign correspondents who begin to fall in love with the country they're in and forget who they're representing," says Howard Simons. "The second danger is that if you do pick up the expertise and the jargon and you know too much about it, subliminally when you sit down at the typewriter you write a sentence and you interpolate in your own mind the next sentence and then you type a third sentence. *You* know what it means when you read the first and third sentences, but the *reader* doesn't because he misses the middle sentence that isn't there but is in your head."

Gerbner's survey of education reporting in 1967 defined reporters' views of the "headline issues in education" as including "the right-wing attacks on education, the movement toward integration and the problem of violence." Doubtless, political conservatives would disagree with this phrasing, if not with the list of issues. So would I. The so-called "right-wing attacks on education" embrace issues ranging from fundamentalist or know-nothing assaults on the teaching of evolution, sex education and *The Lottery* to legitimate concerns that students were being taught Keynesian economics theory to the exclusion of all other theories or even that students were being taught nothing at all. But it is probably true that local school districts, dependent as they often are upon property taxes and other locally raised monies, are especially susceptible to the lowest common denominator of ideological attack from any quarter. This has been demonstrated by the integration question in general and by the school busing issue in particular. I have a large sympathy for the schoolmen on these issues. The schools were forced by the courts to bear the brunt of a social issue which the United States long had neglected and which it was unwilling to confront directly within its less vulnerable institutions. Whatever else it may have done, school busing aimed at securing integration diverted the attention of the American people and the media from the issues of quality education. The post-Sputnik debate, however simple-minded, was at least a debate about what was occurring in the classroom. The busing debate became an emotional, violence-marked controversy about the transportation of school children.

Northern newspapers, by and large, were less equipped to cope with the issues of integration and cross-town busing than were their Southern counterparts. Southern newspapers had been living with the issues of integration for a long time. Early on, such Southern newspapers as the *Little Rock Gazette,* the *Pine Bluff (Ark.) Commercial* and the *Atlanta Constitution* showed great journalistic courage, sometimes at the expense of advertising, in insisting that even the most unpopular court decisions on integration must be obeyed. Later, Northern newspapers — like Northern citizens — had to face the kinds of problems which they had been accustomed to thinking of as "Southern" in nature. Many of these Northern papers lacked reporters with the two distinctive backgrounds that might have been most helpful in coverage. First of all, most papers do not have black reporters.[8] Neither are most papers rich in reporters of working-class ethnic descent whose communities often were most affected by cross-town busing. Nevertheless, the papers usually tried to cover busing issues comprehensively and, in the best journalistic tradition, they caught it from all sides. Blacks often perceive newspapers as being opposed or indifferent to busing, while whites hostile to busing often regard newspapers as unsympathetic to their problems and to their points of view. In a November 1969 article in

---

[8]This is an understatement. Figures provided me by Bob Maynard of the *Washington Post* show that of 38,000 newsroom professionals in the United States only 300 are non-white. Of that number, 28, or nearly 10 per cent of the whole are on the *Washington Post* and disproportionately high percentages of the total also were employed by the *New York Times* and the Louisville and Chicago papers. Most newspapers, as Maynard points out, do not have a minority journalist in their midst. Maynard's figures are based on a report originally made by Norman Isaacs in his capacity as chairman of the minority employment committee of the Associated Society of Newspaper Editors in 1972. It was updated the following year and found no change.

The Quill, Martin Gershen of the *Newark Star-Ledger's*
bureau in New York City charged that newsmen had not
been permitted to report the true story on the violence
which occurred during the New York teacher's strike and
student rebellion of the year before. "Reporters were
beaten up or otherwise harassed, intimidated and
threatened so that they could not see many of the events
occurring or talk to the participants involved," Gershen
wrote. "And their bosses, the editors and news managers,
in too many instances failed to support the working
press. As a result, newsmen after awhile became indifferent to the story and more concerned about their personal safety. Gershen details several instances of violence and threats against reporters, including the beating of an ABC newsman and a death threat against a
New York newspaper reporter. He said that the attitude
of both the political and editorial leadership in New York
seemed to be: "Let's don't rock the boat; let's not blow
things up beyond all proportion; let's pretend that we
don't see horrible things and maybe they'll go away."
Edwin Diamond, a political scientist and lecturer who
examined the performance of the Boston media for the
Columbia Journalism Review, maintained that the press
became the villain for "trying to perform the way the
press is always being told to perform in crisis."[9] The
charge, which Diamond said was repeated both by anti-
busing demonstrators in Boston and by unnamed national reporters, was that "Boston's news organizations
were deliberately censoring the news in order to play
down the city's racial problems." Diamond did not find
the charge valid, and he attempted to prove by arrest
statistics that the violence was far less than many people
outside Boston believed. One reason for this belief, as
Diamond shows, is that the wire service stories from Boston stressed violence even when the violence was very
slight. Diamond quotes one wire service reporter as say-

[9]Edwin Diamond, "Boston: The Agony of Responsibility," *Columbia Journalism Review,* January-February, 1975.

ing that wire service headquarters in New York invariably would ask reporters to move isolated instances of violence higher up in their stories if they filed a lead saying that "classes were generally peaceful." And Diamond quotes one wire service editor as saying:

> In the first four weeks (of the 1974 school year) we were writing one lead every hour, and we got to the point where we'd lead with fights involving five or six people with no injuries. The problem was that some of the stuff wasn't worth reporting. Everybody — New York, the subscribers — was keyed up about "the Boston school situation," and so you've got to come up with a story, even though there wasn't a story there

I share the concern of this wire service editor. Newspapers may cover busing stories in their own communities responsibly, but the notions of domestic "responsibility" rarely apply to out-of-town stories where the standard is the usual one that violent disruption is far more newsworthy than peaceful integration. The trouble with this double standard is that the expectations of the local community are fueled by the stories about busing violence elsewhere. But I also believe that Gershen has a point about the 1968 New York teachers' strike. Even if the Boston papers behaved commendably, it is possible for newspapers to err in the direction of being "too responsible" by suppressing news. Stories of systematic violence in school systems are newsworthy, and newspapers ignore these stories at their own peril. Parents learn what is going on at school from their children and from other parents, whether the newspapers tell them or not. Rumors of racial conflict have ugly potential in a community where a newspaper follows a see-no-evil policy on such stories. Such a conflict can mean anything from a trivial unnewsworthy schoolyard fight to the violent beating of pupils and teachers, and parents should have some recourse other than rumor for distinguishing between the two events. In the long run newspapers are better off if they have the trust of their readers. They are

more likely to gain this trust if they print even the un-
welcome news.

While citizens have other means for checking the validity of local education reporting, they have no such opportunity on many specialty beats. This is true, of course,
for much scientific and medical reporting and for foreign
coverage. It is probably most true of all for a specialized
beat of high importance, the coverage of the Supreme
Court. "Public understanding of the Supreme Court of
the United States depends almost exclusively on the
news media," writes Everette E. Dennis. "For most
Americans what appears in the public press is the sole
source of information about the workings and decisions of
the court."[10] Considering the thousands of reporters in
Washington, suprisingly few people comprise this "sole
source." A January 1974 survey by Dennis found only
seven members of the press corps who had fulltime assignments to the Supreme Court — reporters for three
wire services (AP, UPI and Reuters), the two Washington
daily newspapers, the *New York Times* and the
Newhouse News Service. Eleven other were listed as
"semi-regular," which Dennis defined as "those who
cover the beat assiduously but usually with another
agency, such as the Department of Justice. Five other
news organizations, including the three television networks, were listed as "semi-occasional." This small
number of reporters contrasts with the legions of reporters who regularly cover Congress and the White House
and seems inadequate considering the significance which
decisions of the high court have assumed in American
life. The late Justice Felix Frankfurter once told James
Reston that the *New York Times* would never think of
sending a reporter to cover the New York Yankees who

---

[10]Everette E. Dennis, "Another Look at Press Coverage of the Supreme
Court," *Villanova Law Review*, Spring 1975. I am grateful to Dennis, an
assistant professor of the University of Minnesota's school of journalism and
mass communication, for his helpful letters on this matter and on other
issues of reporting.

knew as little about baseball as its reporters covering the Supreme Court knew about law. "The justice overstated the case against the *Times* but was quite right so far as most of the American press was concerned," wrote James E. Clayton, who covered the court for the *Washington Post* from 1960 to 1964. "The press still does a poor job of covering the courts in general and the Supreme Court in particular."[11] Twenty years ago Max Freedman of the *Manchester Guardian* called the Supreme Court "the worst reported and worst judged institution in the American system of government." It is a judgment that probably would not stand today, although it has since been repeated in many variant forms. "Worst reported" or not, it is remarkable that after so many decisions of vast social consequence — on integration, on legislative reapportionment, on abortion, on evidence in criminal trials, to mention only a few topics — the Supreme Court is covered regularly by so few news organizations.

What has changed in the two decades since Freedman's indictment is the caliber of reporters assigned to the court by the news organizations which do cover it. In the late 1950s, according to John P. MacKenzie, who until 1977 covered the court for the *Washington Post,* only Anthony Lewis of the *New York Times* "really was doing top-notch work." He was joined by Clayton in 1961. "Now half a dozen reporters do very good work, none perhaps doing consistently as well as those two but some approaching it," writes MacKenzie. "The wire service reporters are more serious and better prepared than they were. The court is doing more to make the mechanics easier: (Chief Justice Warren) Burger followed through on Earl Warren's wish and the court now includes the headnote synopses with the opinions when delivered rather than later when published in bound volumes."[12]

---

[11]James E. Clayton, "Interpreting the Court," *Columbia Journalism Review,* Summer 1968.

[12]This quotation and all others by MacKenzie in the chapter except those otherwise identified are from a letter to the author in August, 1975.

Despite this change, the Supreme Court provides very little public information help to the reporters who cover its decisions. "The constraints of this setting and its limited technical assistance stand in marked contrast to other reportorial assignments in Washington," says Dennis. "In the executive and legislative branches the reporter is the target of press releases, special briefings, news conferences and an array of public relations materials designed to assist him in his job. Not so at the Supreme Court. As David L. Grey has written in his useful study, *The Supreme Court and the News Media,* 'The court job in many ways is like no other in Washington. The court is the only part of the federal government where the newsman is left totally on his own.' "[13] While Washington reporters often complain about "PR" in other government agencies, it is significant that the demands of Supreme Court reporters have been for more and better public information assistance. At the onset of the Burger Court twelve reporters drafted a background statement for the chief justice which said that "while we fully recognize that there is a necessary realm of confidentiality within the court, we work under one overriding principle, that the court, like all branches of government, should be an open institution." The reporters made eight specific requests. Among other things they sought simultaneous release of all opinions on a given day, distribution of all opinions a few hours in advance to reporters in a lockup with no access whatever to the outside until a common, fixed release time, advanced notice by docket number on a confidential basis of cases to be decided that day, release of headnotes with opinions and joint release of decisions related to one another. Burger took three months to consider the requests, then held a meeting with the reporters and agreed to release the

---

[13]Dennis, "Another Look at Press Coverage," p. 5. The quotation is from a book by Grey published by the Northwestern University Press in Evanston, Illinois in 1968.

headnotes. He called the lockup idea, which would give reporters a chance to study decisions before writing about them and would be especially helpful to the wire services, "an idea whose time has not come" but said he might eventually redesign the court and provide glass-walled booths where correspondents could telephone directly to their papers and stations.[14]

Secrecy remains the distinctive hallmark of the Supreme Court, a secrecy so extreme that MacKenzie believes it is damaging both to the court and to the press. "The Supreme Court, which can tell a President to divulge his most damaging secrets, is itself one of the most secretive institutions in all of government. The high court, which often lectures Congress and the executive branch on the need to observe due process of law standards, has no rules of its own on such critical matters as when a justice is too ill to participate in cases. And yet the court, despite policies of nondisclosure that would arouse suspicions in any other branch of government, sits astride the judicial branch enjoying broad immunity from criticism over its procedures. It may be the least investigated department in Washington." These were the opening sentences of a news analysis by MacKenzie in the May 11, 1975, *Washington Post* which discussed the secrecy that had shrouded the illness of Justice William O. Douglas. When Douglas left Walter Reed Hospital after three months of recuperating from a stroke, even his departure was kept a secret. The court's press officer Barrett McGurn told reporters that Douglas was using a sling on his left arm without saying anything about the paralysis of his arm and of his left leg. The question of whether Douglas was fit to resume his duties on the bench literally had life-or-death consequences. A number of decisions, including a ruling on the constitutionality of capital punishment, were being held in abeyance in the belief that Douglas' vote could make the difference in the

---

[14]The same, pp. 27-28.

court's decision. The secrecy on the Douglas question was an example of MacKenzie's observation that "jurists habitually confuse the secrecy that's necessary for decision-making with secrecy on matters not related to decisions."

Considering the handicaps, the press actually may be covering the Supreme Court better than anybody realizes. MacKenzie believes that the "regulars" among the court reporters have accurately reported under deadline pressure most of the controversial decisions of the court. But he also thinks that this accurate reporting sometimes has been overshadowed later on by sloppy references to the original decision by non-court reporters, by editorials written by editorial writers who have not read the decision and most of all by politicians who misrepresent a court decision for their own purposes. MacKenzie gives several examples in a December 1968 article in the *Michigan Law Review*. At one point he discusses the reporting of one of the controversial decisions of the Warren Court, *Escobedo v. Illinois:*

> In *Escobedo,* for example, it was widely and correctly reported at the time of decision that the suspect's incriminating statements had been ruled inadmissible because he had been denied access to counsel who had already been retained and who was figuratively beating on the interrogation room door while the petitioner was being questioned in disregard of his express wish to consult his lawyer. Since his release from the murder charge against him, Danny Escobedo has been embroiled with the law many times; finally, in 1968, he was convicted on federal criminal charges. Yet, in most of the news accounts about the later life of Danny Escobedo, the court's initial decision has been described as one which threw out his confession on grounds that police refused to let him see "a lawyer." ... Surely the fact that Escobedo was denied permission to consult a previously retained attorney makes a difference to an evaluation of the situation that confronted the now-notorious petitioner. Given the

actual factual setting, the ruling seems less based on a "technicality" or excessive solicitude for a criminal.[15]

MacKenzie's belief that the coverage of the Supreme Court has improved was shared by the court reporters who responded to Dennis' survey. Twelve of the fifteen reporters responding rated the reporting of the wire services as good or excellent and eleven of the fifteen gave these same ratings to newspaper coverage. (The wires, at the time of the survey, were represented by Charlotte G. Moulton of UPI, dean of the court reporters, Vernon A. Guidry of AP and Tom Stewart of Reuters.) Only four of the fifteen respondents thought that newsmagazines provided good coverage of the court and none thought it excellent. Only two of the fifteen thought that television or radio gave good coverage and none gave broadcast journalism an excellent mark. Five reporters gave examples of a Supreme Court decision during the past five years they thought had been inaccurately reported and three cited the 1973 abortion decision of *Roe v. Wade* as their example.

The level of specialized training is relatively high among Supreme Court reporters. Six of the reporters had law degrees and six also had master's degrees, five of these in journalism. But the debate between specialization versus generalization is as unresolved on this highly specialized beat as elsewhere. When Dennis asked the reporters what educational training they would advise for a young person who aspires to cover the court or other aspects of the legal system, ten said a general liberal arts education, seven said training in a law school, four said graduate work in constitutional law and three said train-

---

[15]John P. MacKenzie, "The Warren Court and the Press," *Michigan Law Review*, December, 1968. A footnote to this article also contains some facetious but useful advice for court reporters: "The word 'landmark' as applied to Supreme Court decisions should be eliminated from journalistic usage and perhaps English usage generally. Another candidate for extinction is the phrase 'in effect,' as in 'The court ruled in effect that . . .' This phrase, as used by journalists, is nearly always followed by a mistake."

ing in a journalism school. Some of the reporters gave multiple responses.

MacKenzie's view is that the press should provide "training and time" for Supreme Court reporters. Anthony Lewis, after a year of legal training at Harvard on a Nieman fellowship, went on to nine years of distinguished Supreme Court reportage and a fine book, *Gideon's Trumpet*. MacKenzie, who I believe is outstanding at translating complex legal decisions into lucid everyday language, also had a year of legal training. Fred Graham of CBS and Carl Stern of NBC, both of whom are lawyers, have given television far more competent coverage of the high court than it has ever had before. "Each paper of any size must, in this day of specialization have at least one well-versed legal writer, able to function not just on the local courthouse level but also on the federal level," believes MacKenzie. "That reporter must be able to interpret decisions coming from distant courts and relate them to local conditions and needs. It's no longer asking too much to have that reporter sent off to school for six months or a year. The investment of *time* is no less significant and no less difficult for management to make. I have to fight for time to keep up with the court's business. Considering their basic impatience, the *Post's* editors actually have been quite good about it but they make it hard psychologically for a reporter to ask for 'dead time' when he knows in his conscience that it's needed. At times the court reporter should be treated the way investigative reporters are, let alone."

This last is not likely to happen. What one hopes *will* happen is that more news organizations will decide to devote more resources in covering the Supreme Court. Dennis, after his analysis of the strengths and weaknesses of Supreme Court coverage, became convinced that it was short-sighted to overcriticize the court's press corps. "Its size and limited resources make impossible the full coverage of one of the most overwhelmingly complex stories in national life," he wrote. "More appropriately,

criticism should be focused on newspaper and broadcasting groups as well as national magazines which have
abdicated their public responsibility by failing to cover
the court. Increasing the size of the press corps would
ease the weighty burden now carried by the wire services, which are the sole agencies covering the court in a
broad sense. Other publications and broadcast outlets are
more selective, relying heavily on the wires for general
coverage."

The argument about specialization versus generalization is never likely to be ended in the news business. One
hopes that it will not end, if only for the reason that it
makes even those news organizations which decide
against hiring specialists aware of the importance of giving their generalist reporters some specialized training.
Ideally, it is not just in writing stories on the specialized
beats themselves that such training becomes helpful. I
have in mind, on the *Washington Post,* then-medical
writer Stuart Auerbach writing the story of the resignation of the emotionally depressed Secretary of the Interi-
or, Stanley Hathaway, and pointing out that one out of
ten Americans suffers from depression. Or of Auerbach
explaining on the sports page of the *Post* the origins of
Baltimore Orioles pitcher Jim Palmer's arm problems.
Such insights by a generalist who has made himself a
specialist can enrich a multitude of news stories on any
given day.

In the final analysis the old editors were right in believing that reporting was a job for a generalist, even if
they underestimated the amount of specialized knowledge this generalist may need. "People do not understand
the basic nature of reporting," says generalist Bill
Moyers. "They do not realize that a person can by research and application master the essentials of a complex
specialized situation and inform others about it. The reporter is an informed citizen who makes himself knowledgeable. A year later he may totally have forgotten the
subject, but that's all right, too, if he has immersed him-

self in it and made it comprehensible while he was reporting about it. Reporters are gifted amateurs, and we badly need their gifts."

CHAPTER NINE

Covering Campaigns

*Riding in crowded buses and cluttered air-
planes, working 18 hours a day, writing stories
on portable typewriters balanced on our knees,
tossing our copy on the run to Western Union
messengers, shabby, tired, frequently dis-
oriented about both time and place, poorly fed
and rarely rested, cranky, crotchety, hungover,
we try to make sense of the most complicated
political system in the world.*

*That we often fail is no surprise; that we
sometimes succeed is a miracle.*

– James M. Perry in US & THEM

On February 9, 1972, the man who had for sixteen
months been described as the front-runner for the Democratic presidential nomination was campaigning in New
Hampshire. An Associated Press story which appeared
that afternoon in the Portsmouth *Herald* and in various
other New England papers described his activities in this
way:

> Sen. Edmund S. Muskie, D-Maine, moved north from
> Massachusetts to New Hampshire today for an early
> morning speech at the Claremont Paper Mill in his quest
> for the Democratic endorsement in the state's presiden-
> tial preference primary next month.
>
> "Something is wrong when six out of every 100 Ameri-
> cans have no jobs," Muskie said in remarks prepared for
> delivery at the mill.
>
> He proposed a five-point program to cut employment
> . . .

The story was correct in identifying Muskie as a
senator from Maine who was seeking the Democratic
presidential nomination. Beyond that, there was nothing

to recommend it. For the facts were that Muskie did not "move north from Massachusetts" (he started in Washington and spent the previous night in New Hampshire), did not make "an early morning tour of the Claremont Paper Mill" (it was late morning, close to noon) and did not make a speech on unemployment. What Muskie *did* do was to walk through the Claremont mill after two question-and-answer sessions at high schools in Keene and Claremont and, to those reporters who were interested, pass out an oft-repeated statement on the ills of unemployment. Outside the mill the senator was cornered by the reporters traveling with him and asked to comment about the remarks of H. R. Haldeman, who had just made a rare television appearance and described critics of the President's Vietnam policy as "giving aid and comfort to the enemy." Muskie denounced Haldeman and the Nixon White House, in terms stronger than he had ever used previously, for trying to suppress dissent. But it was too late in the day for most afternoon papers to "new lead" their stories. As far as most New England readers were concerned, Muskie had "moved north from Massachusetts" to talk about unemployment in New Hampshire.[1]

There was nothing particularly distinctive about the AP story that day. It was a familiar example of the traditional overnight story, in this case written with a fine disregard for geography. It represented the kind of commonplace political public relations triumph regularly achieved by campaign press staffs which take advantage of a wire service's need to be represented by something about a major candidate on every wire cycle. The story had been given out by Muskie's staff in New Hampshire to the AP bureau and rewritten from the handout. On every campaign plane scores of similar stories are ground

---

[1] Portions of this account appeared in an article by the author in the June 1972 issue of *APME News,* the journal of the Associated Press managing editors.

out every day, and not just by the wire services, about
speeches which have yet to be given or which may never
be given. David S. Broder, writing about this practice in
February 1969 in the first edition of *The Washington
Monthly,* said:

> As often as I have seen and participated in this ritual
> of campaign journalism, the artificiality of the process
> never ceases to amaze me.
>
> If the speech is, let us say, prepared for delivery at an
> evening rally in Los Angeles, the stories in the Eastern
> morning papers will be on the newsstands long before the
> event itself takes place. Indeed, the candidate may not —
> if he is as harassed as candidates often are — even have
> seen the speech on which the stories have been based; he
> may not deliver it when the time arrives; but he will, as
> his press secretary assures the reporters, stand behind
> every word of the prepared text.
>
> There is an element of essential phoniness to the whole
> procedure, in which all parties agree to delude the reader
> into thinking he has read something the candidate has
> said and to conceal from him the reality — that nothing
> has happened more significant than the passage of words
> from typewriter to mimeograph machine to typewriter to
> printing press. From beginning to end, the process has a
> life of its own, unrelated to reality, as the word moves
> from the speechwriter's typewriter to the newspaper
> headlines almost untouched by human minds.
>
> Yet, ironically, it is when he is performing this almost-
> imbecile function of digesting and regurgitating someone
> else's thought that the political writer or campaign re-
> porter is in his least controversial role. Almost anything
> else he attempts — and he does attempt other roles — will
> land him in some sort of difficulty.

The reason that these "other roles" get a reporter into
trouble is that most of his readers share with the wire
service the fundamental tenet of objective reporting that
it is the reporter's prime duty to write what the candidate
has said. We have examined the consequences of this
legacy elsewhere, but it is particularly pernicious in

political journalism because the candidate tends to say much the same thing day after day and because he also desires to get his name in print or his head on the television screen with daily frequency. Broder calls this the Nixon School of Journalism, after Nixon's plea in his "last press conference" of 1962 that newspapers should "put one lonely reporter on the campaign who will report what the candidate says now and then." This belief is hardly peculiar to Nixon. In every political campaign which I have covered or know about there have been complaints from the candidate's camp that reporters were ignoring something vital that the candidate had said, usually "something vital" that had been reported ad nauseum. Politics is an ego-generating enterprise, and it is natural for any candidate who sees only a few paragraphs of his remarks in print and even less on television to think that he is being done in by the press. The politician's expectations are fed both by his own ego and by a long tradition in the news business. The tradition is fading now and being replaced by a conviction that reporters should write about the whole campaign, including the character and past record of the candidates and the reaction of the voters to candidates and events. This expanded definition of the political reporter's role is welcome and necessary, particularly in the coverage of presidential elections, because federal funding and the proliferation of primaries has multiplied the number of serious candidates. Not even the most politically oriented newspaper would have the space to cover an early primary — and it is the early primaries that are significant — if it conceived its role to be merely reporting what the many candidates had said. Many of these candidates are likely to be saying the same things, based upon what their pollsters or their instincts have told them about the mood of the electorate. The job of the political reporter is to describe the differences among the candidates, no matter what they are saying.

Political reporting, in its many forms, often has been

compared to sportswriting and with good reason. Political reporters and sportswriters, in Stanley Hyman's phrase about historians, seek "reasoned explanations for random events." Sportswriting is preoccupied with who will win the game and with the "turning point" upon which victory is based. The winning coach (campaign manager) becomes a genius while the losing coach is regarded as an incompetent. Post-game and post-campaign analyses are written as if every move of the winning side pointed to victory and every move of the losers pointed to defeat. But if we are able to tear ourselves out of the context in which the game was played or the campaign run, we know this is nonsense. A strong case can be made that the winning general-election campaigns of Richard Nixon in 1968 and of Jimmy Carter in 1976 were counter-productive and that the losing fall campaign of Gerald Ford in 1976 was exceptionally proficient. In any event, sports writing and political reporting are linked by the common bond which our society places on the competitive aspects of life. Indeed, our politicians emphasize the connection by regularly showing up at football games or, in the extreme case of Nixon, by phoning in dubious plays to the coach of the Washington Redskins on the eve of the big game. After elections political reporters regularly vow, much in the manner of the habitual drinker leaving his favorite saloon, to do less "horse race reporting" the next time and to write more about "the issues" or some other aspect of the campaign. Don't you believe it. The desire of the reader and the editor and even of the campaign reporter's spouse for predictive information is well-developed and persuasive. Let a political writer drop off during a campaign to earn a few extra bucks at some academic grove. The scholars, most of them, will ask the reporter not about issue development or the permutations of campaign organization under the new spending law but about who is going to win the primary the reporter is covering. "The basic American value is to look at the world in terms of win-

ners and losers," says Broder. "Politicians are interested
and the readers are interested in the outcome. I don't
think we ought to deny that basic fact."

One of the dangers for sportswriters and political reporters alike is an enduring capacity for mythmaking or
for believing in myths their predecessors have created.
Some of us think, for instance, that Nixon actually lost
the 1960 election because he failed to have a good
makeup man or because he went to Alaska on the
weekend before the election. Others think that Muskie
was done in during the 1972 primary in New Hampshire
because Donald Segretti sent him pizza pies he hadn't
ordered or because the vulgar attacks by *Manchester
Union-Leader* publisher William Loeb on Muskie and his
wife provoked the candidate to a well-publicized display
of tears. In my view these explanations give Loeb (or
Segretti and the Nixon dirty tricks department) more
credit for influencing events than they deserve. I was in
New Hampshire late in 1971 finishing up a book on Rep.
Paul (Pete) McCloskey, who was challenging Nixon. I
returned early in 1972, writing stories on the campaign
for the Washington bureau of Ridder Publications. It was
decided that on one of these trips I would cover Sen.
George McGovern for a few days and then switch over to
Muskie and accompany him back to Washington. Like
everyone else in Washington, I had been hearing that
McGovern had failed to get off the ground and that Muskie, a favorite of reporters in the 1968 vice-presidential
campaign, was a shoo-in for the Democratic nomination.
But it was a different story in New Hampshire, or so it
seemed to me. Both McGovern and McCloskey had been
campaigning before high-school audiences, a custom in
the New Hampshire primary, and doing very nicely before these forums. McGovern occasionally would be
tossed a hostile question by a Muskie supporter or
McCloskey one by a Nixon backer, but they invariably
answered good-naturedly and usually won applause.
Muskie also was answering questions, but in a different

manner. On Feb. 9, 1972, the same day Muskie arrived at
the Claremont mill, he made a speech at Keene High
School. During the ensuing question-and-answer session
a student haltingly challenged Muskie on the question of
campaign-finance disclosure, then pending in the Senate.
The student said that Muskie had cast a procedural vote
to weaken this legislation. Finance disclosure was a favorite theme at the time of McGovern, who had made his
list of contributors public. Muskie had refused to follow
suit, claiming it would put him at a disadvantage against
Nixon in the fall campaign. The student, a 17-year-old
named Scott Davis, was in the front row of the school
auditorium, near Muskie, and read his question about
the procedural vote from a piece of paper. "Where did you
get that paper?" Muskie shouted at him. Davis, appearing rattled by the intensity of the response, answered,
"From the McGovern headquarters, senator." This provoked an angry denunciation of the youth by Muskie,
which the senator followed with a brief speech asserting
that he favored campaign disclosure and had voted for it
in the Senate. Muskie concluded by charging Davis with
"not doing your homework" and telling him to sit down.

It was by no means an unusual expression of the Muskie temper. A day or so earlier, at Portsmouth High
School, Muskie had been questioned by a black student
about a statement he had made in California saying that
a ticket with a black as the vice presidential nominee
could not win. Muskie, obviously angered, answered that
his questioner was "ignoring reality." And so it went,
Muskie testily fighting off high-school questions any
senator should have been able to field easily. By chance,
on the plane back to Washington, I was invited to join a
poker game in the back of the Muskie plane when an aide
said he didn't want to play. I accepted the invitation. On
the first hand Muskie was dealt four cards to an inside
straight and threw down his hand with an oath when he
failed to make the straight on the fifth card. I like Muskie
just fine but I made a personal decision right then that he

seemed a little temperamental to be President of the United States. What does a political reporter do with this kind of insight? Frankly, I didn't know. Muskie was known to have a temper, but I had yet to read a story saying that he was showing it all over New Hampshire in response to questions asked him by high-school students. I didn't write the story, either. What I did do was to check the Congressional Record and find that Davis had been right and Muskie wrong in their little debate about the procedural vote on financial disclosure. At that point I wrote a weekend column setting forth what I have just described, minus the poker game, and ending with these words: " 'Sen. Muskie doesn't suffer fools gladly,' says (Press Secretary) Dick Stewart. The best guess of the New Hampshire primary is that the 'fools' category includes anyone with the temerity to question the plans or policies of Edmund S. Muskie."

If I had to do it again, and could get away with it, I might lead with the poker game. In my crowd a poker player's blow-up when he fails to draw the statistically unlikely inside straight on five cards is considered more significant than the bawling out of a high-school student. Whatever the lead should have been, I wish I had brought the independent perspective of that campaign trip (where I knew few of the reporters) and that column to more of my political reporting. Usually, we find it difficult to write that most important of all stories: "The emperor has no clothes." If we took that approach we would have written several stories about key political figures at various head tables falling fast asleep, literally, during speeches by Gerald Ford. We might have written, also, as Tom Wicker once suggested, that "Hubert Humphrey opened his 1972 campaign today by misrepresenting his 1968 campaign." And we certainly would have written differently than we did about Nixon in that same campaign.

Early in 1968, Dick Reeves was doing candidate pro-

files for the *New York Times Magazine*. These profiles
often are influential beyond the *Times'* circulation because they are widely quoted and used as research material by other reporters. Reeves in 1968 profiled the Democratic candidates and George Romney and Ronald Reagan on the Republican side. But he did not profile Nixon,
instead electing to do a piece on "the men around Nixon."
It was a prophetic article as those things go, identifying
John Mitchell as the power in the campaign and singling
H. R. Haldeman out for attention at a time when he was
not well known. It did not, however, scrutinize Nixon, an
omission which Reeves still regrets. "Nixon spanned two
generations and I considered him a known quantity," Reeves said. "When he was running for office the first time I
was in the third grade. The New Nixon came from me
and from those like me. Not that I used the phrase, but I
might as well have. The events of his early career were a
long time ago, and we didn't ask questions about them.
Alger Hiss to me was like Dred Scott. So we didn't ask
the essential question. We didn't ask, 'Who is Nixon?' "

Nixon did not, of course, want anyone asking this "essential question." Nor did he really want reporters
around him at all. What he wanted in 1968, more than
anything, was to give the appearance of a New Nixon, an
accessible and well-balanced Nixon, without running the
risks of being provoked. His strategists found the perfect
way to accomplish both objectives with their phony, pre-
arranged "citizens panels" of questioners, a device that
gave the appearance of openness without any of the at-
tendant dangers. But it is doubtful if the panels would
have counted much in the campaign except for the symbolic medium of television. Television places a premium
on campaigns which rely on visual impact rather than
ideas. "The media event has now become almost the total
campaign," says *Washington Star* columnist Jules Witcover. "Let's say a candidate walks through the Manned
Spacecraft Center and meets an astronaut. It takes half
the day. It is done for the benefit of television and noth-

ing has happened. No one learns anything from it. A
campaign at its best is a learning experience for everyone
— the people, the press and not least of all, the candidate.
In 1960 Kennedy campaigned in West Virginia and went
down various mines and for the first time this rich boy
saw what it was to live like that. He learned something
and he did something about what he had learned. His
first order as President was for an expanded distribution
of food to needy families."[2]

Modern candidates believe, with Canadian communications theorist Marshall McLuhan, that "the medium is
the message." The media event has become so central to
presidential campaigning that candidates invariably are
willing to forego the reality of an actual event for the
symbolic reality of the evening news. President Ford,
traveling down the Mississippi during the 1976 campaign, at one point climbed onto a deck chair and started
waving toward the bank of the river. As NBC's John
Chancellor put it, "The trouble was, there were no people
on the bank of the river. Then we noticed the cameras.
You didn't need people for that picture — only the President." Ford's central symbol in the early part of the campaign was the White House Rose Garden. That was
partly because of his aforementioned tendency for becoming a clear and present danger to the sleeping-pill industry while on the campaign trail. And it was a partly
justifiable reaction to the rigors of the campaign against
Reagan and an effort to gain a breathing spell while his
managers tried to get their act together for the fall campaign. But also it was a recognition that the White House
was the most appropriate symbol for an incumbent president, one he couldn't duplicate on the campaign trail.
This symbolism annoyed Carter, who took it as an example of how news coverage favored the incumbent president. But Carter's campaign, which began at the Warm

---

[2] Executive Order 10914 of Jan. 21, 1961, "Providing for an Expanded
Program of Food Distribution to Needy Families."

Springs, Ga., shrine of Franklin Roosevelt, was as dependent upon symbolism as his opponent's. "I don't see much difference between the President coming out of the Rose Garden to sign a bill he's opposed until the moment of passage and Jimmy Carter going to Polish Hill in Pittsburgh and putting on a 'Polish Power' T-shirt to imply that somehow he is more sympathetic to the needs of the Poles than the other guy," says Broder. "Both are essentially propaganda tactics and have to be treated as such."[3]

Not only has television encouraged symbolic campaigns but it has placed a premium on a particular type of candidate described best by Robert MacNeil in his 1968 book, *The People Machine*:

> These, then, are the qualities that the television era demands of political candidates: personality above all else — a personality not too specific and not the least abrasive, a personality which is pleasantly neutral enough to be built upon; a pleasing appearance with no features which may light unflatteringly on television; assurance . . . articulateness — an ability to put anything you say, even if it is "I don't know what we're talking about," in such a commanding and authoritative way that your grasp and

---

[3] Carter made several attempts to enlist the press on his side in the propaganda battle during the fall campaign and succeeded only in making reporters feel uncomfortable. The most overt attempt occurred on Sept. 25, a day when some of the traveling press wrote that Carter had distorted the truth in Houston by blaming *Playboy* for his own comments in an interview with the magazine during which Carter accused Lyndon Johnson of "lying, cheating and distorting the truth." Carter at first blamed this comment on a non-existent "summary" made by *Playboy*, then backed off this comment when it was clear that the press thought he was lying. That night, in San Diego, Carter initiated an off-the-record gripe session with 10 reporters (including this one), which he began by saying: "We're all in the campaign together. We all want what's best for our country." The reporters told Carter that they would be happy to talk with him but couldn't give him advice. Carter's press secretary, the irrepressible Jody Powell, summed up the purpose of the meeting by saying, "We're trying to decide whether to run an open campaign or a closed campaign."

leadership qualities will flow through into every living
room. In other words, you should be an actor.[4]

The last line of this description was aimed at Ronald
Reagan, who demonstrated the advantages of his television training in his successful 1966 and 1970 campaigns
for the California governorship. But one does not have to
be a real actor to qualify. There are many other examples
of what MacNeil calls "the televisible candidate," many
of them alive and well in the U.S. Senate. Such senators
as Charles Percy of Illinois, Robert Packwood of Oregon
and Daniel Patrick Moynihan of New York all qualify as
effective television personalities who understand the
technical requirements of the medium. Another televisible senator is former astronaut John Glenn of Ohio, at
least until he was required to give a lengthy, issues-
oriented keynote speech at the Democratic National
Convention in 1976. Glenn's cool, assured manner and
his celebrity status stood him in better stead when he
was briefly but repeatedly seen on Ohio television
screens during the 1974 campaign.

There also are non-televisible candidates, a category
that I suspect would include the vast majority of Americans. In most campaigns, television tends to be hard on
the old, the overweight, the non-smiler, the strident.
Perhaps the best example of what happens when a televisible candidate meets a non-televisible candidate occurred in the 1964 U.S. Senate race in California, where
Democrat Pierre Salinger unwisely agreed to debate Republican George Murphy on television. Salinger, a journalist who had been appointed a senator, looked jowly
and foreboding as he scowled his way through an inconclusive debate with the affable Murphy, who smiled a lot
and stuck to his basic campaign speech. Murphy was a
runaway winner over Salinger, in a year when Lyndon

[4] Robert MacNeil, *The People Machine: The Influence of Television on
American Politics*, (New York, 1968), p. 162.

Johnson was carrying California by a million votes.[5]
Another non-televisible candidate, even though he certainly qualifies as one of the best informed men in public life, is Sen. Hubert Humphrey. "My problem with television is the nature of my speaking," says Humphrey. "I am an exhorter. I am a dynamic speaker. When they want to pep up a meeting, they call in Hubert Humphrey to give them the political blood transfusion. For television that's not good. Because it looks like you're shouting at people."

The case made for television reporting is verity — that it shows a candidate "as he really is" without the intervention of a reporter. It was this supposed quality of the medium which caused Nixon to praise television coverage of his 1962 campaign in the same "last press conference" where he assailed newspaper accounts of the race.[6] Occasionally, television does perform this function of revealing the inner man, but not usually when he is campaigning for office. The televised glimpses of Sen. Joseph McCarthy badgering Army witnesses or of Richard Nixon battling the press from the San Clemente parking lot told us a lot about McCarthy and Nixon, but these were scenes of the principals as they behaved in office, not in campaigns. The fallacy of the notion that television shows the real candidate lies in the fact that the candidate almost never appears on camera unaided. Serious candidates have advisers who teach them how to simplify their messages for television, what to wear on camera and how to reveal those aspects of their personal-

---

[5] For an intriguing account of Murphy's pre-debate analysis of how to impress the television viewers, see *What Makes Reagan Run: A Political Profile* by Joseph Lewis (New York, 1968), p-89. Murphy anticipated that Salinger would come over as "sly and disrespectful" on television and would be at a disadvantage.

[6] "I think that it's time that our great newspapers have at least the same objectivity, the same fullness of coverage, that television has," said Nixon. "And I can only say thank God for television and radio for keeping the newspapers a little more honest."

ity which television favors. Modern candidates learn this
sort of thing early, much as a candidate of another day
learned to look voters straight in the eye and give them a
firm handgrip. MacNeil, after studying various candidates, came to believe that "television can, in a real
sense, 'create' a personality by filtering out some facets of
a man's own personality and letting through certain
others . . . The television audience is conditioned to expect certain traits as attractive by its prolonged exposure
to the star-oriented entertainment system." He cited the
opinion of Joseph Napolitan, one of the most skilled campaign directors, of what happened to Endicott (Chub)
Peabody, who was elected governor of Massachusetts in
1962. "Peabody was a big handsome guy," Napolitan
said. "Immediately after the election he started holding
press conferences and people said he seemed entirely different than in the campaign. The trouble was he was
getting tough questions and giving bumbling answers.
Not the clean, crisp image of the prepared spots . . . because maybe you waited eighteen times in filming the
spots to get just the right thing. His TV image dropped
afterward like a lead balloon. They had elected him on
one basis and he seemed entirely different."[7]

If a candidate expects to win, it is important to him
that differences of this sort not show up until after the
election. Television therefore encourages candidates,
particularly well-heeled and inarticulate candidates, not
to make any statements to either print or broadcast reporters that might conflict with the images their prepared spots are trying to convey. The best way to succeed
in this objective is to meet with reporters as infrequently
as possible. Even candidates who remain willing to be
challenged by reporters are likely to be inhibited on
campaign planes by a television camera which may show
them rambling on spontaneously in contradiction to a
carefully prepared TV spot into which they have poured

---

[7] MacNeil, *The People Machine*, p. 159.

their campaign funds. "In the old days you would get to know a candidate intimately by traveling with him," says Witcover. "There was a danger to this, but if you were professional you could handle it. Now you're talking to a candidate about something serious, and all of a sudden there are a half-dozen cameras on. Before you know it, you're talking about the weather."

Television also can help an insecure candidate establish an apparent relationship with the people without ever going near them. Nixon particularly liked television, at least when he was on by himself, perhaps because it gave him the feeling of control he sometimes lacked in dealing with newspaper reporters. Nixon's mastery of the medium was demonstrated as early as 1952 when his famous "Checkers speech" saved his place on the Republican ticket. The mastery was absent in the first and fateful debate with Kennedy in 1960, partly because of Nixon's illness at the time, but it returned in the third of the four debates, when Nixon was in a studio in Los Angeles and Kennedy was in New York. ". . . It was as if, separated by a continent from the personal presence of his adversary, Nixon were more at ease and could speak directly to the nation that lay between them," wrote Teddy White.[8]

Nixon's narrow loss to Kennedy in 1960 was followed by his decisive defeat at the hands of California Gov. Edmund G. Brown in 1962. That loss took a heavy psychic toll, as Nixon's press conference afterward revealed. "When he said you weren't going to have Nixon to kick around anymore, he really meant it," his friend Robert Finch said in looking back at that campaign. "He wasn't going to put himself in a position where he could be hurt anymore." Witcover, who covered Nixon's three presidential campaigns and wrote a valuable book about his climb from political oblivion to the presidency, believes

---

[8] Theodore H. White, *The Making of the President 1960,* (New York, 1961), p. 290.

that Nixon from then on resolved to have only necessary
dealings with the press. "Nixon ran himself into the
ground in 1960," says Witcover. "He ran around the
country mindlessly. He was extremely vulnerable to the
press. In 1960 Nixon did himself in by saying and doing
things that didn't advance his candidacy. This happened
again in 1962. What had happened was not lost on Nixon
and his managers in 1968. They decided to keep control
of the press. The 1968 campaign, in contrast to 1960, was
rigidly controlled. Nixon gave the impression of a campaign that didn't exist. He would criss-cross the country,
choosing his speaking appearances carefully. Behind the
appearance of a whirlwind campaign, he would relax on
the plane. He hardly ever spoke at night. He aimed his
campaign at the evening news. He spoke at major air-
ports with direct flights to New York. Hubert Humphrey,
campaigning in the conventional way, would have made
five or six appearances by midday. The odds were that
one of them would be a bomb. Further, the television
networks would select the most provocative item, which
might very well be the one that was the bomb. Then
there would be a need to match Humphrey on the evening news. He would be matched by a Nixon film clip
which showed Nixon doing exactly what he wanted, saying exactly what he had planned to say. The public was
left the impression of a harried candidate who contrasted
to a composed, cool Richard Nixon."

Newspaper reporters covering Nixon, most of them
obedient to the objective forms of journalism, were manipulated along with the television correspondents. With
some distinguished exceptions, most of them wrote the
story of what Nixon said, even if it was what he had said
the week before, rather than focusing on the contrived
emptiness of the campaign. Whatever he may have failed
to understand about the press and the American system
of government after Watergate, Nixon as presidential
candidate in 1968 and 1972 understood the limiting
forms of journalism and the uses that could be made of

them. His understanding in 1972 kept him in the White House and produced a non-campaign. Reporters fumed at Nixon's unwillingness to expose himself but few were able to lodge their protests in print. "One of the reasons I left the *Los Angeles Times* after the 1972 election," says Witcover, "is because of a piece I wrote about how Nixon had freed the press to focus on McGovern by not campaigning. My story went unused on the grounds that it was opinion."

If the politican is both canny and unscrupulous enough, the press also can be manipulated by taking advantage of its better inclinations. Again, Nixon provides the example. When he burst into the Cadoro Room of the Beverly Hilton Hotel on Nov. 7, 1962, to tell the assembled reporters that "you won't have Nixon to kick around anymore" he was acting in defiance of his own accumulated political wisdom and of a standard rule of politics which might be expressed: Never tell reporters what you really think about the press. Because that rule is so rarely violated by major-league politicians, Nixon's supposedly disastrous press conference gave him a rare power over the press in his long climb back to political respectability. The last press conference had been the product of Nixon's human response to his defeat and to the bitterness of his supporters over press coverage of the Nixon-Brown campaign. But in Nixon's careful reconstruction of his political career after President Kennedy's assassination, he saw the benefit of using his celebrated outburst as a means of appealing to the basic journalistic instinct of fairness. It is symptomatic of Nixon's dishonesty in such matters that he appealed to an instinct which he said the press lacked. But it was an effective appeal, both because it seemed unfair to reporters to make too much of a six-year-old temper tantrum and because some reporters thought Nixon *had* been treated unfairly in 1962.[9] Witcover quotes Nixon as saying that

---

[9] Even at this late date, it would be worth systematically reviewing the

the last press conference had worked out well for him. "California served a purpose," Nixon said. "The press had a guilt complex about their inaccuracy. Since then, they've been generally accurate, and far more respectful.[10] Naturally, reporters were even more respectful in 1972, when Nixon was the President and could hide behind the power of his office.

Political reporters may be powerless to force a President out of the White House to campaign. They can have a lot to say, however, about whether a politician gets to be considered "presidential" in the first place. In the 1969 *Washington Monthly* article quoted earlier in this chapter, Broder described the "screening committee of reporters" who perform as talent scouts in determining the potential of various aspirants for national office.[11] Broder found the reporters at that time to be "a narrow and rather peculiar slice of this society," disproportionately white, male, Eastern, middle-aged, Democratic and non-church going. There are a few more women covering politics now, and the Carter campaign has brought a few more Southern accents to the campaign trail on the theory that "it takes one to know one." But it is otherwise much the same and one can still sympathize, as Broder

---

newspaper coverage of that 1962 campaign in an attempt to make a historical assessment of how fairly it was covered. This has never been done, as far as I know. My own impression of the coverage was that it leaned toward Brown but that this was much less important than the diversion of voter attention from state issues in the last weeks of the campaign by the Cuban missile crisis. James Alexander, a Brown aide and former newspaperman told me once that the Brown camp was well aware that reporters disliked Nixon. "This unquestionably was an advantage for us," Alexander said.

[10] Jules Witcover, *The Resurrection of Richard Nixon*, (New York, 1970), pp. 151-52.

[11] The "screening committee" listed by Broder included the three newsmagazines, both wire services, the three television networks, the two Washington papers, the *New York Times*, the *Los Angeles Times*, the *Christian Science Monitor*, the Knight newspapers, the Field papers, the Gannett, Newhouse, Scripps-Howard and Hearst chains and a few columnists. Today one would add the *Boston Globe* and perhaps *Newsday*, the *New York Daily News*, the *Chicago Tribune* and the *Wall Street Journal*.

did, with what it must have been like to be George Romney in politics. "I often thought," Broder wrote, "as I saw Romney during his presidential campaign, surrounded by our circle — men a generation younger than he, many of us with cigarettes in our mouths, drinks in our hands and cynicism in our hearts — that he must have felt as helpless with us as I would feel if my fate or future as a journalist were being decided by a committee of Romney's colleagues among the elders of the Mormon Church."

The screening committee has fallen on hard times in recent presidential elections. We were near-unanimous in missing the McGovern phenomenon and many of us were slow to catch on to Carter. But we are still trying. Within months after Carter's election a number of reporters, including this one, singled out Illinois Gov. James Thompson as a likely Republican candidate for the presidency in 1980 and asked him about his chances wherever he went. Big Jim, a likeable fellow whose candor is exceeded only by his lack of bashfulness, declined the usual dodges and openly proclaimed that he had been interested in running for President since he was eleven years old. Thompson made the point, however, that the continual questions of reporters on the subject made it appear as if he were mounting an early campaign for the White House instead of serving as governor of Illinois.

Nonetheless, Thompson will be thankful for the early attention if he actually decides to run for President in 1980. My own view is that the "screening committee," or at least the attention that the national press pays to one candidate rather than another, is terribly important in determining the options when there are no deep or overriding issues or when there are many candidates occupying the same ground. It was not important in the Democratic primaries of 1972 because of widespread opposition to the Vietnam War, which gave McGovern, as the perceived anti-war candidate, an issue-oriented and loyal constituency. The press was important to Jimmy Carter,

who at first had to work at getting coverage. He was by
no means a consensus choice of the national press, although reporters such as Jack Germond of the *Washington Star* and Johnny Apple of the *New York Times* perceived his potential at an early date. A number of other
reporters regarded him as a substantial candidate if
Humphrey or Sen. Edward M. Kennedy stayed out of the
race, as both of them did. What helped Carter, with both
the press and the public, was that he understood the importance of being seen as a winner. He had much going
for him in New Hampshire, especially a good family organization and the absence from the ballot of Sen. Henry
M. Jackson, who drew votes from some of the same con-
stituencies. But what he had most of all was the perception of coming into the state as a winning candidate. The
winner's image was based, tenuously, on the Iowa caucuses on Jan. 19, five weeks before the New Hampshire
primary. For the meager advertising cost of $8,500, Car-
ter was able to buy well-timed five-minute commercials
describing his life and goals on Iowa television and also
buy newspaper ads telling the readers when to watch his
TV spots. At caucus time the plurality of voters (37 per
cent) were uncommitted to any candidate. Carter had
slightly more than 27 per cent, gaining less than 14,000
votes out of 50,000 cast in the caucuses. It was enough to
get him on all three morning network television shows
the day after the caucuses. Television ignored the huge
uncommitted vote and concentrated instead on "winner"
Carter. And this was enough to help make Carter a real
winner in New Hampshire.

Academicians have deplored the disproportionate emphasis by the press on the early primaries, particularly
on New Hampshire. An analysis by Michael J. Robinson
and Karen A. McPherson of Catholic University in
Washington, D.C. shows that 34.3 per cent of the campaign stories printed in the 70 days between Nov. 24,
1975 and Feb. 27, 1976, were about New Hampshire and
that 53.5 per cent of the television stories during that

period concerned New Hampshire.[12] The concentration of press coverage is so intense and the political stakes so high that any candidate who fails to leave New Hampshire perceived as a serious contender is likely to hold the press responsible. In this vein, the blame William Loeb doesn't get for defeating Muskie in the 1972 primary is likely to be placed on the national press. Muskie, after all, had 46.4 per cent of the primary vote compared to 37.1 per cent for McGovern, who claimed a "moral victory." But it was not the press which had created the expectation that Muskie had to be a bigger winner. That expectation was the work of the Muskie campaign, which operated on the premise that Democrats everywhere were boarding the Muskie campaign train and that it was just about to leave the station. Muskie's operatives used this technique to sign up Democratic officeholders all over the country, oblivious to the fact that rank-and-file Democrats did not always follow their presumed leaders. The impressive-sounding lists of Muskie endorsers also were used to raise financial contributions and to convince an occasionally skeptical reporter that the primary competition was over before it started. It was a gigantic shell game in which the candidate wound up being fooled. But while it lasted, it was bandwagon stories which the Muskie campaign wanted and encouraged. Only after a *Boston Globe* poll showed McGovern gaining and Muskie losing ground in New Hampshire did the Muskie strategists proclaim themselves willing to settle for any sort of a victory. By then it was too late.

A variation of the same theme occurred in the 1976 Republican primary. The state's conservative tradition and Loeb's backing made it seem an ideal arena for Reagan to launch his challenge against President Ford. The

---

[12] Michael J. Robinson with the assistance of Karen A. McPherson, "Television News and the Presidential Nominating Process: The Case of Spring, 1976," Jan. 18, 1977. The paper analyzed stories appearing in the *Washington Post*, the *New York Times*, and Columbus (Ohio) *Dispatch* and on the three television networks.

former California governor's strategists were so confident that Reagan was allowed to campaign in Illinois the day before the primary. He lost New Hampshire by only 1,317 votes, and almost immediately the Reagan strategists began to regret their pre-election candor. Again, it was too late. The press might have been persuaded to accept the "moral victory" standard of earlier Democratic primaries if Reagan had not prepared them for a Ford defeat. The truth is that the Reagan forces didn't want or expect a moral victory until after the vote was counted. They thought they were going to win.

The 1976 primaries did not pose an easy challenge for reporters assigned to cover them on a regular basis. There were too many primaries, and the new federal funding law enabled candidates to stay in the race longer. As a result, the press did its best work when nobody was looking. Recognizing that careful organization would be needed to cover 30 primaries, the networks, newsmagazines and major papers came up with elaborate coverage plans that in many cases included in-depth profiles on the candidates. Many of these profiles were very good, but too many of them ran in the early part of 1976 when few readers or viewers were paying attention to the election campaigns. "In many respects the leading newspapers and magazines are really out of phase with the candidates," says Broder. "By the time the public begins to focus on the candidates, we have written the story so often we're bored with it. Even among those who participate in primaries, the audience is segmented. You can't assume that people in Texas have been paying attention to what was going on in Florida or that the people in California are paying much attention to what was going on in Texas. There's a continual problem of getting information to the relevant electorate that is built into the whole damned nonsense of proliferation of primaries."

Despite the difficulties, Broder believes there were

some discernible improvements in political coverage in 1976. He cites the coverage of issues, a frequent point of criticism in the past. In 1976 a number of news organizations assigned reporters to write exclusively about issues and do comparative pieces about the candidates' stands on various subjects. Broder also thinks that reporters treated the presidential candidates fairly. "I had the feeling that there was less of a problem of personal bias than I've ever seen," Broder says. "There were fewer people rooting for one guy or the other or wanting one guy to lose. That's pretty good when you consider we were dealing with a span ranging from Fred Harris to Ronald Reagan. I don't think any of the candidates feel they were counted out because the press won't let someone from that part of the spectrum have a chance." Perhaps the improvements also reflect an improved attitude of the candidates. In the recent past conservatives often have operated on the self-fulfilling premise that they would not get fair treatment from the national press. Neither Reagan nor his strategists made this mistake, which may have some consequences for conservative candidates in the future. After the election, Reagan's national chairman, Sen. Paul Laxalt of Nevada, appeared before a conservative political-action conference to say that his candidate had been covered "very fairly" and to urge a new attitude of conservatives toward the press. Perhaps this reflects a growing maturity among conservatives, some of whom no longer see themselves as a hopelessly embattled minority. I think it also reflects the background of Reagan, whose first hero was Franklin Roosevelt and whose instincts with the press, if not his philosophy, are those of a Democrat. Reagan knew, for instance, that the press valued accessibility and he made himself accesible during the campaign. As Reagan once put it, "this didn't convert reporters to my beliefs but it showed them I didn't have horns." It had to make a difference in the reporting.

Another improvement in the 1976 campaign coverage

was an increased and more sophisticated use of survey research techniques. This made news organizations less dependent on the candidate's pollsters for predictive information. More importantly, it enabled them to track voter attitudes throughout the campaign. In the California primary I benefited from a survey conducted by the *Washington Post's* Barry Sussman, which showed that an overwhelming percentage of Republican voters in the state approved of Reagan's two-term record as governor. Not only did this point to the primary outcome, in which Reagan trounced Ford. It also demonstrated the futility of Ford's early California strategy, which was based on attacking Reagan's record and making him the issue. A reporter who is armed with the kind of information acquired by the Sussman survey can write with far greater confidence than when he is merely relying on his instincts.

With all of these improvements duly noted, I nonetheless think we did a poor-to-mediocre job of covering the general election campaign of 1976. With Watergate and two Presidents who had betrayed their trust as a precondition, each candidate based his campaign on the proposition that he was the most trustworthy person for the presidency. That was fine, as far as it went. Both parties had rejected issue-oriented candidates in favor of candidates who made "trust me" the central issue, and we were compelled to cover the campaign on these terms. The way we went about doing it, however, suggests a traditional preoccupation with sensation which contrasts oddly with various editorial pleas for a more elevating discussion of issues.

Take the *Playboy* interview with Carter. The interview and an accompanying article by Robert Scheer offered valuable clues to Carter's character. But that's not what sold *Playboys* or what focused the press attention on the interview. Instead, we were tantalized because Carter, making a point about Christian forgiveness, had confessed to "lust in my heart." We were like small boys in

some long-vanished hick town come to see the naked lady
at the carnival. He said it, he really did. It was dismay-
ing, going around the country, to see how much this
phrase was on our minds. Weeks after the interview a
witless local politician in California asked "a lusty welcome" for Carter, and several reporters made a point of it
in their stories. "It was evident," wrote William Lee Miller in *The New Republic*, "that many commentators and
reporters didn't even know that Carter had been applying a sentence from The New Testament; they never
seem to have heard of or read the fifth chapter of
Matthew, although one would be hard put to find a piece
of writing of comparable length more fundamental to the
history of the west."

While we were making too much of the *Playboy* interview, we were making too little of Carter's financial affairs. He withheld records of the contributions made to
his 1970 gubernatorial campaign and his 1975 tax returns after promising to make them public. When he
finally produced the 1975 tax return, revealing a huge
break from the tax system he had repeatedly denounced,
many of the details of Carter's profits were concealed by
corporate returns which the candidate refused to disclose. At the same time he issued a net-worth statement
containing blank items and questionable valuations.
Even some of Carter's aides conceded privately that the
net-worth statement reflected a rather far-fetched effort
to keep the candidate's net worth under a million dollars
so that reporters would not describe him as "a mil-
lionaire." Carter got away with it. A documentation that
Carter was worth far more than this net-worth statement
claimed for him was readily available at the county
courthouse in Americus, but few reporters bothered to
pursue this issue. "Lust in my heart" had more of a ring.

Ford's finances were pursued with the singleminded-
ness that was common to much of the press corps when a
"Watergate" issue was raised. An investigation of an old
allegation that Ford had diverted campaign funds to pri-

vate purposes virtually immoblized the Ford campaign at
a critical point. The coverage, understandably, was av-
idly encouraged by Carter aides. Once the story that the
Justice Department had referred the matter to the
Watergate prosecutor for investigation was broken by
the *Wall Street Journal*, coverage of the allegation was
unavoidable. But the *Washington Post* kept the story
alive with a minimum of information, and we allowed the
allegation — which had been investigated and found
wanting at the time of Ford's confirmation as vice president — to dominate coverage of the campaign. For several days after the *New York Times* reported that nothing had been found to substantiate the charges, by-lined
articles in the *Washington Post* by Bob Woodward and
Carl Bernstein continued to say that Ford had not been
cleared. And the investigation was not the only story.
NBC gave John Dean, whose book *Blind Ambition* was
coming onto the market, a forum to charge that Ford had
been programmed to quash a House investigation in
1972. It would have been a helluva story, if new. But
Dean, a supporter of Carter, had testified to the same
events before the Senate Watergate Committee. Again,
the press reacted breathlessly. The *Los Angeles Times*
published an "exclusive" which told how Ford, as House
minority leader, had sent a letter to Republican members
of the House banking committee describing a Watergate
investigation as "irresponsible." This wasn't new, either.
It had been reported first on Oct. 4, 1972, in the 13th
paragraph of a Woodward-Bernstein story which told
how the House committee had voted against investigating the Watergate incident. Ford's role in this action may
certainly have been deplorable, as I happen to think it
was. But it was not news.

While the press cluttered up coverage of the Ford campaign with old charges, we strangely allowed him to get
away with a tactic we had solemnly vowed to expose after
Nixon used it repeatedly in 1972. This was the White
House political event permitted to masquerade as news.

In Ford's case these non-events were usually held in the Rose Garden because of the backdrop it provided for television. Night after night, Ford's Rose Garden events received their three minutes on the evening news, as the President's strategists had predicted. The low point probably came on Sept. 13, when Ford in the bright sunshine of the Rose Garden signed the "Government in the Sunshine Act" opening the business sessions of government regulatory agencies to the public. My story, in the seventh paragraph, called this performance "another demonstration of a President's ability to use the White House as a platform in a campaign while his opponent is out on the hustings, as Carter was today." The story quoted Ford as saying, in the Rose Garden, that "this legislation should go a long way in reaffirming that government exists for the people, not apart from the people." Alas, the story did not point out that Ford subsequently issued a statement opposing "unnecessarily ambiguous and perhaps harmful provisions" of the new law and it did not tell the readers anything about the administration's support for a more restrictive version of the bill when it was pending before Congress.

We need to do better than this. We need, in our coverage of Presidents and other candidates, to go beyond the campaign rhetoric. We need to tell our readers what the candidates really mean.

CHAPTER TEN

The Cozy
Coverage of Congress

The reporter is the recorder of government but he is also a participant. He operates in a system in which power is divided. He as much as anyone, and more than a great many, helps to shape the course of government. He is the indispensable broker and middleman among the subgovernments of Washington. He can choose from among the myriad events that seethe beneath the surface of government which to describe, which to ignore. He can illumine policy and notably assist in giving it sharpness and clarity; just as easily, he can prematurely expose policy and, as with an undeveloped film, cause its destruction. At his worst, operating with arbitrary and faulty standards, he can be an agent of disorder and confusion. At his best, he can exert a creative influence on Washington politics.

– Douglass Cater in
THE FOURTH BRANCH OF GOVERNMENT

The American political system, more often than not, is a stepladder leading to Washington. Rising politicians, unless they are celebrities or the offspring of a dynastic political family which starts them off on a high rung, most frequently advance to Congress from state or local government. Reporters often climb a parallel ladder, covering a city hall beat or a state legislature before they are assigned to Washington. This parallelism can be enormously beneficial to a reporter, both because he learns about the processes of government and because he gets to know politicians at the lower rungs of the ladder whose rate of climb is approximately the same as his. It was with this latter consideration in mind that editor Dick Harwood called me aside in the early summer of 1974. The House Judiciary Committee was at the time involved in the closed-door phase of its impeachment inquiry, and information was difficult to come by. Harwood was aware that I knew the five Californians on the committee, having covered three of them in the State Legislature and the other two as a regional reporter. He asked me to help, and I immediately sought out one of the Judiciary members, an able and low-key lawyer named George Danielson. He had served in both houses of the California Legislature before being elected to Congress in 1970 at the age of 55. I respected Danielson and liked him, considering him a hard-working legislator who answered questions candidly without overburdening me with stories about his own greatness. But I had seen him only occasionally, usually at social affairs, since he had come to Congress in 1970 as the representative of a Los Angeles congressional district. "What brings you up here?" he asked me over lunch in the House dining room. When I had told him, he flashed a broad grin and said, "Well, I knew we could find something important enough to do up here that would make the press cover Congress."

Danielson was kidding on the square. Politicians who "graduate" to the House of Representatives from a modern legislature — and 19 members of the present California delegation are such graduates — often are surprised to find that they have left a highly visible forum for an almost invisible one. This congressional anonymity is not readily apparent to a visitor who wanders through the often-crowded House press gallery, much less to anyone who glances at the listings of correspondents in the House press gallery. There are some 80 accredited State Capitol correspondents in Sacramento for 120 legislators. In Washington there are more than 2,400 accredited to the various galleries (in round figures, 1,200 to the press galleries, 550 to the radio and television galleries, 525 to the periodical galleries and 180 to the press photographers' gallery) for only 535 congressmen. But numbers often are deceptive in Washington, and these numbers are especially misleading. Congressional press accreditation is the universal badge in Washington, and it is obtained by a variety of editors, bureau chiefs and reporters who rarely or never cover Congress. Robert O. Blanchard, director of the communication department at American University, sifted out these non-congressional reporters along with the cameramen and foreign correspondents and wound up with a list of 750 domestic correspondents, including many specialty correspondents for trade publications and many reporters who spend only part-time on the Hill. Ben Bagdikian uses a commonly accepted figure of 400 correspondents who actually cover Congress. Some 60 individual newspapers have their own correspondents or bureaus and at least another 250 papers are served by correspondents for their chains or groups of newspapers. The bureaus for these chains can be as small as the two-man McClatchy bureau, which serves three California newspapers with exceptional coverage, or as large as the 11-person Gannett News Service, which provides news for 57 papers in 16 states and Guam. There also are a number of one-person bureaus or part-time stringers for smaller newspapers. At the bedrock are the wire services, which furnish the vast proportion of news that is read or heard by Americans. Associated Press assigns 18 reporters to the Capitol; United Press International has 12 regularly assigned Capitol reporters.

These figures are impressive in the aggregate, but they mean that only one-fifth to one-fourth of the nation's 1,768 newspapers have coverage of their own from the Capitol. The Ralph Nader-sponsored Capitol Hill News Service estimates that 72 per cent of the papers have no capitol correspondent of any kind. This also is the case with 96 per cent of the television stations and 99 per cent of the radio stations. And these figures overstate the actual coverage. There is no human way that the seven-person Hearst bureau can actually cover the 145 congressmen who represent the areas served by the nine Hearst papers or that the Gannett bureau can cover 188 congressmen. Despite the impressiveness of the numbers, most newspapers in the country simply have no congressional coverage they can call their own. This is fine with most congressmen. Among the various high crimes and misdemeanors with which they charge the press, non-coverage is not one of them. "I was covered when I returned home to my district," says former Rep. Jerome Waldie of California. "But there was no coverage by papers in my district when I was in Congress except what I told them. Most of the members, I'm sure, would prefer that there *not* be coverage."

That leaves the wires. What they cover, out of necessity and manpower, usually are the big, breaking stories of the day. The wires have some talented congressional correspondents, but most of them lack either the time or the latitude for in-depth coverage. A study by Blanchard of congressional coverage gives this view from a respected congressional correspondent for a daily newspaper: "The wire services are superficial. Congress is like a huge machine of hand-outs, of generated news, and the wire services report this 'news.' "[1] Correspondents for the networks, the national newsmagazines and the handful of prestige papers often stick to the same track of the big story, although they may report this news with added depth and analysis. In the meantime those regional and local correspondents, whom Bagdikian has described as the "diggers and toilers," are preoccupied with the parochial developments of their own congressmen. Between the big story and the local sewer grant lies a vast under-

---

[1] "The Congressional Correspondents and Their World" by Robert O. Blanchard, in *Congress and the News Media,* (New York, 1974), edited by Blanchard, p. 171. This chapter is based on interviews with 31 congressional correspondents and on two questionnaires returned by 227 and 96 correspondents, respectively.

reported landscape of congressional achievements, scandals and intrigue which is almost never seen in the daily paper, let alone on local television. In this wasteland a symbiotic relationship flourishes between congressman and correspondent, a relationship based on mutual need and sometimes on mutual laziness. This relationship permits the typical invisible congressman to become visible in a highly selective way in his home district. In city councils and in the better legislatures a politician who consistently took credit for his colleague's achievements would be scorned by his colleagues and by the press alike. Yet this is the expected and encouraged practice in the House of Representatives. In the 92nd Congress, 20,458 bills were introduced in the House, 7,999 of them identical to the last word. Many more were identical except for minor details. Their purpose, in almost every case, was purely public relations. "This duplication chokes the legislative process," says J. Brian Smith, a campaign consultant and press aide to House Minority Leader John Rhodes. "It is a result of members re-introducing legislation to which they are particularly attracted, under their own names, even though that legislation has been developed by one of their colleagues. The legislation then becomes the property of the member who has most recently introduced it. He gets credit for it in the press, not because he had anything to do with its inception, but because his press release refers to him as the author." Until recently every grant of federal funds in a congressman's district routinely was announced by the congressman, whether or not he had anything to do with it. This, as Smith points out, is because "the system is geared to generate congressional PR." Many regional and local reporters also routinely quote the local congressman on the big story of the day, which gives the story a "local angle" and the congressman a platform. Through this multiple process of press release, grant announcement and involvement in the "big story," even the most invisible congressman can appear to be a potent force in Washington.

The payoff on the symbiotic relationship is news for the correspondent and tenure for the politican. In an age of preoccupation with the presidency, the selective anonymity of the congressman enables him to win re-nomination in his own party easily — usually, he is not even opposed. He is in danger of being replaced only in the general election and then only if he comes from the 40 to 50 districts that can be considered "swing" districts in any real sense of the word. It didn't always work that way. "*Congressional Quarterly* tells us that in the 1870s more than half the members of each session of the House were newly elected, but that by 1900 only a third were first termers and that by 1970 the figure had dropped to 12 per cent," Bagdikian writes. "Of 330 incumbents running for re-election in 1972 . . . only ten incumbents — 3 per cent — were defeated."[2] The percentage was slightly higher in 1974 because of Republican losses in wake of Watergate, but 1974 provides an even more telling statistic about the power of incumbency. At a time when congressmen of both parties routinely were being quoted as saying that they feared the electorate was fed up with everyone, only one congressman in each party lost out in the primaries. Aided by the symbiotic relationship and the congressional reapportionments of friendly legislatures, most congressmen can stay in the House as long as they want.

Not every regional or local reporter is part of the relationship. Some ignore press releases about duplicate bills that have been introduced by other congressmen. Some pay careful attention to attendance at important committee sessions. Some actively pursue any hints of scandal or malfeasance. But relatively few correspondents have the time to do these things, at least not very often. If the correspondent works for the wires or for a major daily newspaper, he is likely to be preoccupied with the complexities of important legislation and with his own news

---

[2] Ben H. Bagdikian, "Congress and the Media: Partners in Propaganda," *The Columbia Journalism Review,* January-February 1974.

organization's deadlines. If he works for a small or
medium-sized newspaper and covers primarily the activities of congressmen in his area, he is apt to be dependent upon the congressman as a news source. Smalltown
newspapermen are even more commonplace and invisible in Washington than low-seniority congressmen, and
they lack the easy access which is common in a state
capitol. In most states any hardworking correspondent
will have little difficulty in seeing an agency head or
even, with a little patience, the governor. But most
Washington correspondents are not going to see the President except on television, and they may sometimes have
trouble in getting even a low-level bureaucrat to return
their telephone calls. The congressman, with his access
and knowledge, can provide tips or information which
may give the regional reporter a story that makes him
look good in the eyes of his editors. If he is too independent, the local congressional correspondent can be left
without any sources at all.

The frustration of being a newly arrived Capitol Hill
correspondent who comes from a legislature where he
had wide access was summed up Martin Salditch of the
Riverside Press-Enterprise six months after he came to
Washington from Sacramento in the summer of 1975.
Salditch was a distinguished reporter in Sacramento,
where he knew most of the legislators and had many
sources in the executive branch of government. "Dealing
with the federal agencies is like dealing with flypaper,"
Salditch said. "It's far harder to find out information here
than in Sacramento. There is an unspoken attitude in the
bureaucracy that the less they tell you the better. The
bureaucracy's credibility is not high with me. I have
learned that in Washington there seems to be two ver-
sions of where anything is at, the official position and the
unofficial one. The unofficial positon, which is the real
one, may not become official for several months, but
that's the one I'm interested in. The General Services
Administration has a gag rule. I have to talk to the press

office, which relays the information to me from the bureaucrat I want to talk to. It's frustrating not to be able to talk to middle-level people and even relatively low-level people directly. And with most of the agencies you have to explain who you are. Riverside, California, is not exactly a household word." It is worth adding that Salditch did not become a part of the symbiotic relationship. When one of the three House members he covers took a trip to South Africa that was sponsored by the government in a disguised form, Salditch found out about it and wrote a story that was picked up by other newspapers. The story demonstrated that, with all the limitations on coverage, it is better for even a small newspaper to have a correspondent of its own in Washington than to be totally dependent upon the wire services and the congressman.

The necessity for newspapers to have their own correspondents is greater today than it used to be because of an unheralded but important development in Washington, the decline of regional news coverage by the wires. AP has 10 regional reporters left in Washington, UPI only four. This is approximately half the resources that the wire services devoted to regional reporting a generation ago, and it is bad news for those organizations which are dependent on the wires. One of the best of these regional correspondents was Harrison B. Humphries of AP, who in 1972 was reassigned to cover the armed services and foreign policy committees in the Senate. Humphries, now in his sixties, is a Depression-era newsman who got his start on the *Muskogee (Okla.) Phoenix and Times-Democrat* in 1933 when the National Recovery Administration required the paper to hire two additional employees. Humphries covered sports and police news for $14 a week and eventually ran the city desk. In 1937 he was offered $37.50 a week, a big salary in those days, to work for AP in Columbus, Ohio. "It put me in clover," recalls Humphries. "I felt I was rich." In 1943 he came to Washington on AP's regional desk, which then consisted of 16

reporters and five deskmen, one of the latter totally assigned to war casualties. Humphries was assigned to
cover California and Hawaii, where he had never been.
The 1940s and 1950s were a time of congressional struggles over water, power and natural resources, and Humphries' stories on these subjects were read by millions of
Californians. But the regional staffs already were being
reduced. Washington and Oregon were added to Humphries' region, then Alaska. The UPI western regional
beat increased to 13 states. And the coverage became
accordingly thinner. In order to compensate for the reduced coverage, the wires gave more control of the news
to the congressional offices, encouraging them to phone
items directly to state bureaus. "I used to insist on being
informed when that happened so I would know what was
going on," said Humphries. "By the time I left the regional beat I wasn't even sure I was being informed."

"The member of Congress is uniquely creator and creature of publicity," wrote Douglass Cater in 1959. "It is
the nature of his job to be concerned with that amorphous
substance known as public opinion."[3] One of the ways in
which that opinion is molded is by the committee hearing, an intensely competitive process since there are 50
committees in Congress, 18 in the Senate and 32 in the
House. Most of these committees have sub-committees,
which also hold hearings, sometimes with virtually no
press coverage. Attracting reporters to committee hearings and keeping them interested once they get there is a
major function of congressional public relations. In Congress a good committee hearing properly is considered a
work of art. When Cater wrote about "government by
publicity" in *The Fourth Branch of Government* he
quoted from a 1943 memo circulated by the counsel of a
House investigating committee which advised members
on ways to get maximum publicity for their investigations. Along with some helpful hints on press releases

---

3 Douglass Cater, *The Fourth Branch of Government*, (Boston, 1959), p. 47.

and recesses, the memo suggested that the committee should decide in advance "what you want the newspapers to hit hardest and then shape each hearing so that the main point becomes the vortex of the testimony. Then *adjourn.*" While this advice is still relevant, the memo seems almost innocent today. The late Sen. Estes Kefauver of Tennessee once was the marvel and complaint of his colleagues for his skill at adjourning hearings at the point of maximum impact with some tidbit that would insure Kefauver a prominent place on page one of the next day's newspapers. That technique is now routinely practiced by almost all Senate committee chairmen, who have found it especially suitable to the compressed narrative required by the evening network news. Frequently, this technique is augmented by a leaked document from the public relations-oriented committee staff which finds its way onto the front page of the *Washington Post* or the *New York Times* and begets some additional stories.

But the big change in Congress during the last decade and a half has been the extension of the congressional powers of publicity from the committee chairmen and the leadership to the ordinary member of the House. Each house of Congress now has a $500,000 broadcast studio which enables members to make their own video, film and audio tapes. These are sent to the home districts as weekly or monthly reports, frequently disguised as interview news programs. Some stations run these reports in toto; others excerpt a question-and-answer for use on a local "news" program. (The campaign version of this practice is to have an aide provide "beepers" for local radio stations in which the candidate comments on issues of the day, ostensibly in response to questions.) Bagdikian found that 352 of the 435 House members used this broadcast service in 1973. Though the Federal Communications Commission has said that stations are subject to fines if they use these congressionally produced programs as their own, no station ever has been fined for failing to comply with this supposed FCC policy. According to Phil Tracy, writing in *MORE,* congressmen who use the recording studios pay about one-tenth of the private production costs and can mail the tapes free to stations with their franking privilege. This process of presenting the congressmen's propaganda as news is not limited to the broadcast media. In 1975 Tracy described his conversation with Rep. Jerry Litton, a Missouri Democrat who had a televised show which ran once every three weeks on stations in Missouri, Illinois and Kansas:

> I asked Litton if he didn't think it was unethical for TV stations to take raw film clips and insert them into news programs without identification. Litton said he didn't see how it was any different than a press release that newspapers use. "But at least the newspapers don't use the press release verbatim," I told him, somewhat naively. Litton smiled and then showed me his scrap book. At the top corner on one page was a photo of Litton and President Ford with a six-line caption explaining why they were shaking hands. Then Litton pointed to the six newspaper clips with the same photo and the six-line caption. On the next page was a news release which was made up to look like a news story. Below it was the same news release, printed word for word by five different newspapers. "Oh yeah?" said the congressman from Missouri.[4]

This practice is not peculiar to the state of Missouri. Bagdikian gives an example of a release sent out by Rep. Les Aspin (D-Wis.), which praises a particular natural gas company for not raising prices. The release ran as written in at least four Wisconsin papers. Sometimes congressmen themselves are at first skeptical that any newspaper will actually run their own releases as news. When Jerome Waldie first arrived in Congress in 1966 he did not believe in press releases. Back home he had been majority leader of the State Assembly and widely

---

[4] Phil Tracy, "Canned Goods From Capitol Hill," *MORE,* September, 1975. Litton was killed in a plane crash in 1976.

covered. "I used to think that press releases were non-sense," Waldie recalls. "I don't think that now. Some-where somebody is going to print your press release no matter how absurd. You have the frank, so there's very little expense to it. So you send out the press release."

Sometimes, relationships between congressmen and correspondents can go beyond symbiosis to collusion. Bagdikian gives the example, which he credits to the Capitol Hill News Service, of Rep. Joseph M. McDade of Pennsylvania, who after he was elected in 1962 went to the editors of his hometown *Scranton Tribune* and said he wanted to put a *Tribune* reporter, one Bob Reese, on his payroll. The arrangement was that Reese would remain on the paper, where he covered city hall and the police beat, and would also write news releases for McDade. According to Bagdikian, the *Tribune* editor usually hands Reese back his own release to write for the paper as a news story.[5] I have no reason to think that the dual employment of newsmen as reporters and congressional flacks is common on Capitol Hill. A reporter covering Congress who did this would, in fact, be violating the rules of congressional correspondents and would lose his accreditation for taking any income from a congressman. But the very existence of the practice at all is an uncomfortable reminder of how cozy the relationship between the covered and the coverers can become.

The consensus of the Blanchard study was that the wire services and the prestige newspapers do a good job on the routine legislative congressional stories. A number of reporters, however, were skeptical about how well Congress, and particularly the House, is covered on difficult and complex institutional issues. Blanchard quotes one prominent correspondent on the quality of congressional coverage:

> There's a decided failure of the congressional reporters themselves to know what they're writing about. There's a

---

[5] Bagdikian, "Congress and the Media: Partners in Propaganda."

tendency among the reporters to take a pretty superficial
view of Congress. They don't understand the rules, the
history of American politics. In all journalism, it is a
tendency to be superficial, popular. At one time there was
a basic fault in the understanding of the editors of how
important the congressional news really is. I suspect that
30-40 years ago the congressional reporter had more in
print. But since the time of Roosevelt, the President has
sort of preempted Washington affairs.[6]

This comment tells a lot. Congressional correspondents
once were at the top of the heap in Washington, occupying the place taken over successively by White House
correspondents and foreign correspondents and now by
investigative reporters. Fletcher Knebel quotes
Raymond P. Brandt as saying, "We never covered Washington in the 20s. We covered the Senate. You wasted
your time downtown." This changed, as the correspondent quoted by Blanchard observes, with the New
Deal. Journalists are attracted to power and the appearance of power. It is no accident that in four decades of
retreat and acquiescence by Congress to the claims of the
executive branch the press developed a preoccupation —
some would say an obsession — with the presidency. Nor
is it any accident that Congress, in the wake of the impeachment inquiry and the subsequent resurgence of the
Democratic caucus, is becoming a focal point for coverage
again. "As it was perceived that the Congress, and particularly the House of Representatives, was losing power,
it tended also to lose visibility," says David Broder. "Now
these are interacting processes; we are not outside of the
power process as much as we would like to pretend that
we are in journalism. So the very fact of this coverage
becomes an additional tool of power for the person who is
being covered. The two things have fed on each other."

The congressional hiatus obscured both achievements

---

[6] Blanchard, "The Congressional Correspondents and Their World," p.
219.

and failures. Many Americans who watched the impeachment hearings on television discovered that the large majority of committee members on both sides were intelligent, fair-minded and well-prepared. While the House Judiciary Committee is one of the best committees in Congress, the performance was no surprise to reporters who had been watching the steady improvement of Congress for a decade. Increasingly, old members in the getting-along-by-going-along style of Sam Rayburn retired and were replaced by younger, more independent congressmen. During the congressional hiatus, however, the national impression of Congress was more likely to be based on voter perceptions of House Speaker McCormack or his successor, Carl Albert. There was a basic validity in regarding these men as symbols of the House, since they had been chosen by their fellow Democrats as leaders. More precisely, it might be said that they had been chosen by the congressional system, which values time spent on the job far more highly than it does competence. The seniority system has fostered habits of thought and behavior among congressmen which are inimical to democratic governance. Within the House, even now, a member customarily refers to the head of his committee not by name but as "the chairman" and behaves toward him with a deference suitable for an underworld don. Many members after they have been in Congress a few years, become so accustomed to talking about "the chairman" and "the speaker" in quasi-reverential terms that they become unaware of how obsequious this sounds to ordinary citizens. In an extreme example, a few years ago in the House, members had to ask former Interior Committee Chairman Wayne Aspinall, a legendary autocrat, for permission to go to the bathroom.

This sycophancy sometimes finds its way into the symbiotic relationship between Congress and the press. Michael Green, formerly a reporter for the McClatchy newspapers, has written about a 1970 incident where the

then 78-year-old House Speaker John McCormack lost
his temper. "Turning on a reporter who had written a
matter-of-fact, even sympathetic account of McCormack's years in Congress and current troubles, the
Speaker denounced the newsman as 'a goddamned
sonofabitch.' The reporters seemed stunned. None was
sufficiently stunned, however, to write anything about
the outburst. No one seemed sure exactly why, except
perhaps that McCormack is an old man, given to frequent outburst these days over both real and imagined
slights, and it did not seem the tasteful thing to do."[7]
Perhaps the non-coverage of this incident also can be
explained by the traditional reluctance of reporters to
write about incidents involving the press, but the same
solicitude, bordering on cover-up, extends to other incidents. Brit Hume, examining the problem of reporting
the private lives of public figures in the April 1975 issue
of *MORE,* tells of an incident where Walter Taylor of the
Washington Star talked to 81-year-old Wright Patman
after Patman had visited Albert's office in an attempt to
save his chairmanship of the House Banking Committee.
Taylor asked Patman how he had come out with Albert
and received the reply, "Yes, Speaker Rayburn will vote
for me." Rayburn has been dead since 1961. When Taylor
asked Patman some further questions, Patman again referred to "Speaker Rayburn." Taylor did not report the
incident, but, as Hume points out, "he did a more forth-
right job than most of his colleagues" in writing about
Patman. What he did was write a long analytical piece
which, among other things, quoted Rep. Richard Bolling
as saying: "The old man has always been a rattlesnake
and now he is senile." Presumably, it was the latter perception which finally caused Patman to lose his chairmanship.

Reporters certainly can be forgiven some tenderness

---

[7] Michael Green, "Nobody Covers The House," *Washington Monthly*, June
1970.

for the aged, a quality which is in short supply in American society. But how do we answer for the coverage of Wilbur Mills, a heavy drinker whose reputation as a sage and power broker was inflated beyond all reality until he had the political misfortune of encountering the "Argentine Firecracker," Fanny Foxe? For the most part, before this incident, we did not write about either the personal problems of Mills or about his tax policies and his conflicts of interest during a long career. Instead, we created the picture of a loveable gnome, a trifle unpredictable perhaps, but wise in the ways of Congress and the tax structure. The plain truth is that we protected Mills from the scrutiny which the chairman of a congressional committee writing tax laws for the nation both needed and deserved. Then we took him down for the wrong reasons because of an incident which conformed to the prejudices of the news business in behalf of public scandal. The nature of Mills' decline and fall is a rebuke to all of us about the shallow and misleading ways in which we cover Congress.

One answer to the "Mills problem" is to write more frequently, and with less deference to influential chairmen, about the personalities of congressmen. Most of our newspapers betray a double standard on this issue. We write ad infinitum, ad nauseum about the jeans-wearing and muffin-making proclivities of presidents and their families, behaving as if they were American royalty. We also glamorize a few senators, although these are most apt to be persons who are considered "presidential" (Kennedy, Humphrey, Muskie et al) and hence suited for such treatment. Mostly, we do not personify the run-of-the-mill congressman at all. As we have seen, this leaves the congressman free to create his own image back home with the help of the House Recording Studio and sometimes of his hometown correspondent. But there is an even more harmful consequence, which is that most readers never learn to develop a serious interest in Congress. "What is generally omitted from coverage of Congress, almost alone of the categories of people and events with which a newspaper regularly deals, is journalism that might portray congressional life so as to engage public interest," writes Michael Green. "The human face of congressmen and their aides, in all the day-to-day expressions of their small human foibles and unreported triumphs, mirrors the forces at work in the population as a whole. They color the story and, in so doing, reveal it. But the public is not allowed to know this story. Readers are told only in dry, clipped accounts the numerical fate of legislation. They are shown the final score, seldom the action itself. The smells and faces and humanity of the players is lost to them and with it the opportunity for interest. The daily weather report is more interesting to the public and seemingly has more demonstrable relationship to their lives."[8]

Green believes that people would lose interest in sports overnight if sportswriters adhered to the style of public affairs reporters. The sports interest is more durable than that, but there is much to be said for Green's corollary point: ". . . For their news about government, the American people must suffer the dullest, driest and most dehumanized accounts being published in the English language." What we badly need to do is to harness some of the institutional stories, and the endless stories about bills being passed or rejected to the human dimension of Congress." Another reason for humanizing the coverage of Congress was pointed out by Martin Salditch in the September 1975 issue of *California Journal*. Salditch observed that only 4 per cent of the bills introduced in Congress are passed compared to 45 per cent of the bills in the California Legislature. Many congressmen, particularly those in the minority, never get a bill passed, and it is almost impossible to assess their performance simply by writing about legislation. One Republican congressman, Clair Burgener of San Diego, succeeded in get-

---

[8] The same.

ting more than 300 laws through the Legislature during a decade in Sacramento. He has yet to get a bill through Congress since he came there in 1973, and Salditch quotes him as saying, "You find you can do more in solving constituent problems through agencies than with lawmaking." It was possible, covering Burgener in Sacramento, to inform readers of his public service by writing about the bills he submitted and about his voting record. This is not enough in Washington. We need a human record to tell us how well our congressmen are doing.

CHAPTER ELEVEN

The Sad State
of Public Affairs Reporting

*Understanding the news situation in a city
like Los Angeles, the politican and bureaucrat
can adjust to it. Important matters sneak
through in government meetings, unnoticed because they are sandwiched between overwhelming amounts of trivia. Operating unnoticed,
county supervisors turned over land of unparal-
leled beauty to favored land developers, doing it
in bits and pieces, in actions recorded only
briefly in the* Times *and with a few exceptions,
untouched by the powerful television stations.*
– Bill and Nancy Boyarsky in
BACKROOM POLITICS

Congress, despite everything, is one of the best-covered
institutions in America. It is penetrable, for one thing,
and it has a diverse collection of reporters and news organizations doing the reporting. Off Capitol Hill, with
the exceptions of the White House, the State Department
and the Defense Department, coverage of the vast, overlapping federal bureaucracy is sporadic at best and non-
existent at worst. "Reporters are fragmented much along
the lines of the federal bureaucracy," says former *Washington Post* and *New York Times* reporter Peter Braestrup. "There is no systematic intelligence at work. At its
basest what is reported are competing claims of rhetoric.
The managerial function is insufficiently covered. We get
a fragmented, hit or miss view of the world." Many bureaucratic decisions are buried from public view until
long after the fact, sometimes emerging as a historical
exercise in an investigation by a congressional commit-

tee. Such investigations often reveal the tremendous power possessed by bureaucrats to pursue their own priorities irrespective of the orders of their superiors or the express will of Congress. The CIA investigation of 1975, for instance, produced the story of the middle-level bureaucrat who had declined to carry out a 1969 order of President Nixon's to destroy certain deadly poisons. This incident was unusual only in the dramatic character of the subject matter. "Getting a handle on the bureaucracy" is a familiar battlecry for political orators and a persistent frustration for Presidents of the United States. It also is one of the unmet challenges for the press.

There are a number of reasons why the bureaucracy is poorly covered, but perhaps the most compelling is simply that few journalists are management minded; they do not really know very much about how operational decisions are made and carried out. "One example of that," says David Broder, "is that while every reporter in Washington recognizes that the Office of Management and Budget is a very important decision-making place, there is almost a total aversion to finding out just what it is exactly that they do there. We probably ought to encourage the development of internship programs that would put journalists inside the Office of Management and Budget for six months or a year at a time, simply so that we have that kind of expertise available. I think government is going to operate very much in terms of budgets and management techniques from this point on. If we're going to cover government, we're probably going to have to learn something about those techniques." Elliot Richardson, speaking of the days when he was secretary of health, education and welfare, makes a similar point. Richardson believes that the central issue of whether government should intervene to help people in need was decided during the New Deal. In his view the really important questions facing HEW are issues of process relating to "decentralization of programs, simplifications, citizen involvement and the like." But he found that repor-

ters were far more interested in ideological issues and
that they tended to think of all issues in ideological
terms. "I never found a major issue confronting HEW
while I was there where the distinction between 'liberals'
and 'conservatives' routinely used by the press was even
relevant," says Richardson.

It is not surprising that we resort to political labels for
operational questions. It is a hangover from our preoccupation with politics at the expense of government. And it
is a reflection, too, as Broder observed on the Medicare
issue, that we tend to judge people in terms of their
stated aspirations rather than on their capacity to de-
liver. "I think you have to take seriously the testimony
that comes from every former journalist that I can think
of who has ever gone to work for government, particularly for the president," says Broder. "All of them say
that the operation on the inside is not at all what they
had assumed it was when they were covering it from the
outside."

From the vantage point of the Washington reporter the
federal government often appears to encompass the entire range of public affairs coverage. In fact, it is only a
small part for most American news organizations, which
are rooted in their community and not in Washington.
The localness of the American newspaper is its unique
characteristic. Strictly speaking, there is no "national
press" in the United States unless one has in mind the
Christian Science Monitor, the *Wall Street Journal* or the
National Observer. All are fine newspapers, but the total
circulation of the three is a tiny fraction of American
newspaper readership, and none of them are national
papers in the sense, say, of several of the British dailies.
Given the realities of our geography and our history, it
could not be otherwise. While there are students of communication who believe that cable and perhaps the use of
satellites someday will make it commercially feasible to
produce a daily national newspaper in various cities of
the United States, it is safe to predict that most newspa-

pers will in the foreseeable future continue to regard their own communities and possibly their own states as their arena of public affairs responsibility. How well these local newspapers meet this responsibility is of special concern in a nation where many of the fundamental public decisions are made at the state and local levels. In 1946, a year after World War II ended, state and local governments in the United States spent 11 billion dollars, which was then 5.3 per cent of the gross national product. In 1972 these governments spent nearly 160 billion dollars or 14 per cent of the gross national product. While federal spending is a familiar political target, it increased less both proportionately and in absolute terms than did state and local government spending. Federal spending in 1946 accounted for 17 per cent of the gross national product, in 1972 for 21.6 per cent. Furthermore, if expenditures for defense and international efforts are taken out of the federal total, we find that the federal government in 1972 spent 107 billion dollars for civilian-domestic purposes, about two-thirds of the state-city total.[1] The trend is toward an even greater proportion of state and local government spending. And this means greater challenges for newspapers that take seriously the public affairs coverage of their own communities.

How well do newspapers meet these challenges? It is difficult to generalize, given the wide variety of competence and interests which newspapers display in covering their own local governments, but there are some disturbing indications. The New England Newspaper Survey found a "don't-rock-the-boat" attitude prevailing on many of the region's daily newspapers. Similarly, a study by William L. Rivers and David M. Rubin of the San Francisco Bay Area press in 1971 found serious deficien-

---

[1] Advisory Council on Intergovernmental Relations, *Federal-State-Local Finances: Significant Features of Fiscal Federalism*, (Washington, 1974), p. 5.

cies in local reporting.[2] The *San Francisco Chronicle*
stressed entertainment at the expense of news and ran
stories favorable to local, cooperating businesses. The
San Mateo Times had a "news blackout" on stories about
filling San Francisco Bay, a controversial issue on which
the company seeking to fill a substantial area of the bay
was represented by the publisher's law firm. The *San
Jose Mercury* engaged in "civic boosterism" and respected "many sacred cows." I have written elsewhere in
this book of my experiences with *Mercury* policy stories;
it is worth observing here that the Rivers-Rubin study
quotes the curious defense of a since-retired editor that
"there are no more policy stories in our papers than in
any others."

For all I know, the retired editor was right in his belief
about the widespread existence of policy stories. I can
remember, from the other side of the fence in 1956, when
it was virtually impossible for Phil Burton, now a congressman, to get his name into either the *San Francisco
Chronicle* or the *San Francisco Examiner*, then vigorously competitive, until the campaign was over and he
had become the youngest member of the State Legislature. I know of the difficulties experienced by *Sacramento
Bee* reporters who tried to get anything into their stories
which suggested that the California Water Plan, with its
program of high dams on many of the state's few remaining wild rivers, was anything less than perfect. And I can
remember, not so long ago, the difficulties experienced by
blacks who tried to get their side of the story about Oakland's racial unrest told in the *Oakland Tribune*. It
wasn't very long ago, either, that spokesmen for the radi-
cal left or, later, for the John Birch Society automatically
received negative treatment from most newspapers.
Generally, the papers were hardest on those who were
"fighting city hall," which usually meant they also were

---

[2] William L. Rivers and David M. Rubin, *A Region's Press: Anatomy of
Newspapers in The San Francisco Bay Area*, (Berkeley Calif., 1971).

fighting the dominant economic interests of the community. ". . . Too often," wrote Bill Boyarsky, "the publisher is part of the backroom crowd that runs the city or county, a businessman who feels his fortunes are tied to those of the real estate, industrial or business interests in the area."

Boyarsky went to the *Los Angeles Times* in 1960 after covering state politics for the Associated Press. He found there were only two *Times* reporters covering the Los Angeles County government and only three covering the city government compared to 19 in Washington and five in the state capitol in Sacramento. "At the *Times*," wrote Bill and Nancy Boyarsky in their book, *Backroom Poli tics*, "readers are given long in-depth stories about subjects the editors believe are of interest to the Southern California community. They are deliberately written in a lively or dramatic style by reporters chosen as much for their writing ability as their reporting skill. Reporters, themselves, think of many of these stories, and their suggestions are usually accepted by editors who pride themselves on running what is known as a 'reporter's paper.' As a result, the staff spends long hours on a relatively small number of stories that interest the reporters or editors. The day-to-day run of news is often neglected in favor of a lengthy piece on a single subject."[3]

I favor such an approach to the news, particularly if it is contrasted with the box-score or bulletin-board approach to city council actions common on so many newspapers. But Bill Boyarsky makes the point that selective reporting is carried to such an extreme in Los Angeles that citizens interested in reforms are left ignorant of important governmental actions and that "many boards and commissions feel free to act without much thought of public reaction." He believes that it is possible for the *Times* to behave this way because of its near-monopoly position. (The afternoon *Los Angeles Examiner*,

---

[3] Bill and Nancy Boyarsky, *Backroom Politics* (Los Angeles, 1974), p. 264.

weakened by a long strike and an unwillingness to devote resources to news coverage, does not offer serious competition.) The Boyarskys contrast the Los Angeles situation with the competitive one in Chicago, where there is a long tradition of robust muckraking journalism. "Chicago papers are blunt in their accusations," write the Boyarskys, "often drawing damaging conclusions about public officials that papers in most cities would refuse to publish for fear of lawsuits. But in Chicago, the heat of daily competition forces publishers to be more courageous." The attitude of the Chicago newspapermen about their work is summed up in a quote from Chicago columnist Mike Royko: "The fact of the matter is that it is damn hard to libel people."[4]

Even newspapers which attempt serious and comprehensive coverage of their local government do not find their intentions easy to accomplish. Often, newspapers are hampered by the step-ladder tradition of news organization promotion in which city government is likely to be near the bottom rung. If a young reporter assigned to city hall proves to be a hotshot, he is apt to demand and get promotion to a "higher" beat, a decision which keeps him on the newspaper but does nothing for the coverage of city hall. In many places the same pattern prevails at the state capitals, where good reporters are apt to move to Washington just as they have begun to master the intricacies of state government. Reporters of my middle-age generation grew up learning that Washington was "where the action is" and naturally gravitated to what seemed to be the more glamorous and significant arena of national public-affairs reporting. I first covered a police beat and city government, then county government. After two different editing jobs I went to Sacramento for four years before coming to Washington. Except for the editing, this is a fairly typical pattern. The pay scales as well as the prestige follow the same step-

---

[4] The same, p. 267.

ladder, which is a further incentive for reporters to leave the city hall and statehouse beats as soon as they can. Sacramento is supposed to be one of the best-covered state capitals (partly, I suspect, because Californians have a state rather than a federal focus), but many of the best reporters there — people like Boyarsky, Martin Salditch and Norman Kempster, then of UPI and now of the *Los Angeles Times* — left and went to Washington. Bill Stall, the knowledgeable AP bureau chief, quit to become press secretary for Gov. Edmund G. (Jerry) Brown Jr., then also joined the *Los Angeles Times*. The only daily newspaper bureau in Sacramento from out of town that has maintained both continuity and excellence is the *Los Angeles Times* bureau, headed by Tom Goff. The *Times*, which once had an inferior bureau in Sacramento, might be a model for other metropolitan papers that desire a similar high level of state capitol coverage. Its pay scales are high, probably the best in California and certainly the highest in Sacramento. The paper consistently gives good play to state government stories and shows a balanced interest in both the Legislature and the governor's office. The bureau also has an investigative reporter, Robert Fairbanks, a competent and experienced newsman who used to cover state government for UPI. And the *Times* is willing to devote the space to intricate and important stories about the way state government operates. The result is a very high order of coverage.

The decades since the end of World War II have been an explosive period of growth for state and local government. This growth also taxed the historic coverage practices of metropolitan newspapers, which found their circulation fleeing to the fast-growing suburbs. Usually, the people moved more quickly than the newspaper coverage did. "The *Washington Post* was slow to read the census," says Herbert Denton, a former *Post* Maryland editor who is now District of Columbia editor. "We were perfectly geared to cover the Washington area of 1950." The Boyarskys quote Jean Packard, a supervisor in Fairfax

County, Virginia, as believing that the *Post* regards the
county as "low on the totem pole of training." Another
unnamed Fairfax County supervisor is quoted as saying
of *Post* reporters, "Generally speaking, I think they are
very good but usually they don't stay more than a year,
and it takes six months to learn the lingo . . ." Until
recently, this was a fair assessment of the coverage. But
the *Post* is changing. The paper now has 11 reporters and
two editors assigned to Maryland coverage and is putting
particular emphasis on suburban Prince George's
County, a complex area of cultural, racial, environmental and political conflicts. "Prince George's can be an important beat and it can be a stepping stone, too," says
Post metropolitan editor Leonard Downie. "What is bad
is to exile people to counties, which we used to do. We
don't do that anymore. People are exiled, if at all, to late
night duty. And we've been getting some of the brightest
young reporters on the toughest county beats."

One consequence of the post-war government growth is
that a proliferation of public agencies has made local
news coverage an almost impossible task for smaller
newspapers. When I was editor of the *Contra Costa
Times*, I once estimated that half the agencies in that
important suburban California county never were
covered by any newspaper on a regular basis. Boyarsky,
assigned to a local political campaign by the *Los Angeles
Times*, found he often was the only reporter present at
public meetings. Newspapers which try to cover a multitude of city and town meetings out of a sense of public
responsibility often find themselves in a "can't win" position. Long, routine meetings can chew up hours of a reporter's time without producing anything resembling a
significant story. On the other hand, a public body may
operate more responsibly simply because the reporter is
present — and it may take an unscheduled action of
great significance if he is not. It is a dilemma for the
reporter, too. On newspapers where he is allowed to
make his own decisions, sometimes he must gamble that

"nothing will happen" to find time to work on a longer, more reflective piece. The problem was summed up by Douglas L. McMillan, a young reporter who formerly covered the Palm Springs area for the *Riverside Press-Enterprise*. "The one thing that bugs the hell out of me is the daily demand for copy," said McMillan in his Palm Springs days. "They'll tell me to work on a story for two or three days but every day they want copy. It gets to the point where editors are just looking for copy to fill up space between the ads — and yet I have myself to blame, too. I follow the path of least resistance. It is easy to go to a meeting or down to City Hall and find something that I can file. And that stuff should be reported, too." One answer to the problem of government multiplicity that would be of enormous benefit to newspapers, and indirectly to the public, is the development of regional agencies to deal with those issues, such as transportation and smog control, which do not respect local government boundaries. The trend to regionalism in the United States, although advanced in a few metropolitan areas, has been slowed by the ideological opposition of those who regard "regional government" as weakening the fabric of representative government. If public awareness has anything to do with the effectiveness of government, the opposite is true. There is little question that people would know more about what their representatives did if what they did was done by fewer governments.

State governments may be neglected even more than the Washington bureaucracy or city hall. A study by the Citizens Conference on State Legislatures (now Legis 50-The Center for Legislative Improvement) found that the press coverage of legislatures in the 50 states was "generally poor." Norman E. Isaacs has referred to legislative coverage as "the soft underbelly of journalism." And Al Hester of the University of Georgia, former city hall reporter and city editor for the *Dallas Times Herald*, has called legislative reporting "the journalistic stepchild." These are merited descriptions. State government spends the largest share of public dollars on highways and welfare, and in many states on education as well. State governments also serve as laboratories for innovations which, if they work, can be adopted by another state or by the federal government and which, if they fail, can be discarded without becoming imbedded into national policy. But state government reporting suffers from all of the problems which beset public affairs reporting on any level — and from some special problems of its own. Few papers follow the example of the *Los Angeles Times* or the Miami newspapers in giving both good coverage to the Legislature and good play to legislative stories. Fewer still follow the example of the *Houston Post*, which in 1972 devoted page-one space for a reflective eight-part series on legislative reform written by Felton West and Henry Holcomb, or the example of the *St. Petersburg Times*, which in 1973 decided to give magazine treatment to legislative news by capsuling stories on a single page with eye-catching headlines and a modern makeup which defies the tradition that such news must be presented in a dull "inside baseball" style. Most papers rely on the wire services for their state government news, or on a small and overworked bureau which sometimes must duplicate the wire service stories. Too often, the result is a superficiality and a neglect which mocks the notion of the federal system.

"All but the larger newspapers and broadcasting stations receive most legislative news from Associated Press or United Press International or both," wrote Tom Littlewood in 1972. "Yet wire service bureaus in state capitols are disgracefully understaffed. The Harrisburg, Pa., bureau of AP was reported to have fewer newsmen now — five — than in 1935 (six). UPI has two newsmen in Trenton, two in Madison and makes do with a stringer in Annapolis when the legislature is not in session. During a session a single reporter is usually assigned from the UPI Baltimore bureau. In the smaller states, especially, it is a common practice for the wires to use one newsman to cover both houses — assigned, perhaps, by an editor who was home ill the day the teacher explained the bicameral system."[4] Littlewood gives the example of a UPI bureau chief, Richard Adorjan, who resigned as head of the Springfield bureau in 1970 after the Chicago regional office took away the fourth man in the bureau — the teletype operator. This meant that reporters would have to transmit their own copy onto the wire.

After Adorjan's departure, the bureau consisted of three newsmen, none of whom had covered a legislature before. At that time the three were coping simultaneously with: a special session of the Legislature; a constitutional convention; all of the other facets of state government, including the Governor, the Supreme Court, and the administrative agencies, processing the high school basketball scores and weekly team ratings for the entire state; handling the daily "interior Illinois livestock market"; covering fatal highway accidents and other spot news happenings for the middle one-third of Illinois; and responding to the special service requests of clients for coverage of events such as the tedious rate hearings before the state regulatory agencies. "Chicago kept saying just handle it the best you can," Adorjan recalled.

The attitude described by Adorjan is not limited to the wire services. More often than not, state government reporters on newspapers find themselves dealing with city desks oriented to local issues and to local coverage. The editors are likely to be unfamiliar with the issues and personalities of state government. Frequently, they are indifferent to them. And newspapers which are serious about state government coverage sometimes find it difficult to keep qualified correspondents in a distant

---

[4] Thomas B. Littlewood, "What's Wrong With Statehouse Coverage," *Columbia Journalism Review*, March-April 1972. Littlewood covered the Illinois capitol in Springfield for 10 years. See also Littlewood's article, "The Trials of Statehouse Journalism," in the Dec. 10, 1966, issue of *Saturday Review*.

state capital remote from any population center. "When Illinois legislators decided in 1837 on the new location for the state capitol, one farsighted legislator voted for a small community in Lawrence County called Purgatory," wrote Paul Simon. "There are times when that seems appropriate. Too often good reporters view the state capital as an unhappy stopping place on the way to Washington or some other assignment."[5]

The failure of state government reporting begins in the journalism schools, few of which offer any training in this coverage to prospective public affairs reporters. A survey by Al Hester, assistant professor at the University of Georgia School of Journalism, shows that only 18 per cent of journalism schools give a high emphasis to state government coverage in public-affairs reporting courses. Four-fifths of the schools gave their highest emphasis to local reporting, an action which they justified with the observation that most beginning reporters usually start on the local government beat. "It is obvious from the responses of educators and legislators that state legislative reporting is a journalistic stepchild and that improvement in such training is needed," Hester wrote. "Journalism educators, harried by severe limitations on the number of journalism courses they can offer, generally have relegated legislative reporting to a low priority."[6]

Better training is especially needed for television reporters covering state government. Because television

---

[5] Paul Simon, "Improving Statehouse Coverage," *Columbia Journalism Review*, September-October 1973. Simon, now a congressman, served 14 years in the Illinois Legislature and four as the state's lieutenant governor. As a cure for the "purgatory complex" problem he suggests higher pay for statehouse reporters, better play for legislative news and improved journalism training in statehouse reporting.

[6] Dr. Al Hester, "The Journalistic Stepchild," a working paper prepared for Legis 50. Hester, who also surveyed a number of legislators, in 1973 sent questionnaires to 81 journalism schools with enrollments of 200 or more. He received responses from 43 schools, or 53.6 per cent.

stations have a job-demand far exceeding the supply and because few of these stations value state coverage, the reporters assigned to state capitols frequently are beginners lacking essential knowledge of state government. Often, they have no one to learn from. "Much of TV reporting was pretty awful," says Ann Compton of ABC, in looking back on state government coverage in Richmond, Virginia. "People didn't take the time to prepare. At best it was what I call adequate reporting. So-and-so legislator is going to introduce a bill banning no-return bottles. You report this, and what the soft-drink lobbyist says against it. You don't fill out the story. You don't tell them that the chairman of the committee to which the bill has been assigned is a thirty-year friend of the lobbyist and that the legislator who introduced it is simply going to get the business. Most TV reporting simply doesn't have the knowledge."

However, even superficial television coverage is preferable to the absence of any coverage at all. Since Littlewood evaluated statehouse coverage in 1972, a number of newspapers with a history of indifference to state government coverage, have decided that it is important to cover the state capitol. The trend in commercial television has been the other way, leaving public television to fill the vacuum (as it does in Albany and Harrisburg) or abandoning coverage largely to radio (as has been the case in Sacramento). First, broadcasters were caught up in the mystique of "happy talk," which meant that the viewers weren't supposed to be burdened with the serious and deadly dull coverage of public events. Then the trend was toward "action news," which stressed spot-news coverage of breaking local stories. At one time during the Reagan administration as many as nine California television stations had a crew assigned to Sacramento. Now, KNBC in Los Angeles is the only one of the state's 67 television stations to cover the state capitol. As Ed Salzman observed in the Feb. 14, 1977, issue of *New West*:

The decisions to abandon Sacramento aren't being made by newsmen — they are being made by marketing-research firms, armed with computer printouts which supposedly prove that serious analysis of government does not sell purring automobiles or the latest erotic shaving products. But "action news" — whatever that is — does. One of the former Sacramento television reporters was told upon being assigned to the capital beat that his reports should be a cross between the kind of material published in the *Reader's Digest* and the *National Enquirer*.

Not surprisingly, the diminished interest in serious state government coverage also has been reflected in reduced coverage of state political races. A study conducted by the California Center for Research and Education in Government under the direction of Mary Ellen Leary had some critical things to say about both newspaper and television coverage of the 1974 gubernatorial campaign in which Edmund G. (Jerry) Brown Jr. was elected governor. But though it found gaps in the newspaper coverage (principally by the *San Francisco Chronicle*), the study also concluded that the *Los Angeles Times*, the Copley papers in San Diego and the *Sacramento Bee* provided adequate-to-good coverage of the campaign. This could not be said for the television coverage, which Leary found severely distorted the campaign by too little coverage and by emphasis on entertainment values and candidate events at the expense of any substantive discussion of the political issues. In effect, candidates were left to communicate with their 20 million fellow Californians through the medium of paid television advertising, if they could afford it. This performance by the television stations was of enormous benefit in the Democratic primary to Brown, whose name was familiar to voters because of his father's eight years as governor. On the basis of name recognition alone he figured to win a primary where other candidates were unable to command the attention of the media for serious political discussion. I wrote some stories on that primary for the *Washington Post* and found the campaign the least informative one since the pre-television days of crossfiling, when the law encouraged candidates to hide both their specific views and their party identity. Brown's chief opponents, San Francisco Mayor Joseph Alioto and Assembly Speaker Bob Moretti, became so frustrated at the lack of coverage that they attacked both Brown and the news media in the hope of "making news" that would attract some interest to their campaigns. They succeeded only in making themselves appear combative and unsportsmanlike. The other principal candidates, William Roth and Rep. Jerome Waldie, had even more difficulty in breaking through the television news blackout. I doubt whether any of these candidates could have beaten Brown, given the size of the field, but the fact remains that millions of Californians were scarcely aware there was a primary, let alone of what the issues might have been. Not surprisingly, many of them did not vote. And television coverage remained conspicuously poor until the final month of the general election campaign.

"The effect in the 1974 campaign was to deny television coverage to the viewer other than through the paid commercial," wrote San Francisco television reporter Rollin Post.[7] "Had coverage been extensive I think it is not unrealistic to believe that either Houston Flournoy (the Republican candidate for governor), or Bill Bagley (the Republican candidate for state controller), or both, might have been elected in November. If the system doesn't change, then the continuing blackout obviously helps the well-known candidate."[8] Post, who has an en-

---

[7] In an Aug. 25, 1975, letter to the author.

[8] Flournoy, who had trailed in published polls by margins ranging from 14 to 30 per cent, lost by the close margin of 178,694 votes out of 6 million votes cast. The narrow race was anticipated by Flournoy's pollster, the Orange County-based firm of Decision Making Information, which found that Flournoy conformed more closely to Californians' image of "the ideal governor" than did Brown. DMI also found that the undecided voter more closely re-

cyclopedic knowledge of Northern California politics, was considered during the years I covered state government to be the best of the state's broadcast journalists on public affairs. He was one of perhaps a half-dozen commercial television reporters in the state who spent full-time on politics or public affairs coverage. The commercial stations, emphasizing "happy talk" and de-emphasizing public affairs coverage, have moved their political reporters to other assignments. This also happened to Post. He quit commercial television and went to work for KQED, a San Francisco educational station which has a serious commitment to the coverage of politics and government.

The federal government bears a hefty share of the blame for the sad state of TV public affairs coverage. One of the worst consequences of the so-called "Fairness Doctrine," a Federal Communications Commission requirement that stations present both sides of controversial issues, is that it has provided timid broadcasters with an alibi for not providing public affairs coverage at all. To be sure, this same doctrine also requires a certain amount of public-affairs programming on controversial issues, but this usually is satisfied by formally balanced panel shows which satisfy the requirement while simultaneously inducing mass sleeping sickness. In practice, as Fred Friendly has pointed out, the Fairness Doctrine had been used by the Kennedy administration to restrict right-wing commentary and then by the Johnson administra-

---

sembled the Flournoy supporter than the Brown supporter. The *Los Angeles Times*, in a story published the day before the election said that its own poll of registered voters showed that Brown continued to hold a "commanding" lead in the race. To the credit of the *Times* it published another story after the election confirming the accuracy of the DMI survey. This post-election story also quoted San Francisco pollster Mervin Field, whose last published poll had shown Brown with an 8 per cent lead but Flournoy gaining, as saying: "The public didn't start sizing up Jerry Brown until the remaining days of the campaign. If they had a few more days, the election might have gone the other way."

tion to inhibit pro-Goldwater broadcasts.[9] The Nixon administration added to broadcasters' fears by threats to monitor programming and by a politically inspired effort to challenge the licenses of stations owned by the Washington Post Company. The fruit of this governmental pressure at most stations has been public-affairs programming of uninformative and deceptive blandness. Television stations, and not entirely without reason, just don't want to get involved.

The California political campaign of 1974 demonstrated that this broadcasting quiescence extends even to the First Amendment. Despite the Supreme Court's upholding of the Fairness Doctrine, most broadcasters argue — and I agree with them — that the First Amendment should apply to electronic journalism as fully as it does to the "print media." The broadcasters had a chance to translate their brave words into action in California. It was provided them by the two nominees for governor, both of whom were acting in what they perceived to be their own political interests. Republican Flournoy, trailing Democrat Brown in a state where Democrats have a big edge in registration, had a typical underdog's anxiousness to debate his opponent. Brown's strategists, seemingly secure in their lead, did not want a debate but they also did not want to give an impression that Brown was ducking Flournoy. The result was a contract between the two candidates for six scheduled debates, some of them in unlikely places at obscure times. The contract contained this unique clause: "*No other television or radio use may be made of all or any part of the program by any person, including a candidate or the stations, except for normal news coverage.*" "This provision," wrote Ed Salzman in the November 1974 *California Journal,*" was strictly for the benefit of front-runner Jerry Brown, who had a strategic interest in preventing

[9] Fred W. Friendly, "What's Fair on the Air," *The New York Times Magazine*, March 30, 1975.

radio and television stations from broadcasting the debates live and on tape in their entirety. And the broadcasters knuckled under." The stations were not a party to this agreement, and it was clear they were not bound by it. Brown's chief aide, Tom Quinn, told me candidly before the contract was signed that Brown would have no recourse against a station that decided to re-broadcast the Sacramento or Fresno debate so that it could be seen, say, by voters in Los Angeles. The only thing that Brown could have done would have been to use the re-broadcast as an excuse to cancel the remainder of the debates, an action which would have reinforced the point that he was ducking Flournoy. As it was, Brown had the best of both worlds. He was able to use the debates as evidence of his willingness to meet Flournoy, but he avoided the risks of a well-publicized television confrontation on a statewide network. It was a brilliant stroke by the Brown camp, and a sad example of broadcasting gutlessness. "The fact is that the radio and television stations were not anxious to devote time, money and effort to the campaign," wrote Salzman, "and they took the easy way out."

Another example of broadcasting timidity occurred in Washington a few months later when the House Ways and Means Committee was considering proposals to televise its hearings on national energy policy. Traditionally, the House has prohibited television coverage of its committee meetings and floor debates, but it changed this policy in 1974 and allowed each committee to set its own rules. This change permitted the House Judiciary Committee to televise the hearings on Richard Nixon's impeachment but few other committees have opened their meetings to broadcast coverage. The members of Ways and Means — for a variety of personal and partisan reasons — were unwilling to permit television coverage unless it was gavel-to-gavel, a restrictive prohibition which prevented excerpts of the hearings from being shown on the nightly news. "Reporters working for newspapers and magazines have no Hill-passed direc-

tives governing how they cover open congressional committee sessions . . ." wrote Walter Pincus in the *Washington Post.* "By establishing a specific set of rules applying
only to radio and television newsmen, Congress has limited their First Amendment rights. Ironically, television
news officials, who continually argue that they should be
protected by the First Amendment as their print brothers
are, have behaved miserably in the present situation. No
television network, for example, went to see Ways and
Means Chairman (Al) Ullman in January to work out
coverage of his initial hearings on the emergency tax bill
although ABC's Washington bureau chief did send him a
note." When the networks were given a brief moment
before the committee on February 26, 1975, to present
their case for selective coverage, no network official
asked to be heard. Only John Chancellor of NBC, in his
"Editor's Notebook," mentioned the committee's decision
against the networks. As Pincus observed in his March
19, 1975, editorial page article in the *Post*, a similar action directed against newspapers would have provoked
an editorial outcry and stories about the abuse of press
freedom. But the networks did nothing.

For the most part, these exercises of timidity, are those
of network and station management, not of the television
correspondents themselves. Many TV reporters push as
vigorously for access and full rights of coverage as any
newspaperman; most of them also would be willing, at
least in Washington, to depart from the beaten track of
public-affairs coverage and explore the ideas of candidates and officeholders if they were given half a chance.
They do not have that chance now. Nor, in many cases, do
the people who report public affairs for newspapers have
much say about the direction their coverage should take.
The typical legislative reporter, and often the reporter
who covers Congress or city hall, is a "grunt" who operates within news definitions narrowly prescribed by
journalistic forms and works long, uncertain hours in the
pursuit of the routine. Too often, his organization looks

for early copy and old ideas rather than for comprehensive coverage or creativity. The modern citizen, meanwhile, is bombarded with a bewildering variety of "facts" and conflicting stimuli. Every year this citizen becomes more dependent on isolated fragments of electronic reporting, arranged in the entertaining narrative form of television news. Frequently, he feels powerless to influence events in the face of this news. Even more frequently, he suffers from an overload of information. And yet, amid all the information presented to him, the citizen often is provided next to nothing on which to base a judgment of the performance of his representative institutions of government. "A popular government, without popular information, or the means of acquiring it, is but a prologue to a farce or a tragedy; or perhaps both," wrote James Madison in 1822. In the modern age we have the means of acquiring the necessary popular information. Whether or not we actually acquire it, depends upon whether news organizations at all levels accept the responsibility for providing serious coverage of public affairs.

CHAPTER TWELVE

Presidents
and Other Manipulators

*Power is poison. Its effect on Presidents has
always been tragic, chiefly as an almost insane
excitement at first, and a worse reaction afterward; but also because no mind is so well balanced as to bear the strain of seizing unlimited
force without habit or knowledge of it . .*

— Henry Adams in
THE EDUCATION OF HENRY ADAMS

Every president of the United States, beginning with
George Washington, has complained about the press. "It
is much to be wished," Washington wrote the president of
the Continental Congress in 1777, "that our Printers
were more discreet in many of their publications. We see
almost in every Paper, Proclamations or accounts transmitted by the Enemy, of an injurious nature." Thomas
Jefferson, the patron saint of press freedom in America,
the philosopher who preferred "newspapers without a
government" to "governments without newspapers," as
President declared that "even the least informed of the
people have learned that nothing in a newspaper is to be
believed." He suggested that editors divide their papers
into four chapters, headed truths, probabilities, possibilities and lies and added, "the first chapter would be
very short." Other presidents followed suit. John Tyler
suspected that the words "editor" and "blackguard" were
synonymous. Ulysses S. Grant called the publisher of the
New York Sun a blackmailer. Theodore Roosevelt, who
liked reporters and cultivated them, barred from the
White House some reporters who wrote stories he regarded as unfavorable. His distant cousin Franklin told a

reporter who suggested he would run for a third presidential term that he should wear a dunce cap. John Kennedy set the FBI on the trail of reporters in an effort to find out their news sources. Lyndon Johnson once told the King of Thailand, while showing him the press lobby, "This is the press room. This is where they try you and convict you and execute you all at the same time."

It would be tempting to say that the press gave as good as it got. Tempting, but untrue, at least until Richard Nixon came along. It *is* true that the descriptions of presidents in the press often have been unflattering. Washington was described as an atheist, Tyler as an "executive ass," Grant as "Kaiser Ulysses," Theodore Roosevelt as a drunkard[1] and Franklin Roosevelt as a would-be dictator. Kennedy, for all his popularity with the working press, repeatedly was denounced for "news management." But these descriptions were mostly by editorialists, often far removed from the scene of action. Presidents always have held the upper hand over correspondents who tried to cover them directly. This has been especially true in this century, when the modern concept of "news" won ascendancy over the expression of editorial opinion. James E. Pollard, writing during the Truman administration, listed 25 specific devices available to the president for public information purposes, ranging from the State of the Union message to "unofficial reports and rumors" deliberately given by a presidential appointee or supporter.[2] Pollard was writing before Presidents Ken-

---

[1] And had the satisfaction of winning a libel suit against the *Ishpeming (Mich.) Iron Ore*, a weekly which said during the 1912 campaign that Roosevelt "lies and curses in a most disgusting way; he gets drunk, too, and that not infrequently, and all his intimates know about it." The publisher, George H. Newett, admitted in open court that he could not substantiate the charge and the jury returned a verdict for six-cent damages after Roosevelt told the jury that he wasn't interested in money but in his reputation.

[2] James E. Pollard, *The Presidents and the Press: Truman To Johnson*, (Washington, D.C., 1964), pp. 13-15. This is the sequel to Pollard's earlier book, now unfortunately out of print, *The Presidents and the Press*, (New York, 1947), which is a valuable source book for this chapter.

nedy and Nixon set up series of meetings with newspaper publishers, or before President Carter answered the people's questions directly on CBS radio with Walter Cronkite serving as his dutiful interlocutor. In an age of instant communication the president is the supreme communicator in the American system of government. His role has been assured by the U. S. Constitution, which made the president both head of state and head of government, and by an early tradition of strong chief executives who grasped the public relations aspect of their leadership roles more surely than did the leaders of other branches of government. Congress contributed to the ascendancy of the executive branch at the very outset, when for a time it adopted the practice of the British Parliament and prohibited coverage of its proceedings. The judiciary, from the earliest days of the republic until the present, remains an essentially closed and secretive institution. But presidents from the beginning established a relationship with the press. George Washington, although generally aloof, summoned David Claypoole of the *Pennsylvania Packet and Daily Advertiser* to discuss publication of his Farewell Address. A significant achievement of the most recognizable ancestor of the modern newspaper, the *New York Herald*, was an "interview" with President Van Buren by its publisher, James Gordon Bennett. Read today, it seems more like an audience than an interview, but it both fed on and perpetuated a popular interest in Van Buren. By the time of the Cleveland administration the *New York World* could assert, in defense of its coverage of Cleveland's marriage, "that the President is public property." He was not, in fact, such "property" during the administration of the suspicious and secretive Cleveland, but he would become so. The late Gould Lincoln of the *Washington Star* liked to tell how he went over to the White House one Saturday afternoon during the Theodore Roosevelt administration to check on a local news development. He found no one about and started through a corridor which led to the

White House living quarters. While he was walking through the corridor, the President himself came out through a side door, dressed in a sweat suit after working out in the gym. Roosevelt asked what he wanted, and Lincoln wound up with an exclusive Sunday story.

Such approachability was useful to Theodore Roosevelt in reminding his fellow citizens that he remained "a man of the people" in the White House. It formed the pattern for the modern presidents who have been most successful in their press relations — Franklin Roosevelt, Harry Truman, John Kennedy, Gerald Ford. The presidency is uniquely suited among American institutions to personification, and access to the White House increased journalistic interest in the lifestyle and personal habits of presidents and their families. For reporters who enjoyed this access, the personal relationship with the nation's most powerful citizen encouraged coverage that could border on flattery or even sycophancy. And the relationship encouraged presidents who were accumulative of power to assume that the press, as a body, could be co-opted for the greater good. Lyndon Johnson's dangerous notion that Americans should form themselves into a great consensus led by the president was revealed most consistently and damagingly in his relations with the press. "His problem was that he wanted the press to collaborate in the building of the Great Society," says Bill Moyers. "He could never accept that the press was unwilling to play the role."

Johnson, carrying the notion that knowledge is power to absurdity, installed teletypes upon which he could instantly read the wire-service reports as they were sent out to the newspapers of the nation. His sensitivity was demonstrated by his immediate reactions to stories he regarded as critical or inaccurate. When Richard Nixon became President he made as much of removing these teletypes as Johnson had of having them installed. A public official who knew Johnson well and had also worked for Nixon told me that it was Nixon who needed the teletypes and Johnson who did not. In his view, Johnson cared too much about what was said about him and over-reacted to trivial criticisms when he would have been better off devoting himself to essential policy. This official regarded Nixon as a calculating and lonely man who badly needed to be more in touch with the outside world. As another former Nixon aide put it, Nixon "really thinks he can go over into that little office in the Executive Office Building of an afternoon and solve a world problem by a feat of concentration and thought." It would have been better, surely, if LBJ had spent more time in that little office and Nixon had begun to read the wires before they carried stories calling for his impeachment.

The presidency is an intensely personal office operating under an intense public glare. Journalism, for all its faults, shines when it focuses on personality. Reporters who wouldn't know an international monetary policy from a foul pop fly often are quick to spot the fraud, the self-aggrandizer, the phony. Along with most other human beings, they also are able to perceive whether someone genuinely likes them or is insecure in their presence. I would argue that the Washington press corps has an almost indefinable sense of the substance of those with whom they deal. "In a very gross way we do make judgments as to who is a heavyweight and who is a lightweight," says David Broder. "And I think those judgments even in retrospect tend to look fairly substantial. This does not have anything primarily to do with the use of language or of ideology. It has to do with how seriously the politicians take themselves and how much weight they carry in terms of direct relationships with other politicians. Goldwater was a serious person in terms of presidential candidacy. Nixon was not popular personally, but he was a person of substance and weight. McGovern, though many people agreed with his position on the war, was never regarded as a heavyweight politician. I think that judgment ultimately was reached by the people."

Ultimately, Nixon's substance was insufficient to over-
come his insecurity. This, too, showed most of all in his
relationships with the press. Nixon had been capable of
cultivating reporters when they were necessary to him,
most of all in the period of his "resurrection" of the mid-
1960s when another blowup of the "last press conference"
variety would have proven fatal to his political ambi-
tions. But Nixon always knew that he was disliked by the
press. Like Lyndon Johnson, Nixon did not recognize
that the press had an independent purpose. Unlike
Johnson, Nixon held no personal affection for reporters.
Perceiving that few reporters liked him and that many
detested him, Nixon wrongly blamed their attitude on
their liberalism or their presumed Democratic sym-
pathies. A Republican president certainly is not without
his ideological handicaps, but both Dwight D.
Eisenhower and Gerald Ford enjoyed favorable press relations. What happened in Nixon's case was that reporters resented his lack of respect for them, his manipula-
tiveness, his debater's tricks and, above all, his revealing
rhetorical device of describing whatever it was he was
trying to accomplish as the very thing he was *not* doing.
". . . I have to use the press conference — I don't mean the
reporters, but use the press conference — when I believe
that is the best way to communicate (with) or inform the
people," Nixon told reporters on June 29, 1972, in trying
to explain why he had been unwilling to hold press conferences. Similar verbal constructions abounded in any
Nixon meeting with the press. Contending, on October 5,
1972, that the national press had wrongly said that
"South Vietnam was down the tubes," Nixon interjected
a comment that "I am *not* referring, of course, to you
ladies and gentlemen, who are reporters." In the same
press conference, when Phillip Potter of the *Baltimore
Sun* asked Nixon why he couldn't hold more press conferences before the election, the reply began, "Well, Mr.
Potter, the press conference to me is *not* basically a
chore." Replying to a question from Dan Rather of CBS

on October 26, 1973, Nixon said he had been described as "tyrant, dictator, he has lost his senses, he should resign, he should be impeached." In the middle of this tirade Nixon remembered to say, "I don't mean you," to the television reporter he detested most of all. The contempt which blazed through such statements was made worse, in the viewpoint of reporters, by this mealy-mouth quality. Of course, Nixon considered press conferences "a chore," and worse. An aide who had seen him prepare for them many times told me that Nixon often vomited before them and was always tense. Of course, Nixon was referring to the "ladies and gentlemen who are reporters." Of course, he had Rather in mind instead of some television correspondent on another planet. The patronizing little verbal tricks of Nixon are what made him unbearable to the press. We had long since grown used to his hostility.

Every modern president has found press conferences at least occasionally burdensome, and every president has sometimes given in to his temper in dealing with the press. On December 19, 1942, while the United States was at war with Nazi Germany, Franklin Roosevelt sent the Iron Cross to *New York Daily News* columnist John O'Donnell in response to a light-hearted column complaining about the censorship of U.S. correspondents in Australia. O'Donnell had written that "the boys have turned to flutes and piccolos just to keep their fingers nimble for the time when the censorship lets them beat the keys of their portable typewriters to turn out a tell-all story." For sheer vindictiveness Roosevelt's action has not been matched by any of his successors. Harry Truman is famed for his blunt letter to *Washington Post* music critic Paul Hume, but that was at least in defense of his daughter. More revealing of how wildly inaccurate an aroused Truman could be was his remark to reporters on January 18, 1951, that not a single newspaper had printed his statement of a week before that he was ready to consult with congressional committees before sending troops to Europe. The statement had been carried accurately by all the major papers and the wire services. According to the late Jack Bell of Associated Press, President Eisenhower once told J. Russell Wiggins of the *Washington Post* that "some of these fellows are not reporters but district attorneys." Bell and other reporters who covered Eisenhower regularly wrote that the general's face would quickly redden whenever he was asked a question that he didn't like. And John Kennedy was described (anonymously) by a White House correspondent as reading everything that was written about him and having a "skin as thin as cigarette paper."[3] In an April 1962 article in *The Reporter* magazine, Worth Bingham and Ward Just described "a truly monumental display of presidential anger" when *Time* was critical of the appointment of Gen. Maxwell Taylor to Kennedy's staff. The *Time* White House correspondent, in a preview of what was to come in the Nixon administration, found that his sources were "out" or "busy" and that his telephone calls were not returned. Kennedy subsequently engaged in a more public display of temper when he ordered cancellation of the 22 White House subscriptions to the *New York Herald-Tribune*. His successor's skin was even thinner. Along with many other presidents Johnson believed that true patriotism involved no skepticism. "He had a warped view of the press and saw it as the press's duty to support the U.S. undertaking in Vietnam as part of the national interest," says Moyers in retrospect.

All of these modern presidents, however, also valued the press or some conspicuous part of it. Explicitly or otherwise, they accepted the unwritten adversary relationship by which the press, in the American system, performs some of the function which British members of Parliament exercise in their questioning of government ministers. These modern presidents either had strong personal friendships with certain reporters or editors

---

[3] The same, p. 103.

(true for all the Democratic presidents, especially Truman and Kennedy) or a well-developed understanding of the role of a free press (true, especially, for Truman and to some degree for Eisenhower and Roosevelt) or an appreciation of the strengths and weaknesses of the press and a desire to use them for their own purposes (in particular, Kennedy).

Nixon did not understand the purpose of the press. He lacked the friendships, and indeed went out of his way to prevent them. While he certainly desired to use the press for his own purposes, and showed great skill at this in his last two presidential campaigns, his appreciation of the press in any larger sense of public policy was almost non-existent. In a remark apparently directed at James Reston, Nixon once said: ". . . All that matters is that it comes out all right. Six months from now nobody will remember what the columnists wrote." And on June 29, 1972 — twelve days after the Watergate break-in and Nixon's first press conference in a year — the President left the impression that the press's evaluation of his performance didn't make much difference one way or the other. "Now if I do a good job, the fact I get a bad press isn't going to help." It did not occur to Nixon that the press could tell him something, as Woodward and Bernstein would shortly do in the Watergate case, that might help determine whether or not he was doing a "good job."

Probably it goes too far, at least in any evidentiary sense, to say that this lack of understanding cost Nixon the presidency. Despite the published revelations in the *Washington Post*, Nixon would have remained in office had not it been for John Sirica and John Dean and the special prosecutors and the congressional committees. Some think Nixon would have survived even then if he had not preserved those self-accusatory White House tapes or if Alex Butterfield had not revealed their existence. Survive or not, however, Nixon's presidency was irrevocably tarnished once the various congressional hearings began to demonstrate the truth of Woodward

and Bernstein's stories. And it is not too much to say that
the qualities which prevented Nixon from understanding
the importance of the press were the same qualities
which brought him down. "President Nixon's relationship with the press exhibited the same strengths and
weaknesses that he brought to other situations as well,"
says Elliot Richardson. "His most fundamental flaw was
an unwillingness — or an inability — to give trust. He
came, I think, psychologically to perceive himself as an
outsider who had to establish his own place by sheer
stamina, intellectual resourcefulness and manipulative
capability. There was always an 'us and them' perception
on his part, as between himself and the press, himself
and the Congress, himself and the bureaucracy, himself
even and the American people — certainly the American
establishment, whatever that is, whatever he thought it
was."

This "us-and-them" quality became the yardstick of
the Nixon White House and was the measurement used
by the man who led it. Reporters were slower to see this
than they should have been. In cases of great scandal, for
all its attractiveness to the press, many reporters always
are ready to blame the "men around the president," even
the men around Nixon, rather than the president himself. For one thing, it makes their jobs easier. For
another, they are citizens first and reporters second and
most of them would prefer to believe that the president
would not permit great wrongs "if he only knew." Reporters also naively believe that the White House has
magic power to change the character of presidents. But it
was the men around Nixon who were changed by the
atmosphere of power in the White House, not Nixon.
H. R. (Bob) Haldeman defended the right of an editor to
print an article favoring civil disobedience when Haldeman was president of the UCLA alumni in the mid-
1960s; in the bitter controversy between Ronald Reagan
and Jesse Unruh on the University of California Board of
Regents over higher-education tuition, Haldeman

emerged as one of the reasonable regents. John Ehrlichman was a well-regarded Seattle lawyer whose only real political experience was as a Nixon advanceman; he was an exemplary family man until the troubles of Watergate. What these men became in the White House reveals not only that they were secret monsters but that they were limited people with limited experience working for a president almost totally lacking in trust. They were badly affected by the power they came to wield, which is certainly no excuse for their crimes. But I think these crimes also perfectly reflected the attitude of their president that no one outside the inner circle could be trusted. This was Nixon's attitude before it was theirs. "Nobody is our friend, let's face it," said Nixon to John Dean. If nobody is your friend, you can lie to anyone, and the necessity of lying was a premise that the president's men took for granted in their dealings with the press. Ehrlichman, testifying before the Senate Watergate Committee on July 30, 1973, was incredulous when Sen. Lowell Weicker braced him about lies he had told the *Chicago Tribune* saying that the administration continued to support L. Patrick Gray for director of the Federal Bureau of Investigation. The testimony shows that on March 7, twenty days before he lied to the *Tribune,* Ehrlichman had acknowledged to Dean that the administration was no longer committed to Gray. He added the words, "Well, I think we ought to let him hang there. Let him twist slowly in the wind." When Weicker pressed Ehrlichman about the difference between what he had said in private and what he had told the *Tribune,* this exchange took place:

> MR. EHRLICHMAN: . . . Now senator, I am sure you realize that when a nomination is still up here and still before the Senate, we support that nomination right down the line. What I may say to John Dean privately, the inhouse disenchantment with that nomination, certainly would never be reflected in statements to the press. Until the President decides that he is going to have to withdraw

that nomination, then by George, we are going to root for
the — we are going to root for the team.
   SEN. WEICKER: Can we paraphrase 'by George, we
are going to lie to the press?'
   MR. EHRLICHMAN: We are certainly not going to indicate to the press our disenchantment, that is right.

I cultivated as many sources in the Nixon administration as I could, from Ehrlichman on down. Some of them
were truthful, some not; some of them were voluble about
certain subjects and would not talk about others. (Inci-
dentally, it is always permissible not to talk about something; every reporter I know draws a distinction between
a refusal to comment, which Ehrlichman could have done
in the Gray situation, and a willingness to lie.) But most
of them, consciously or otherwise, came to reflect the
prevailing untrustingness of their chief. It showed up in
little things, like the time I was skeptically questioning
the President's legal authority to take some minor action
and an aide replied to me, "That's up to the President.
The President can do anything he wants." It showed up
in the press office, too, or more specifically, it showed up
with Ron Ziegler, the White House press secretary.
Ziegler, of course, was a hired hand who worked for
Nixon and not the press, and he should be judged in this
light. There has been a fair amount of sanctimonious
nonsense written about Ziegler's supposed loss of credibility after Watergate by people who had doubted
Ziegler's credibility from the beginning and who knew, in
any case, that he wasn't going to confess to the crimes
(and blunders) of his employer. What bothered me about
Ziegler wasn't the protection of Nixon at all costs, which I
expected, but the unnecessary little lies about Nixon not
getting angry or not watching television football games
or the impeachment hearings. Ziegler, like his boss, did not
recognize the importance of trust. I doubt he ever realized
that putting out wrong information which could be checked
elsewhere undermined his credibility even with reporters
who were slow to wake up about Watergate.

One of the staples of Ziegler's informal conversations with reporters was that Nixon "always had been hated by the press." This was dogma in the Nixon administration and usually didn't seem worth arguing about. Once, however, mostly out of curiosity, I asked Ziegler, "Since when?", and he replied, "Since the Hiss case." Ronald L. Ziegler was nine years old when Nixon undertook this particular investigation and it required no brilliance on my part to realize that, as usual, Ron was just telling me what he had been told. In this instance, however, Ziegler shared a common misconception about the source of Nixon's hostility toward the press that is shared by some of Nixon's critics as well as his apologists. The truth is that Nixon hated the press long before he heard of Alger Hiss. He was raised with this distrust, raised that way by a father whom even Nixon's most sympathetic biographer, Bela Kornitzer, describes as "tough, opinionated, capricious, argumentative and unpredictable." This is an understatement. The father, Frank Nixon, an uneducated handyman who had been orphaned at the age of nine, was a rough disciplinarian who beat the Nixon boys and brooked no back talk. Dick Nixon learned to avoid the beatings (learned, perhaps, to be devious) at the cost of repressing an already inward nature. "Dad was very strict and expected to be obeyed under all circumstances," Nixon told Kornitzer. "If he wanted something, he wanted it at once. He had a hot temper, and I learned early that the only way to deal with him was to abide by the rules he laid down. Otherwise, I would probably have felt the touch of a ruler or the strap as my brothers did." One of Frank Nixon's favorite targets for his opinionated arguments was the press. Once, when the father was seriously ill and his son was vice president, Frank Nixon proposed that some reporters be kicked out of the house. Dick Nixon demurred in this instance, but he had learned early on to share his father's antipathy to the press. In a prize-winning speech which Nixon gave as a high school junior on "Our Privileges Under the Con-

stitution," he attacked misuse of "privileges" by the press
and asked rhetorically: "Should the morals of this nation
be offended and polluted in the name of freedom of speech
or freedom of the press? In the words of Lincoln, the individual can have no rights against the best interests of
society." Nothing that happened to Nixon, including the
Hiss case, changed his childhood perception of the press. I
have written elsewhere[4] how the Hiss case ratified an
inner feeling for Nixon that the Ivy Leaguers, the "better
people" with money were wrong about what was going on
in the world and that Whittaker Chambers, fat and ugly
and relentlessly honest, was right. But it was not during
the Hiss case, where essential help was provided to him
by Bert Andrews of the *New York Herald-Tribune*, that
Nixon's essential view of the press was formed. He had
brought that with him from Yorba Linda.

Nixon's early life was not well known to most White
House correspondents, partly because Nixon did his best
to conceal it but mostly because he had been around so
long that reporters tended to assume that his origins
were well-known. This was a mistake. Had the stories
out of the White House in the palmy days of Nixon's
administration been infused with more understanding of
his boyhood, the country might have had distant early
warning of the Nixon revealed on the White House tapes.
This is not an advocacy for reporters to become psychia-
trists. It *is* an argument for the necessity to report, as
best we can, about the real personal lives of public figures
rather than resubmitting the carefully bowdlerized accounts offered to us by the presidential hagiographers or
by such autobiographies as *Six Crises* and *Why Not The
Best?* In trying to determine why the man who followed
Nixon was perhaps the most open of presidents a reporter
does not consult the *Congressional Record*. He goes instead to the early days of Gerald Ford in Grand Rapids

---

[4] Cannon, "The Forces That Forged the Future," in *The Fall of a President*,
pp. 53-54.

and examines what happened to him there. "I believe this (openness) is something that I grew up with," is Ford's own account. "My parents were always open. We lived in an open family. I lived in a community where there were open attitudes towards virtually everything. I participated in activities where openness was respected and not condemned. So my whole life style from the beginning has been predicated on an environment that was open, frank and candid."[5] I always thought that the most revelatory action taken by Ford as President was one he never announced — ordering that cartoons be included in the daily White House news summary. Editorial cartoons, by their nature, inevitably are more critical than editorials, because cartoons are not the place for saying "on the other hand." When I asked Ford why he had called for the inclusion of cartoons in the summary at a time that many cartoonists were depicting him as both clumsy and insensitive, Ford replied simply: "I think cartoons have a great impact on the newspaper reader, and our news summary is a depiction of what is said. As long as cartoons have an impact, I think they ought to be in the summary."

On the other hand, what happened to Ford in the White House demonstrates that even the least ostentatious and most secure president can succumb to the temptations of the imperial presidency. There are several illustrations of this, but the one I remember best occurred Easter Week of 1975 when the South Vietnamese armies were in retreat and the collapse of the U.S.-supported regime in South Vietnam was imminent. Ford wanted badly to spend the holiday in Palm Springs, Calif., where golf courses abound. His press secretary, Ron Nessen, and other aides argued that the President would appear to be having a holiday while South Vietnam burned. But presidents come quickly to believe that

[5] These remarks and the subsequent comment in this paragraph are from an interview with the author aboard Air Force One on July 3, 1975.

they can do whatever they want to do whenever they want to do it. Ford flew to Palm Springs for what Nessen called an eight-day "working vacation." He rented a $355,000-Mayan style home in the desert for $100 a night and played golf almost daily. In an effort to convince reporters that he was really working, Ford also scheduled a series of meaningless "media events," including inspection tours of The Geysers, a geothermal steam-producing area north of San Francisco, and the Elk Hills Naval Oil Reserve ("one of the few places," said Ford aide Bob Hartmann, "where you could put up an oil derrick and improve the environment.") The President and Betty Ford also greeted a planeload of arriving Vietnamese orphans. Except for this last quick sentimental journey it was a week when Ford never saw a person in distress or even an ordinary citizen experiencing the economic crisis through which the nation was then passing. There were a lot of unemployed working people in California, and lots of Mexican-Americans and black people, too, but they weren't in Palm Springs. Behind the facade of the presidency, Ford was almost as totally isolated from the realities of the outside world as Palm Springs was remote from the events of Vietnam. Reporters were fed with media events, a presidential press conference in San Diego, occasional presidential golf scores, a briefing by Nessen where he announced a non-existent peace initiative and a briefing by Henry Kissinger, closely resembled a filibuster, where the secretary of state and national security adviser to the president explained that the Paris peace accords would have worked if only North Vietnam had lived up to the agreement. In dull moments reporters feasted off pool reports like this one:

> The President finished playing golf at the Thunderbird Country Club around 1:20 p.m. After posing very briefly for pictures for the benefit of club members, he went into the locker room, where he stayed until 2:10 p.m. We're told he had a cheeseburger for lunch.

The President was dressed in grey checked slacks, a light blue polo shirt and a white hat. One of those who followed him around the course said Ford "indicated he didn't shoot too well on the front nine, but on the back nine did okay." The club pro, Claude Harmon, reported the President was "good driving, but had trouble with his short irons and putting." We weren't given his score. Harmon followed him around on the course.

Motorcade left the Thunderbird at 2:15 p.m. Drove to Collector's Corner, a combination office and shop run by the Eisenhower Medical Center Auxiliary . . . Alice Fay Harris (wife of Phil) and Dolores Hope (wife of Bob) were signing autographs in a cookbook called "Five Star Favorites . . . Recipes from Friends of Mamie and Ike." The President, still in his golf clothes, sat at a table and signed about a dozen of the cookbooks. The cookbooks sell for $12.95, and we're told all the proceeds go to the Eisenhower Medical Auxiliary. The only thing we heard the President say: "Could I sit down to sign. I'm a left-hander." All small talk. He posed for pictures with the two ladies and the small group of people inside. He kissed Mrs. Hope and Mrs. Harris, upon leaving, and returned to the residence at 2:30 p.m.

This was on April Fool's Day. Two days before, on Easter Sunday, the President and Mrs. Ford had attended an Episcopal service and heard Bishop Robert Wolterstorff say: "God's message is the same the world over. It is an Easter message not only for the affluent of Southern California, but for arid, drought-ridden Africa, strife-torn and starving Bangladesh and Vietnam." These words also were in the pool report, and some reporters tried to use them as a lever to prod Ford into talking about the rapidly approaching Vietnam collapse. They did not succeed. On the plane coming out, when Ford was asked about Vietnam, he replied, "Let's talk about Easter." The day after the Easter service he jogged good-naturedly away from CBS reporter Phil Jones when Jones tried to question him about Vietnam on the Bakersfield Airport runway.

Reporters, some of whom had looked forward to their own vacation in Palm Springs, worked ten or twelve hours a day regurgitating all the managed news material that was served up for their benefit. In our spare time we composed our own leads about the more memorable Ford utterances of the week, leads such as "Ford reveals that American population reached 213 million" (by James Deakin of the *St. Louis Post-Dispatch*) or "A mysterious sleeping sickness today struck 3,000 delegates gathered to hear President Ford at the Broadcaster's Convention in Las Vegas," where Ford stopped on his way home. The only defense for the last mythical lead, which is one of mine, is that the Western Union operator who was waiting for our telex copy actually did fall sound asleep while Ford's speech blared into the press room over the public address system. He was the envy of the press corps.

The above is typical of what happens when the White House goes on the road with its press entourage. Such trips nearly always produce a torrent of stories, especially the "picture stories" beloved by television. In the communities the president visits (which is one of the reasons he visits them) these trips also tend to resurrect gee-whiz journalism, including a flood of sidebars celebrating the president's first visit to Lower Ishmingle since the last campaign. Sometimes these stories come complete with bewildering headlines, such as this two-line banner in *The Cincinnati Post* for July 3, 1975: "Ford Arrives Smiling But Is Stingy With Autographs." It gave the traveling press a good chuckle, but some of our stories are as dubious as that headline, particularly when we are forced to digest a complicated or controversial story on the road. "I remember when Pierre Salinger handed out the first government press release announcing federal support for the supersonic transport," recalls Tom Wicker. "I was the *Times'* White House correspondent and I was sitting with the White House press corps in the football stadium of the Air Force Academy, listening to President Kennedy make a speech. As soon as he had finished, we were going on west; so in a few minutes, we had to file some kind of story on a complex technological and financial story like that. Salinger knew we couldn't do any more in those circumstances than rewrite his self-serving press release, which is what we all did."[6]

White House correspondents, once overpraised and now overcriticized, have a mixed reaction to such accounts. Most White House reporters are dedicated, hardworking journalists, and they resent being depicted as lazy seekers of handouts and persistent transmitters of managed news. In fact, few of them are lazy. Many are relentlessly hardworking, filing both the announced "day story" on a regular basis and adding stories of analysis or interpretation gleaned from their own private conversations and phone calls. The problem, particularly on the president's many trips, is not laziness. It is hyperactivity, which allows scant time for thought or evaluation. The institution of the presidency, as practiced in the jet age, envelops everyone in motion for the sake of motion, in reams of paper, in too much waiting, in big meals at infrequent intervals, in the shared camaraderie of a campaign. It is missing the mark to call this "handout journalism." It is worse than that. It is mindless journalism. The plain truth, as the late, great Peter Lisagor of the *Chicago Daily News* has said, is that we over-cover the White House. "I honestly believe that we, the press, created the imperial presidency," said Lisagor. "Richard Nixon did not. When John Kennedy came in with that attractive family, he was on the cover of *Life* or *Look* every third week, or whatever. In the American personality somewhere there must be a royal itch, a kind of an imperial itch. We feed on the gossip about Jackie and about how she made the souffle. Perhaps the last non-regal president we've had in my experience was Harry

---

[6] From a speech at the University of California, Riverside, February 29, 1972.

Truman. From that moment on we began to give the presidency monarchial overtones. And by the time Nixon came along, he believed that, by God, he was to the manor born. He didn't have to tell you a damn thing. Now presidents, I've always thought, and here maybe I am a little cynical, are people who elbowed and gouged and struggled and fought their way into the White House. Nobody carried them in there kicking and screaming. They get a helluva good wage. They get a damn good expense account. They've got a fleet of helicopters and planes at their disposal. They are politicians who managed to get to the top of their trade, and they're not divinely ordained. When they go into the job they don't suddenly get touched with a wand and become different than they were when they were struggling and gouging and fighting their way in. But American people get tongue-tied in the presence of presidents and flock around them like they were some strange creature. We ought to have a healthy wholesale skepticism and sense of irreverence about them. In an egalitarian society like ours it would be better to treat them that way than like an imperial presence that has come into our midst."

This imperial treatment has a negative effect upon presidents, as well as on the reporters who cover them. Why shouldn't the president go golfing, if he wants to, without a reporter tagging along for a pool report? Why shouldn't he go to dinner? Why doesn't he have the right — a right we have challenged at White House briefings — to have a private social gathering without it becoming the property of the press? I say these things in the belief that the president becomes less imperial to the extent that he becomes more human — and in the related conviction that all human beings need a certain amount of privacy. When Carter's press secretary, Jody Powell, said that he didn't give a rat's ass what Carter was eating for Thanksgiving Dinner, it seemed to me he was striking his own small blow for reducing the presidency to human scale. Presidents need and deserve some privacy. And readers, who elected a president and not a "First Family," deserve to be spared stories abut Tricia and Jack and Betty and Amy. The same point was made, in a more traditional way than Jody Powell made it, by then-Gov. Daniel Evans of Washington during the Nixon administration. "In my view there is nothing more essential than that the President of the United States be given the opportunity to see and be seen by the people," said Evans in a speech to the National Press Club. "The modern day tragedy of the presidency is that he is quite literally the prisoner of Pennsylvania Avenue."

Our fascination with the presidency, as we have observed, has much to do with the historic interest of journalism in personalities. It also has much to do with the unique character of the presidency itself. An Englishman, Harold Laski, said it best in his classic book on *The American Presidency*:

> No one can examine the character of the American presidency without being impressed by its many-sidedness. The range of the President's functions is enormous. He is ceremonial head of state. He is a vital source of legislative suggestion. He is the final source of all executive decision. He is the authoritative exponent of the nation's foreign policy. To combine all these with the continuous need to be at once the representative man of the nation and the leader of his political party is clearly a call upon the energies of a single man unsurpassed by the exigencies of any other political office in the world.

Laski wrote these words in 1940, when the very life of Great Britain depended upon Franklin Roosevelt being "the authoritative exponent of the nation's foreign policy." If the president's authority in that sphere has now been diminished by the Vietnam War and its aftermath, it has been enhanced in all others by an invention which was in the trial stage when Laski wrote. That invention is television, which more than anything else has changed the coverage of Washington. "The whole character of a press conference was changed by television because people were then put on stage and not for the audience in front of them," said Lisagor. "In their mind's eye they were on stage for the millions of people who watch it on the evening news or maybe even live." In a similar vein, columnist William S. White concluded after covering seven presidents that the introduction of live television was "a bad thing" for presidential press conferences. "It enormously increased the number of participants, people being human and not adverse to getting onto the tube," White said. "It gave unfair returns to the more aggressive correspondents by way of presidential recognition of them, and penalized the more thoughtful and less elbowing sort of reporter."[7]

The presidential press conference is a relatively recent institution. Begun in a desultory fashion by Wilson and continued by Harding, it persisted under Calvin Coolidge, who demanded written questions from reporters. Richard L. Strout of the *Christian Science Monitor* has recalled the time when a dozen correspondents agreed to ask Coolidge if he would be a candidate in 1928. Coolidge looked at the first question and put it aside. He looked at the next and put it aside. He went on from the third to the 11th question. At the 12th, he paused, read it and went on drily, "I have here a question on the condition of the children in Poland. The condition of the children in Poland is as follows . . ." He then talked for several minutes and concluded, "That's all the questions." Herbert Hoover somewhat ineptly continued the tradition of the press conference, which came to its finest flower of the newspaper age during the Roosevelt administrations. (We should remember, however, in making historical comparisons the considerations that were extended to Roosevelt. Following the tradition of his prede-

---

[7] In a speech to a symposium on "The Presidency and the Press" at the Lyndon Baines Johnson School of Public Affairs, University of Texas, April 23, 1976. White, a frequent defender of Johnson's policies, also concluded that "Johnson was not a press conference type of politician."

cessors, he was never quoted directly except at his say-so. And he was never photographed in any way that would show he had been crippled by polio.) Truman, despite problems of saying both too much and too little, continued the press conference in the Roosevelt tradition. Douglass Cater wrote that "no man . . . enjoyed his press conferences more and none fared worse" than Truman.[8] Maybe, but Truman also understood the value of a press conference. He said that the president should meet reporters once a week, which he usually did, so that he could find out "what's on the public's mind." Eisenhower, ridiculed by some writers for his tangled syntax, nonetheless took the decisive and related steps of allowing nearly unlimited direct quotation and permitting television coverage. The televised press conference came to maturity under Kennedy. With it came the opportunity for the president to talk directly over the heads of the reporters to the American people.

Television is an enormous advantage for a president, indeed for any public official who knows how to use it. "A public official who is a skillful man, who's bright, quick and articulate can answer the questions in his way on television," maintained Lisagor. "There is absolutely no way you can cut through that unless you choose to be prosecutorial, and you can't do that in the mass. If there are more than five or six people in a press conference, or briefing, you're at the mercy of the fellow you're questioning. That's true of presidential press conferences. It's true, also, of congressional people who hold press conferences in the mass." Reporters who attend televised press conferences become participants in the play. Except for an occasional reporter who relishes a curmudgeonly reputation or being thought of as a character, reporters often refrain from asking the "impolite" questions they would put with little hesitancy at a non-televised press conference.

---

[8] Cater, *The Fourth Branch of Government*, p. 36.

This hesitancy is reinforced by the rigidity of the formal press conference, which follows a precise format and is usually limited to a half hour. President Ford and Nessen made a mildly useful change when they initiated the practice of follow-up questions, a practice which Carter has continued. A report by Prof. Lewis W. Wolfson of American University commissioned by the National News Council suggested a number of other changes, among them longer and more frequent press conferences and the opportunity to question the president and his aides in a variety of settings. I question whether these proposals, desirable though they may be, will do much to change the impact of the press conference when conducted by a president skilled in communications techniques. The presence of the television cameras makes the press conference almost entirely an instrument of presidential public relations rather than the useful exercise in probing ideas and policies that it was once reputed to be.

No president since Kennedy has demonstrated the advantages accruing to a skilled television communicator better than Carter. He is an indifferent stump speaker, but his quick wit and ready smile show to good advantage at a televised press conference. "Jimmy Carter met the press and they were his," concluded Haynes Johnson of the *Washington Post* after Carter's first presidential press conference on Feb. 8, 1977. Except for a few effective questions on foreign policy, reporters were mostly foils for Carter, as he good-naturedly answered 16 questions in the 30 alloted minutes. Amidst the century's worst winter and the nation's worst energy shortage, not a single question was asked abut energy issues unless a radio reporter's self-styled "philosophical question" about nationalization of the oil industry qualifies. "It was a Carter victory almost by default," wrote Johnson. "That may not be so monumental a feat, either. The format of these televised jumping-jack affairs is now part of presidential tradition. In the nature of the beast, the televised conference transforms the press into a clamoring pack shouting for attention and a chance to ask a quick question. The format hardly permits serious discussion of issues or provides fresh insights into a president's thinking."

Perhaps fortunately, most White House news does not originate with press conferences. It comes out of the daily White House briefings, a forum for presidential PR that also has been affected by television even though the briefings themselves are rarely filmed. Briefings can serve a useful purpose, and sometimes do. As Adam Clymer of the *New York Times* points out, "When they won't answer a normal question, that's an alarm bell." One such briefing clue, Clymer recalls, came during the Nixon administration when press briefers refused to say whether John Dean had sat in during FBI interviews of White House aides investigating the Watergate case. More often, briefings simply constitute the presidential statements of the day and the response of the White House to whatever issues or charges have been raised concerning the president. Well into the Nixon administration, the White House usually held two briefings a day. Ziegler reduced the number to one and this practice has peristed under Nessen and Carter's press secretary, Jody Powell. Usually the briefing is held late in the morning or at midday, and it often provides the staple for the evening news and two cycles of wire service stories. This is because of the nature of television news, not because of laziness on the part of the television correspondents. "We are hemmed in by the mechanics," says ABC's Ann Compton. "Because of the pressures of time we do things on a simple level. We want to get the film in very early. The film editor may be all thumbs. The videotape machine may break down. If the president does anything at three in the afternoon, we're in a real press. The closer something happens to noon the better. What happens in the afternoon often never sees the light of day." Because of the expense, networks maintain television crews in only a limited number of cities, principally

Washington, New York and Chicago. Each network always has a crew on duty at the White House. "The White
House has become a kind of convenient well for television
news programs," says NBC's Tom Brokaw. "We've always got our apparatus in place here. It's always a place
of some interest to the country. And it's too easy for the
programs to just turn to the White House whether or not
we have a meaningful piece that deserves to get on the 22
minutes that is reserved for network news each night."
This phenomenon is understood by the White House.
Each day Powell will try to say something that can be
used on the evening news, perhaps with the addition of
some background or a congressional response. The
briefings are even more important for the wire services,
though the wire correspondents assigned to the White
House have a wide range of sources outside the press
office. But the wire services operate under the severest
time constraints. Four of every five dailies in the United
States are afternoon newspapers, and those in the Eastern and Central time zones are likely to be on deadline
when the daily briefing concludes at noon or later. So the
information which comes out of the briefing, even if it is
afterwards filled out for the next day's morning papers,
usually goes on the wires for the afternoon papers pretty
much as the press secretary gives it. What all this means
is that the briefings, scorned though they may be, provide
the vast bulk of the White House news.

Most White House correspondents, and all of the good
ones, get out of the briefing room as much as they can.
They develop their own sources and try to resist chan-
nelization of the news. But in most administrations there
are a limited number of people who know what is going
on and a far greater number of people who have a need to
show that they know something. A reporter learns the
real sources from the uninformed ones by painstaking
trial and error. He values the truly informed sources like
they were solid gold and is apt to become dependent,
sometimes too dependent on them. When Ziegler and

other Nixon spokesmen denounced "source stories" during the Watergate coverup, they were simultaneously demonstrating presidential PR and revealing a certain ignorance about the way Washington works. Washington lives on source stories, and has throughout most of its existence. The practice is an important part of presidential, as well as journalistic, tradition.

In an effort to protect their sources, reporters in the 19th century frequently used the "it was learned on highly reliable authority" approach still favored by their British counterparts. Often this became simply "it was learned." During the administration of Theodore Roosevelt many reporters were told important news by the President himself — but nearly always on the condition that Roosevelt not be quoted directly. Theodore Roosevelt really is the father of modern presidential PR. He was the first president to admit reporters to the White House on a regular basis and the first to hold periodic not-for-attribution briefings, a practice he had developed when he held two-a-day sessions for the working press as governor of New York. These meetings with the press, though not press conferences as such, set the tone and the ground rules for the press conferences that were held from Wilson through Truman. Reporters who broke the rules and quoted Roosevelt without his permission, either in Albany or Washington, were banished from further such sessions, a most effective form of punishment then and now. One of the levers a president has for obtaining favorable coverage is his own high value as a news source. Reporters do not cast away valuable news sources lightly. "The first rule that I learned covering Washington was to ration your sources and ration your enemies," says Russell Baker. "This is the first sound rule, and every reporter who works effectively in Washington knows this, or should. He knows, also, if he is honest with himself, that there is always the potential for compromise if the source is a valuable one. Kennedy, with a keener insight into the mores of journalism than any other president, understood this and succeeded in compromising several journalists. "Information is to any journalist what water is to a perpetually thirsty man, and when a politican or official is a supplier of information as well as a friend, it is impossible to be objective," wrote Stewart Alsop in discussing Kennedy's relationships with reporters.[9]

In official Washington the reliable high-level sources are heavily outnumbered by the journalists, reliable or otherwise. When Ron Nessen sought to refute an accusation by *New York* magazine columnist Aaron Latham that the Ford White House was battening down the information hatches, he visited White House senior staff members and asked them for a list of reporters they had talked with the previous week. Then, in violation of the ground rules of some of these conversations, Nessen sent the list to *New York*, where it was published subsequently as part of a letter to the editor. The compilation showed that Donald Rumsfeld, then Ford's chief of staff, had talked to five reporters for as many publications, and that his deputy, Richard Cheney, had talked to 15 reporters for 13 news organizations. Seven other officials listed by Nessen had talked to 28 different reporters, some of whom were also on the Rumsfeld-Cheney list. This may not quite boil down to single-source journalism, but it suggests that many reporters are going to the same few high-ranking sources for their information. Since most of these sources are not quoted by name, Washington stories often have one meaning for insiders and another meaning for everyone else. But it is not only ordinary readers who wind up feeling left out of secrets. Other reporters also are affected. Bob Woodward remembers that he felt like an outsider in the early months of the Watergate story when he was working on leads that few people in Washington took seriously. On August 1, 1972, in the middle of the front page of the *Washington*

---

[9] Alsop, *The Center*, p. 173.

Post which was led by the story of Sen. Thomas Eagleton dropping off the Democratic presidential ticket, Woodward and Bernstein ran their first big break in the Watergate case. It was a story which told how a $25,000 cashier's check signed by Kenneth E. Dahlberg, Nixon's midwest finance chairman, had been deposited in the bank account of Bernard L. Barker, one of the five men arrested in the Watergate break-in. That night Woodward talked to Clark MacGregor, who had recently taken over from John Mitchell as chairman of the Committee for the Reelection of the President. MacGregor was friendly, as Woodward recalls it, saying that he had just come aboard, didn't know anything about it and would talk to him the next day. For a week thereafter Woodward tried to get him, finally succeeding on August 10. "He really lit into me," Woodward recalls. "He said, 'How can you do this? How can you ask these sorts of questions?' And I said, 'Look, it's your goddamn campaign money that went to one of the Watergate burglars. Now what's the explanation?' And he really got angry. Then I knew. Then I sort of said, you know, something's here. Even when I had done very hard investigations on the (Washington) restaurants or some of the other local stuff, no one had castigated me. But MacGregor did and that was a very big tipoff to me. It made me much more of an outsider. I felt exluded. I couldn't even get the damn guy on the phone." The reaction of MacGregor, the official source, left Woodward with no choice but to develop his own sources or to give up on the story. He did not, of course, give up. What Woodward and Bernstein were doing that was unusual was not that they were writing "source stories" but that they were writing source stories from sources which were theirs exclusively. The careful protection which Woodward gave to "Deep Throat" and to other sources was not unusual, either. Most reporters have highly valued personal sources which they will not share with their editor or their colleagues. The best recourse for the editor, if his reporter has a hot story, is not

to insist upon disclosure but to do what Ben Bradlee and
Howard Simons did and require the reporter to confirm
his story from more than one source.

The corollary of this protectiveness is that many reporters also will refuse to include material in their own
bylined stories which comes from a blind source, i.e., is
furnished by another reporter without attribution. I
broke this rule once, with Bernstein, and wish that I
hadn't. It happened in the tense weekend before Nixon
left office after I was called at home and tipped that a
speechwriter had been told to begin work on a Nixon
resignation speech. The source was one I valued, but he
did not have any details. Both Bradlee and Dick Harwood
happened to be away. I called Peter Silberman, then the
national editor, and told him what I knew. It was late on
Sunday, and both of us thought that the information was
not enough for a story in itself. Nixon and his top aides
were at Camp David, returning late that night. Early the
next morning Silberman and I met with Simons, the
managing editor, who asked me if I had been able to
confirm the story elsewhere. "Not for certain," I answered, but I was convinced the story was true. Simons
wanted to stick to the prudent policy which had brought
the *Post* that far and insist on two sources, and he did.
But we were putting together a story on the Camp David
meeting, and my checks with sources had confirmed that
resignation had been discussed as a possibility, although
Nixon apparently had not then decided to quit. Woodward and Bernstein, making their own checks, had come
up with similar information. So, too, had Dave Broder.
Simons, who has a preference for pulling information together rather than scattering it through the paper as the
Post sometimes does, wanted one story and decided I
should write it. I did, also putting Broder's name on it
because of information he had contributed. (Woodward
and Bernstein had their names that day on the lead story
telling about three new White House transcripts which
showed that Nixon had covered up a coverup on Watergate

six days after the break-in.) But Bernstein provided "source information" for my story, including an account of the Camp David meeting where Nixon supposedly had met in the same room with his top aides and discussed, then rejected, resignation. The only trouble with this information was that the meeting had never taken place. We found out the day after the story ran that the aides had been closeted in separate cabins and that chief of staff Alexander M. Haig had taken material from them to the President. Broder and I talked to Bernstein about it afterward, and he seemed uncertain whether the mistake had been his or his source's. Either the source or Bernstein had assumed the meeting into existence. I felt particularly bad about putting Broder's name on the story, which ran as the "off lead" in columns one and two of page one. The story as it ran had made mincemeat of my own original accurate tip, saying that Nixon had weighed resignation and rejected it. I made a mental reservation never again to accept anonymous information of any consequence for a story with my name on it, no matter who it comes from.

Many sources, of course, belong to fifteen or twenty reporters at the same time. I am talking now of the pernicious Washington practice of the "backgrounder," a session where an official briefs a group of reporters with the understanding that his remarks will not be quoted directly. There are as many different types of backgrounders as there are Washington publications, and nearly as many ground rules. A 1972 survey by Courtney Sheldon, chief of the *Christian Science Monitor* Washington bureau, on the value of backgrounders listed these seven different types of rules for briefings and interviews:

1. Completely on the record, everything fully quotable.
2. On the record, but check quotes with interviewee before using.
3. On the record, but paraphrase or indirect discourse only.

4. Background with direct quotes attributable to a source such as a White House official.

5. Background with indirect quotes attributable to a source such as a White House official.

6. Deep background, no quotes, use with attribution such as it is understood or without attribution and "on your own."

7. Off the record, information not publishable.

The sixth rule, which requires a reporter to write as if possessed by divine revelation, is sometimes known as the "Lindley rule" after former *Newsweek* columnist Ernest K. Lindley. In most of the transactions between reporters and officials in Washington with which I am familiar there are fewer options than the above list would suggest. The second rule, for instance, is limited primarily to tape-recorded interviews. And the third rule is primarily a presidential device; I do not know of any instance where it has been used by another official. Reporters generally recognize four categories — on the record, not for attribution, background and deep background. I naively supposed when I came to Washington that everyone was as familiar with these rules and their meaning as a baseball team is with the ground rules of its home park. Unfortunately, such is not the case. Continually, supposedly sophisticated public officials say they want to talk "off the record" when they mean "not for attribution." The best guide for a reporter — and I would presume for a public official, as well — is to be sure that both parties mean the same thing when they use a particular phrase. It is clear enough, I think, what at least three of the four phrases are supposed to mean. "On the record" and "off the record" mean exactly what they say and as they are defined on Sheldon's list above. "Not for attribution" usually just means, "keep my name out of it."

The main problem lies in the "backgrounder." I am refering to the group backgrounder, rather than an interview "on background," where the source and the reporter can easily work out their own ground rules. Group backgrounders have all manner of ground rules, most of them insidious. No matter how scrupulous the official and the reporters, group backgrounders nearly always are a mechanism by which a public official can say something anonymously which he ought to say openly, if at all. Ben Bradlee, confessing to a quarter century of profiting from backgrounders as both a reporter and government official, called backgrounders what they really are in a January 2, 1972 editorial page piece in the *Washington Post*: A conspiracy in the restraint of truth. Bradlee's piece signaled the end of the *Post's* acquiescence in the policy of going along with background briefings. He related that in the Kennedy administration, when Kennedy called reporters and told them on background "what a hell of a legislative record his administration had chalked up in its first year," a spate of unattributed stories appeared the next day listing the supposed accomplishments. And he told how Orville Freeman held a background briefing because his stenotypist was sick. And how three high officials in the Johnson administration — McGeorge Bundy, Robert McNamara and George Ball — briefed the press for 45 minutes on a Johnson speech on "deep background" and then said much of the same on the record into television cameras without protest from the writing press. Background briefings are both seductive and convenient to the press, Bradlee said. The stories they produce are "easier to write, easier to edit, easier to read and often easier to understand" even if they also are "incomplete, misleading or even false." Above all, background briefings are useful to the government. "By its control of the briefing, it can withhold whatever information it wants to withhold, and by forbidding identification of the briefer it prevents accountability," Bradlee wrote. "They may be a legitimate aim of government, but it is a perversion of journalism. Government is a noble career. So is journalism. They are not the same."

Bradlee's declaration of policy by no means met with unanimous approval from the Washington press corps. Some reporters felt that it was all well and good for the *Washington Post* or the *New York Times* to take a high-minded stand on backgrounders. They contended that the smaller newspapers, which did not possess similar clout with government officials, sometimes needed backgrounders as a condition of access. I worked for Ridder newspapers longer than I have worked for the *Post*, and I do not believe this to be true. It *is* true, of course, that there are some public officials who are not going to talk for the record when a reporter calls them, no matter what the newspaper, but this occurs in a one-on-one interview, not in a group orgy at which the government anonymously puts out its story. And it is also true that sometimes reporters for smaller newspapers have to band together to make a public official think it is worthwhile to give any of them time. It is clear, however, that officials who are willing to have such meetings do so because there is a story they want to get out — and that they are not likely to stop telling their story if the Washington press becomes insistent on attribution. I see signs we are moving in that direction, if the increasing number of guests who talk on the record at the famous breakfast sessions organized by Godfrey Sperling of the *Christian Science Monitor*, is any indication. At the first of these sessions which I attended, late in 1969, a couple of reporters suggested to California Assembly Speaker Jesse Unruh that he might want to talk on background, but Unruh declined the offer. "I learned the hard way that it is better for me to talk on the record," Unruh said. We need to learn that, too.

The master background briefer of them all, in the Nixon and Ford administrations, was Henry Kissinger. Sheldon's survey found that Kissinger's briefings were "the lightning rod for press criticism." It quoted Max Frankel of the *New York Times* as saying, "Henry Kissinger's background briefings are such largely as a matter

of administrative convenience, not public necessity."
This was 15 months before Kissinger became a vastly
more powerful official by adding the secretary of state's
post to his portfolio while continuing in his role as national security adviser to the President. When Kissinger
succeeded William Rogers as secretary of state he lost
little time in taking firm control of the entire foreign
policy public relations apparatus. In celebration of his
own proclaimed status as peacemaker, Kissinger also
took the press along with him from capital to capital so
reporters could see how he did it. This occurred with the
encouragement, not to mention the connivance, of the
Washington press. John Foster Dulles, considered in his
day to rival Kissinger in power, traveled alone. "Mr. Dulles," wrote Murrey Marder of the *Washington Post*,
"would have goggled at the uninhibited sweep of Dr.
Kissinger's travel, leaping all boundaries." Dean Rusk,
too, was a solitary traveler, believing that privacy and
diplomacy were closely connected. Rogers began the policy of taking reporters with him, but they lost interest in
his trips because Kissinger was apt to be making policy
in Washington while Rogers was on the road. But when
Kissinger, in September 1973, added Rogers' duties to his
own, reporters urged him to continue his predecessor's
travel policy. "Try it, you'll like it," is the way Marder
described the appeal from the diplomatic press corps.
And Kissinger did. He made his first negotiating trip to
the Middle East in October 1973 without the press. But
when he returned a month later to repair his ceasefire he
took with him 14 reporters and three television cameramen. What resulted, said diplomatic correspondent Marder, was "a rush of hard and interpretive news, emanat-
ing from or authorized by Kissinger . . . from each capital
along the route, supplying the Nixon administration, at a
time of urgent need, with a public display of action in
world affairs to set against the miasma of Watergate."
Kissinger had become, in Marder's words, "the biggest
permanent, floating foreign policy establishment in our

history — in the air or on the ground." When Kissinger
was in Washington the news flow was accomplished by
interviews, source stories, tips, and State Department
briefings that once had been "backgrounders" before the
outcry from the *Post* and other publications convinced
Kissinger to put them on record. But while Kissinger
controlled the news flow in Washington, there always
was at least the theoretical danger that an enterprising
reporter might balance what he was given from some
hostile source. No such danger existed aloft. As Marder
described it in a December 8, 1973, column in the *Washington Post*:

> Dr. Kissinger found . . . that even with a platoon of
> reporters riding in his plane he was readily able to close
> them off for secrecy and privacy. The plane is divided into
> three compartments, for press, staff, and a separate section
> for Dr. Kissinger, similar to the sectionalizing of
> President Nixon's travel aboard similar aircraft, although
> only a small press "pool" is on the President's
> plane, and they infrequently talk with the President at
> any length.
>
> Dr. Kissinger, by contrast, was a frequent caller on the
> press aboard his plane. In addition to the advantage of
> supplying newsmen with his own interpretation of the
> news he made in each capital, he had a captive audience
> for exchanges of levity to break the tension and enhance
> his reputation as a raconteur . . . Dr. Kissinger would
> tease the press about "cutting off the caboose," meaning
> the press end of the aircraft, if anyone wrote anything
> unfavorable about him. The aircraft returned intact.
> There was so much news generated during the journey,
> and the trip was so physically exhausting that there was
> little time or energy for drawing critical balance sheets.
> Occupants of the White House, several administrations
> back, discovered the guiding formula: each hour that you
> keep the press occupied, or in motion, eliminates an hour
> for critical thought.

Kissinger was aided, particularly in the image-
conscious and disintegrating days of the Nixon adminis-

tration, by his own larger-than-life reputation. On the popular level, if not the scholastic one, this was largely a reputation wrought by television. "Men of the stature of Dean Acheson and John Foster Dulles could not have hoped to achieve in this world what Henry Kissinger did in terms of identity," said Peter Lisagor. "The difference is television. Television made Kissinger into a figure of national and international identification instantly, and, without it, even the cartoonists would have problems drawing him, as they did with Acheson and Dulles in their time." In a larger context Kissinger once wrote that Bismarck's talent was his ability to manipulate antagonisms, and I think this explains a good deal of his own success. As a student of history, he understood that reporters often have less latitude in writing about foreign policy than they do on other subjects. "There are special mores concerned with foreign policy ever since World War II," says Leslie H. Gelb, former diplomatic reporter of the *New York Times.* "You are talking about the national security, about the defense of America. On the government side that puts a low emphasis on truth telling — you can lie if necessary. On the journalistic side there is a disposition to accept the same kind of morality."

Kissinger also kept track of the other players in the bureaucratic drama. I remember a sunny day in San Clemente — it must have been a day when they were trying to keep the Eastern Establishment press in the same room — when John Herbers of the *New York Times* and I simultaneously were interviewing Al Haig. Suddenly the door burst open and Kissinger appeared. He smiled at us and said to Haig, in what seemed to me to be a thicker-than-usual German accent, "Ah, when I heard you talking in those dulcet tones I knew that you either must have a woman in here or that you were talking to the press." The analogy of seduction was a vivid one and it applied even more to Kissinger than it did to the embattled White House chief of staff. The comment also was

a reminder, as if his former deputy Haig needed any, that
Kissinger keeps tabs on other senior staff members. In
the spring of 1975 I undertook a study of White House
Press Secretary Ron Nessen's briefings for *Columbia
Journalism Review* and concluded that Nessen was doing
a good job of supplying information on domestic affairs
and a poor job of supplying information on foreign affairs.[10] With some shading, this conformed closely to
Nessen's own view at the time. But the White House
press secretary dissembled about the reasons for his
foreign policy problems, blaming them on insufficient information from the National Security Council staff. This
insufficiency was demonstrated on Ford's Palm Springs
trip, when Nessen announced a peace initiative which
never existed that supposedly was aimed at stopping the
North Vietnamese drive. Nessen blamed this faulty report on a supposedly inept member of the National Security Council staff, who unfortunately was the NSC
press liaison. He refused for a long time afterward to
accept any information from this individual. But my own
sources found Nessen's explanation for the error laugha-
ble, pointing out (once they were suitably assured of not
being quoted) that the National Security Council told
Nessen exactly what Kissinger wanted it to tell him,
which was very little. In this case there was the suspicion
that Nessen had been given a trial balloon.

One interesting account of the way Kissinger worked
has been provided by William Safire, the former Nixon
speechwriter who is now a columnist for the *New York
Times*. Safire had written in *Harper's* that it was Kiss-

---

[10] Lou Cannon, "Ron Nessen's Briefings: The Missing Questions And Answers," *Columbia Journalism Review*, May-June 1975. This article was
based on a contention by Nessen that he has material in his briefing book to
give to reporters about which he is never asked questions. To check the
thesis I examined the briefing book on random days and wrote a story about
it. Most of the reporters rejected Nessen's premise, saying he should announce something if he had it to announce and wasn't asked about it. In the
article I quoted Nessen as saying, "The quality of my foreign-policy statements is far below the quality of my domestic statements."

inger who early in the Ford administration had inspired talk by Nessen, on the President's trip to Vladivostok, that the strategic arms limitation (SALT) agreement was "something that President Nixon could not do in three years but Ford did in three months." Kissinger described Safire's accusation as "a malicious canard" and said that Nessen had made his statement on Air Force One returning from the Far East while Kissinger lingered in Japan, "preparing to go to China and therefore thousands of miles from the event." Safire, admitting he was breaking a "deep background" rule, then goes on to tell in a Feb. 17, 1975, column in the *New York Times* how Kissinger, on the Anchorage-to-Tokyo leg of the flight *to* the Far East, had told the press that "in terms of personality, Ford and Brezhnev are better matched than Nixon and Brezhnev." Under the ground rules this statement could not be attributed to Kissinger. Then, continued Safire:

> While in Vladivostok, Ron Nessen extended the theme in conversation with a few reporters. At 2 a.m. Sunday morning in the press hostel, Nessen said that "Nixon could never look Brezhnev in the eye" as Ford could. When asked how Nessen, new to international diplomacy, could be aware of this, the press secretary replied: "I dunno — that's what Henry tells me."
>
> This Kissinger line, dutifully unsourced, appeared in *Time* magazine later as, "While former President Nixon was often nervous in summit negotiations and had trouble looking his adversary in the eye, Ford . . . never wavered from eyeball-to-eyeball contact."
>
> Subsequently, while still in the Soviet Union, the presidential party rode Siberian rails from Vladivostok to a Soviet airbase. In the dining car, obviously acting on instructions, Nessen said on the record that Ford had done in three months what Nixon could not do in three years. Kissinger was on the same train, not "thousands of miles from the event."

Safire, of course, is an old Kissinger foe, and the columnist is not known for charity toward those whom he

considers his enemies. Nevertheless, I am satisfied from
my own inquiries that Safire's account was basically accurate. His account differed from others chiefly because
Safire broke the ground rules and thereby revealed that
Kissinger's fingerprints were on the Nessen statement.
What struck me about the incident was Kissinger's
transparent confidence that reporters would not betray
his rather crude attempt to elevate his present boss by
denigrating his former one. Kissinger was never a fool.
His confidence was the result of a long stretch of being
the anonymous "senior official" who emerged into the
light of attribution only when he wanted to be identified.
In fact, it is not too much to say that Kissinger enjoyed a
"presidential" press, indeed a presidential press which
compared favorably with such master users of the
medium as the Roosevelts and Kennedy. Like some of
these presidents, Kissinger was preoccupied with power
and obsessed with secrecy (characteristics in which he far
more resembled Nixon than Ford), and his assumption of
the dual foreign policy positions made it possible for him
to achieve the power and to secure the secrecy. Kissinger
believed that he and he alone must provide public information on foreign policy, a notion which he brought with
him into government. "The chief substance of Kissinger's
first staff meeting in January, 1969, was that there
would be no White House mess privileges and *nobody
was to talk to the press!*" wrote former Kissinger aide
Roger Morris.[11] " 'We are not going to repeat the experience of the Johnson administration,' Kissinger wishfully
told us. 'If anyone leaks anything, I will do the leaking.'
Over succeeding weeks, one saw some discreet infrac-
tions of the rule, but for the most part it stood. Members
of Kissinger's staff were authorized to explore secret
negotiations, even to edit the ceaseless outpour of his
diary. But none of us was trusted to deal with that most

---

[11] Roger Morris, "Henry Kissinger and the Media: A Separate Peace,"
Columbia Journalism Review, May-June 1974.

sensitive and perilous phenomenon of them all — a journalist."

Sometimes Kissinger's obsession with secrecy just for the hell of it became pretty silly. The night that Nelson Rockefeller was sworn in as vice president I was a pool reporter attending a champagne reception given for Rockefeller by Senate Minority Leader Hugh Scott. The pool report had been filed, and I went back to the reception to talk to some of the Rockefeller aides. Kissinger came by beaming, and said something about it being a wonderful event. Then, as if by reflex, he added, "You understand, that's on background of course." I mumbled something about not being able to get it in the paper even if it was on the record and moved on. But the same obsession with secrecy can in other circumstances undermine the processes of representative government. The most significant aspect of the secret minutes revealed by Jack Anderson of the Nixon government's "tilt to Pakistan" in 1971 was not Nixon's unfeeling concern for the Bengalis who were then being murdered but Kissinger's readiness to accept an actual policy that was at variance with the professed one. We have paid insufficient attention to this aspect of Kissinger's personality. "Partly as a result of Kissinger's energetic accessibility," says Morris, in the process of criticizing his failures on economic issues, "the media, while covering Kissinger and what he has concentrated upon, have a tendency to ignore what he ignores."[12]

"Everyone sees what you appear to be, few know what you are, and those few dare not oppose the opinion of the many, who have the majesty of the state to defend them. . ." wrote Niccolo Machiavelli. Kissinger understood the meaning of these words. To reporters covering the Nixon administration, Kissinger seemed a truly towering figure, superior in intellect and certainly in character to other officials of that sorry presidency. This

---

[12] The same.

presumed superiority, when added to the constraints of covering foreign policy, meant that Kissinger never received the personal or political scrutiny which his role and his policies warranted. On a rare occasion when Kissinger's credibility was challenged, at a news conference in Salzburg, Austria, on July 11, 1974, where he was pressed about the wiretapping of National Security Council staff aides, Kissinger responded emotionally and threatened to resign. It was an effective response. Willing as many of us were for Nixon to step down, we shared the belief of then-Vice President Ford that the nation could not do without Kissinger. Whether or not this was true, Kissinger was just too much for the press. Understanding us better than we understood ourselves, making useful captives of those who traveled with him, paying court to publishers and editors, he made the press dependent upon him, as he made the nation dependent on the success of the agreements he negotiated for Vietnam and the Middle East. In the process Kissinger became the only truly glamorous figure of two administrations, and his darker side was kept from public view much as it used to be with Hollywood celebrities. The last night of his vacation at Palm Springs, President Ford was host to the traveling press at a cocktail party at the lavish desert home he had rented. It was something his predecessor never would have done and, for all that had gone wrong that week, it reflected the genuine friendliness which Gerald Ford holds for reporters. Henry Kissinger came to this cocktail party, indeed he was the life of it, and he entertained the correspondents with tales of his negotiating prowess and other incidents from the now-punctured Paris peace accords on Vietnam. One of the stories which Kissinger told was about Le Duc Tho, the North Vietnamese negotiator. Kissinger said Le Duc Tho was "queer," illustrating what he meant by relating how the North Vietnamese negotiator always put his hands on Kissinger when they met at the peace talks. Afterward, some reporters said they found this description both irrelevant and offensive, but none of them conveyed their view to Dr. Kissinger. What they did convey, at this pleasant cocktail party in the desert, was the impression that they regarded Kissinger as being more influential than their host. Many of the reporters who came shook hands with the President, politely greeted Betty Ford and had a drink. They spent the rest of the evening across the room from the President, listening to the stories of Henry Kissinger.

CHAPTER THIRTEEN

Suppression and Distortion

*News is like sausage – a lot of meaty ingre-
dients go in one end of the machine and come
out, it is hoped, at the other. But to the extent
that information from the Government is one of
the ingredients, we cannot be sure that what is
going into the sausage is wholesome, untainted
and unadulterated.*
                    *–A. M. Rosenthal, Managing Editor
                        of the NEW YORK TIMES*

On May 7, 1975, the deputy director of the Central
Intelligence Agency, Lieutenant General Vernon A.
Walters, appeared in the musty ballroom of the National
Press Club to discuss national security issues before the
Washington chapter of Sigma Delta Chi, the Society of
Professional Journalists. Dick Walters is an accomplished raconteur who speaks eight languages and likes
to regale after-dinner audiences with his experiences as
interpreter for Vice President Nixon on his South American trip in 1958, when the Nixon party was stoned by an
angry mob in Caracas. On this evening Walters was in
good form. He mingled anecdotal accounts of his Army
days with a plea for civil liberties for the CIA ("intelligence people have rights, too") and with a shrewd admis-
sion of past illegalities ("the CIA might have gone to the
edge and even over it"). The latter statement became the
platform for an assertion that the CIA is now a law-
abiding agency which tells the truth to the American
people ("I would like to see it written about as it is rather
than as it was"). Up to this point the speech was at least a
mild triumph for Walters, particularly in view of the
skeptical nature of the audience. Then the deputy director turned to questions. He was sailing along unscathed

until Jack Nelson, the blunt-spoken Washington bureau chief of the *Los Angeles Times,* asked Walters why, if the CIA doesn't lie anymore, the editors of the *Los Angeles Times,* the *New York Times* and the *Washington Post* had been given conflicting details by CIA officials about Project Jennifer, the attempt by the agency to raise a sunken Soviet submarine in the Pacific Ocean using a deep-sea mining ship built by Howard Hughes. Walters' response undid most of the good impression of his speech. He apologized, but said he wouldn't comment on any aspect of the submarine story. A follow-up question came from the audience. Since the Russians knew what we were up to and we knew that they were watching us and they knew that we knew they were watching, was the submarine story being concealed from anyone except the American and the Russian people? Again, Walters answered with a polite no comment. Finally, after another variant of the same question produced a similar no-response, David Murray of the *Chicago Sun-Times* asked Walters for an example of an occasion where newspapermen had been trusted by the CIA or another government agency and had given away a national security secret. If there were no such cases, asked Murray, why shouldn't the press rather than the government be allowed to make the decision to publish? "That, of course, is one view," said Walters in response. He gave no examples of a situation where the press had been trusted and then had betrayed the confidence. The question-and-answer session ended with the skeptical reporters in the audience as skeptical as they had been before.[1]

The questions which Walters declined to answer raised some of the central issues concerning national security and the press: Does the government lie for bureaucratic,

---

[1] I attended this dinner and my account is from notes made at the time. The CIA was not anxious for newspaper coverage of Walters and did not make a speech text available. A CIA public-information official accompanying Walters said that he would send me a text of the deputy director's remarks but never did.

partisan or other reasons and then use "national security" as a means to cover up? Can the press be trusted
with national security information? Even if the press can
be trusted, should it be allowed to makes its own decision
about what to publish when national security issues are
at stake? Many of the reporters who were in the room
with Walters and many other reporters presumably
would answer "yes" to all three questions. But the answers often given by their editors and publishers, as the
story of the Soviet submarine demonstrates, are quite
different.

Seymour Hersh of the *New York Times,* to no one's
surprise, was a light year ahead of everyone else on the
story of the 1974 CIA-sponsored expedition of Hughes'
mining ship, the Glomar Explorer. But he was not the
first to get the story into print. Hersh turned in a detailed
story early in March 1975 but it was withheld by *Times*
managing editor A. M. (Abe) Rosenthal. CIA Director
William Colby had talked to Rosenthal and told him that
the CIA had not succeeded in obtaining code books and
other information aboard the sunken sub and was planning to make another attempt in the summer of 1975.
"After consideration I decided the government's ration-
ale was sensible," Rosenthal said. "There was no coer-
cion. The idea of Colby's being able to pressure me is
ridiculous. What's he going to do? Take away my
passport?" Rosenthal is one of the editors in this country
who is most consistently dedicated to a literal interpretation of the First Amendment. But he also believes, as he
expressed it in a February 11, 1973 article in his own
newspaper, that the same amendment which gave the
press the right to examine the judgment of the president
and his servants "imposed an ethical obligation on the
press to use the right decently and in the public interest
. . ." Rosenthal put Hersh's story on the shelf without
discussing it with the reporter.

Colby was not talking to the *New York Times* alone.
On February 13 he paid a visit to the *Washington Post*

where editor Benjamin C. Bradlee was out of the country. Colby talked to managing editor Howard Simons and to publisher Katharine Graham. Again, he found a receptive audience, this time made more receptive by the fact that the *Post* at the time had virtually no information about the incident. "We didn't know enough and we still don't know enough," Simons said four months after Colby's visit. But the *Post* called a reporter who had made preliminary inquiries. There was a strong presumption in Colby's favor, expressed most strongly by Graham, who was concerned that the ongoing scandals involving the CIA might destroy the agency's effectiveness. "Obviously, when the CIA does something wrong it ought to be clipped for it," she said in a June 1975 interview. "But it's just unarguable that this country has to have a functioning, strong, able CIA and I don't want to demolish it. I thought there was a valid national interest at stake." This view apparently was shared by the executives of the eleven major news organizations which *Newsweek* said were visited by Colby or other CIA officials. As always when "national security" is the byword, Colby found a receptive audience in the executive offices of these news organizations.

Hersh and at least one other reporter known to the author had been hearing about the salvage operation since it was in the planning stage late in 1973. So had other people in Washington, including Charles Morgan, an attorney for the American Civil Liberties Union, who shared his information with his friend Jack Nelson. The *Los Angeles Times,* aided by some leaked information about papers that had been stolen from a Hughes-owned corporation on February 8, 1975, printed the first story on the operation, a sketchy and somewhat inaccurate account which placed the sub retrieval operation in the Atlantic. Nevertheless, the story was close enough to the mark to worry Colby. After the first edition appeared with the story prominently headlined on page one, CIA officials called the newspaper's editors and urged them to

withdraw it. The presumption of CIA legitimacy existed
at the executive level of the *Los Angeles Times*, too, but
not as strongly as it did at the *New York Times* and the
Washington Post. The story was not withdrawn in later
editions but instead was tucked away to the safe middle
ground of an inside page. Bill Boyarsky of the *Los
Angeles Times*, in a story published in that paper March
20, 1975, about the reasons for the newspaper's action
quoted editor William F. Thomas as saying that he believed the story could jeopardize completion of the salvage operation. "There was the entire matter of international relations," Thomas also said. "The Russians were
not likely to look kindly on this."

The story of Project Jennifer remained a secret to most
Americans until columnist Jack Anderson made it public
in his radio broadcast of March 18. Anderson also had
talked with Colby, whom he afterward called "the most
candid CIA director I've ever dealt with." But Anderson
had talked too, with Navy sources of high rank who told
him that the secrets which the eighteen-year-old Soviet
sub contained were of no military significance. Anderson
had crossed Hersh's trail several weeks behind him and
he courteously decided to inform the *New York Times* he
was breaking the CIA embargo. The *Times* let him break
it, allowing, in *Newsweek's* words, Anderson to take "the
ethical heat . . . while the *New York Times*, from a stance
of responsible citizenship, reaped recognition for the
most comprehensive coverage." Hersh's stories about the
salvage operation clearly were superior to any others,
but the simultaneous publication of varying accounts
raised questions about the game Colby had been playing.
Considering that the CIA had volunteered details to
newspapers about which the papers knew nothing, it
seemed remarkable to some reporters and editors that
the stories that were published in various papers differed
in significant details, such as how much of the Soviet sub
had been recovered, the number of bodies found and the
information which had been on the portion of the sub

brought up by the Glomar Explorer. Hence, Jack Nelson's question, which also was on the minds of his colleagues. If the CIA was playing straight, how come the newspapers which the CIA had briefed didn't have the same story? Important as this question was, it soon became secondary. Former Defense Secretary Melvin R. Laird, questioned by Peter Lisagor of the *Chicago Daily News*, said that the Russians were watching when the Glomar Explorer brought up portions of the Soviet submarine and that the U.S. government was aware of the surveillance. I happened to have placed a call to Laird on an unrelated matter the same day Lisagor talked to him. Twenty minutes before Laird returned my call a *Post* editor who knew I was trying to reach Laird placed on my desk a copy of Lisagor's story for the next morning, received over our own wire under a cooperative arrangement with the *Chicago Daily News*. After discussing the matter which originally had prompted my call, I asked Laird about the Lisagor story. He readily confirmed it and hinted that there had been other reasons for concealing the excavation attempt. I formed the opinion that these reasons had to do with Hughes' involvement and the $350 million cost of the operation, although Laird never said so directly. What Laird did say directly was that the Defense Department was very interested in the operation because of the need for developing a capability of recovering our own lost submarines, a naval concern ever since the loss of the *Thresher* on April 10, 1963. Laird's statement raised serious questions about what Colby had been attempting. Though the CIA director had given different details to different editors, his basic argument had been the consistent one that the Russians were ignorant of Project Jennifer, which was as yet uncompleted, and that publication would jeopardize a future salvage attempt. Had Colby, the new-look director of the CIA and the man who had candidly admitted past illegal domestic spying activities first revealed by Hersh's stories, been lying as past directors had lied?

This question troubled editors who had suppressed the story, including Howard Simons at the *Washington Post*. He evolved a theory, at least partially in earnest, that the CIA, "in deep trouble for its nefarious domestic activities," had pretended to suppress a story it knew would come out. In Simons' mock scenario Colby "goes to several news organizations and gives them more details about a secret operation that is to remain secret than has any master spy in recent memory — details, in some instances that the news organizations did not have before Colby came to them. And Mr. Colby knows that it is just a matter of time before one of them publishes. The outcome, of course, is a rash of editorials favorable to the agency. The *New York Times* concludes editorially: 'the CIA is only to be commended for this extraordinary effort to carry out its essential mission.' The *Washington Post* editorial begins: 'In retrieving parts of a sunken Soviet submarine from 16,000 feet down in the Pacific, the Central Intelligence Agency was performing its prime function brilliantly.' The *Washington Star* in its editorial says: 'We regard Project Jennifer, as the submarine operation was known in official circles, as a tremendous feat.' And finally, columnist Smith Hempstone of the *Star* claims that given the Kremlin's arms build-up and intentions, '. . . the CIA would have been derelict in its duty had it not tried to procure the intelligence sealed in the sunken sub's crushed hull.' "

Whether there really was such a "scenario" even Simons doubts. Certainly, if Colby wanted the story to come out, he went to a lot of extra trouble with his telephoning, including the call to the editors of the *Los Angeles Times* on February 8 after the presses were running. Information obtained recently suggests that the CIA actually was after a Soviet cipher machine and that Colby was worried this might get out.

Granted that the CIA undoubtedly was performing its essential purpose in trying to recover the submarine, should the news organizations that knew about it have suppressed the story? Ben Bradlee, back on the job, had his doubts. He conceded that the *Washington Post,* at least initially, had scant choice because the *Post* knew so little about the story. But he thinks that the *Post* went too far in going along completely with Colby and that it should have put reporters on the story immediately. "The only thing I would have done differently," said Bradlee, "is that instead of calling a reporter off I would have put two reporters on it and said, 'There's no fucking way this thing is going to stay out of print.' " Bradlee's approach would at least have given the *Post* a competitive story when Anderson broke the embargo. But his concern goes deeper than a single story. Though he has sometimes had his doubts about the quality of Anderson's reporting, Bradlee thinks there is merit in the columnist's complaint that the press has begun to wear a hair shirt in an effort to demonstrate its post-Watergate responsibility. Simons is not so sure about this. "Anderson has been more responsible, certainly, than his predecessor (Drew Pearson)," says Simons. "But I read his columns and we edit his columns and some of it is very wild stuff that we don't publish. That's the other extreme of not publishing material that we should. And I worry as much about that as he's worried about me getting up tight about responsibility."[2]

Simons has a point. Nevertheless, I think that Anderson was right in breaking the story of Project Jennifer and that the newspaper publishers and editors were wrong in suppressing it. I am not an Anderson fan, considering him at times irresponsible and at other times self-righteous. But the incident demonstrates the necessity of having a Jack Anderson around to print a story

---

[2] The comments by Katherine Graham and Ben Bradlee about the CIA sub story are from interviews with the author. The comments by Howard Simons also are from interviews except that the "scenario" about what the CIA was up to is from a speech given by Simons at Stetson University on April 11, 1975. The comments by Rosenthal are from an account in *Newsweek* on March 31, 1975.

when newspapers won't do it on their own. "The old pre-Watergate, pre-Vietnam ideals of partnership with government, of cozy intimacy with the high and mighty, of a camaraderie of secrets shared by this peerage but kept from the public, begins to appeal once more to a press concerned that its abrasive successes have earned it a bad name and a hostile reception," Anderson wrote in his column of March 25, 1975. "At such time we reporters need a reminder that we exist not to lie down with the lions but to fend them off, to cause the turmoil by which the free system cleanses and energizes itself." Anderson then inserted into his column a self-serving letter he had received from Colby on another matter in which the CIA director complimented him for protection of intelligence sources. "But this time," Anderson continued,

> Colby's arguments for secrecy were not compelling. It was hardly a secret that the Glomar expedition was still a secret from Soviet intelligence. Thousands of people in our government and industry had played some part in it over a seven-year span; some of them were leaking it out; newsmen were asking questions; a ring of thieves and blackmailers had broken into the Hughes offices in Hollywood and had stolen documents describing the Glomar operation . . . So the Russians knew. We knew they knew. They knew we knew. But, as Colby told us, it would be "rubbing their noses in it" to let the American people know.
>
> What was at stake in publishing, then, was not national security but international etiquette, not American secrets but Soviet face, not the sabotage of a second Glomar mission but the ruffling of Russian tail feathers if we should go ahead with it. These are considerations not to be mocked, but we hold them to be insufficient reasons for renewing the dread precedent of cutting off the news — the windpipe of the American system.
>
> All right. If there is no compelling reason to suppress, is there a public need to know a story that might inconvenience the conduct of our diplomacy? We think so. An estimated $350 million was spent outside of the legitimate

appropriations process — in a gamble to recover an archaic diesel sub, obsolete missiles and outdated codes. No doubt this submerged museum piece would have been of some intelligence value had it not fallen apart. But was it worth a sum that, for instance, could have financed the down payment on 100,000 new homes? Was it a national necessity or was it an admiral's toy?

One does not have to regard the operation as an admiral's toy to accept the thrust of Anderson's argument. If Mel Laird is right about the need to develop a submarine salvage capability — and the loss of the *Thresher* is a powerful argument for this need — then Project Jennifer is a story about which the American people and especially the families of those who go to sea should know. I also think there is justification for Anderson's fear that the press may be overeager to demonstrate its responsibility at the expense of its independence and its judgment. As David Murray's question to General Walters suggested, the track record of American news organizations in suppressing material when the government has taken the press into its confidence is good, perhaps too good. After the ill-fated Bay of Pigs invasion President Kennedy said that the *New York Times* might have saved the administration from itself by completely exposing the invasion before it happened.[3] Certainly, the history of government-press relations ever since World War II suggests that the press keeps both diplomatic and military secrets when asked to do so. Press violations of national security confidences are so rare that advocates of greater suppression always wind up citing a World War II incident, the publication by the *Chicago Tribune* on

---

[3] The late Stewart Alsop in *The Center*, (New York, 1968), p. 189, gives an account which he attributes to Clifton Daniel, now chief of the Washington bureau for the *New York Times*. According to Alsop, Kennedy convened a meeting of press executives in the White House two weeks after the Bay of Pigs and castigated the press, especially the *Times,* for prior disclosure of the government's plans for the invasion. But then he said to Turner Catledge, the *Times* managing editor: "If you had printed more about the operation, you would have saved us from a colossal mistake."

June 7, 1942, of information which might have led the
Japanese to conclude that the United States had cracked
their naval fleet code. This achievement had made it possible for the U.S. Navy to secure a dramatic victory in the
just-concluded battle of Midway Island, one of the turning points in the Pacific war. Contrary to many references to this incident, the *Tribune* did not say that the
code had been cracked. Instead, the newspaper reported
that the Navy had guessed that Dutch Harbor and Midway might be the targets of an invasion fleet and then
gave a detailed description of the Japanese forces. This
was too far to go in wartime. "The Navy feared that the
release of such accurate information would alert the
Japanese to the fact that their code had been broken,"
wrote John Toland. "The fear was groundless; the
Japanese Navy, convinced their fleet code was unbreak-
able, attributed the rout at Midway to overconfidence."[4]

So far, we have been discussing secrets which the press
was asked to keep or which, as in the case of the Midway
incident, it was clear the government wanted kept. The
record of the press is quite different on those matters
where no request has been made or where the military
importance of the secret is less clearcut. President Truman once claimed that "ninety-five percent of our secret
information has been published by newspapers and slick
magazines," and President Eisenhower maintained that
"technical military secrets" of value to the Soviet Union
had been made public.[5] Every president since has made
some complaint about the difficulty of protecting secrets,
and President Nixon ordered an intensive investigation
to find out the source of Jack Anderson's revealing story
about the Nixon adminstration's "tilt to Pakistan" during the Bangladesh war. Reporters, by and large, have
been unimpressed with the presidential complaints in
any administration, and with good reason. They know

---

[4] John Toland, *The Rising Sun*, (New York, 1970), pp. 241-42.

[5] Cater, *The Fourth Branch of Government*, p. 118.

that the published "leaks" which presidents like to blame on the press more often are the fault of bureaucratic or inter-service rivalries or of Congressional opposition. Usually, a secret gets out because someone in government wants it to get out, or is willing to have it come out, to influence policy considerations. Testifying before the Joint Atomic Energy Committee in 1960, Admiral Hyman Rickover said that a toy manufacturer had produced a $2.98 plastic model of the Polaris submarine complete with a sheet of instructions stating that it was in strict accordance with official Navy blueprints. A Soviet ship designer, he said, could "spend one hour on the model and tell he has millions of dollars' worth of free information." The model was built with Navy permission. "I personally am aghast that this was done," Rickover testified, "but our internal military controversy is so great that there is a tendency for each service wholeheartedly to fight the others in order to achieve its own objectives."[6] The government often takes a benign view of the unnecessary release of such secrets when it is the government that does it; it is quite another matter when even trivial secrets are published in the press. Douglass Cater, in *The Fourth Branch of Government,* quotes these 1955 words of Robert Cutler, who had been a special assistant to President Eisenhower on national security matters: "I am convinced that leaks to the press of matters in a discussion stage, of working papers, or oral (National Security) Council deliberations, of bits and pieces of the vast paraphernalia that goes into careful, reasoned, sensible policy-making, play into the enemy's hands. Publicized differences of view among the president's chief advisers afford a ruthless enemy the rarest of chances to make trouble — drive a divisive wedge between friends, between counsellors, between allies. In the face of the Soviet will and power and fixed determination, to give such a chance is to flirt with survival." What

---

[6] Cater, "News and the Nation's Security," *The Reporter,* July 6, 1961.

strikes a reporter about these words two decades later is the apocryphal premise that the American government is in danger of going down because its secrets are being exposed. Cutler's fears, if not his doomsday rhetoric, have been shared by his successors. In Bill Moyers' White House days he once explained President Johnson's view in these terms: "It is very important for a president to maintain up until the moment of decision his options, and for someone to speculate days or weeks in advance that he's going to do thus and thus is to deny to the president the latitude he needs in order to make, in the light of existing circumstances, the best possible decision." James Reston, writing in his 1967 book, *Sketches in the Sand,* about Moyers' comment, said:

> No doubt this is true in many circumstances, but not in all. Is absolutely nothing to be printed about clandestine plans by the President to mount an illegal invasion at the Bay of Pigs in Cuba for fear of interfering with the President's option to humiliate the country? Are the people to be denied information about Presidential options that will involve them in a war they have to finance and fight? If all Presidential options are to be protected from speculation "until the very last minute" what redress will there be the next day after the President has opted to dispatch the Marines or bomb Hanoi, or publish a request to wage war as "he" deems necessary all over Southeast Asia?

Ten years later one might amend this last rhetorical question by asking: what redress was there? "The History of U.S. Decision-Making Process on Vietnam Policy," better known as the Pentagon Papers, contained much material which previously had appeared as driblets of information. But the publication of these papers by the *New York Times* on June 13, 1971, in defiance of "top secret" classification, showed, as Abe Rosenthal has written, "how deeply secrecy had become a pattern of living in our government, simply accepted as an assumption as so many other assumptions were accepted. The Papers showed clearly that one administration after another carried itself and the country into a constantly escalating series of wars: a political war against the Geneva accords of 1954, a counterinsurgency war, a land war, an air war, a mass land war, the greatest bombing war in history. And the Pentagon Papers show that each step was taken because the government knew the preceeding step had failed. Yet the public never knew that each step had failed."[7]

This last sentence is an exaggeration. A variety of newspapers, especially the *Times,* reported cogently about the failures of some of these escalating steps. Nevertheless, Rosenthal is right in suggesting that the Pentagon Papers gave a comprehensive picture of the progressive failure of policy which contrasted with the. picture being presented to the American people by its government. On April 23, 1975, the *New York Times* printed a useful postscript to these conflicting pictures of reality in an article written by one Paul P. Brocchini, a businessman who in 1966 had been an official in the United States Information Agency. Selected for Vietnamese-language training, Brocchini was sent to the Foreign Service Institute in Arlington, Virginia, across the Potomac River from Washington. In the jargon of the bureaucracy he thus became a member of "the pipeline," the government network which one entered in Washington and emerged from in Saigon. Each day, in an Arlington basement, Brocchini and his colleagues studied Vietnamese history and culture "and had access to an amazing amount of intelligence that painted an accurate picture of what was really happening throughout Indochina:"

> It was strange there in the basement. While great moralizing and hard-sell campaigns emerged from myriad Administration sources, peddling dominoes, World War II fears and Red threats to the public, there

---

[7] A. M. Rosenthal, "The Press Needs A Slogan: Save the First Amendment!," *New York Times Magazine,* February 11, 1973.

was no one trying to sell us, the pipeline people. On the contrary, in an age of institutionalized deceit, it was a refreshingly honest place, that basement. No pep talks. No rah-rah about saving democracy and freedom in places where neither had ever existed. But lots of straight talk.

Bernard Fall, the writer and historian who had devoted his life to the affairs of Indochina, would come in every week or two to tell it like it was.

Rand Corporation confidential reports on Vietcong morale made it devastatingly clear who was motivated in Vietnam, who fought with conviction and who did not.

Foreign Service officers coming back from Southeast Asia rarely covered up: It was bad out there and getting worse. But they had finished their tours and were relieved to be able to pass on the mess to us.

For the most part, however, the people in that basement were reluctant to pass on the same information about "the mess" to the American people. Deeply conditioned by the dogmas of secrecy, they accepted as an article of faith the destructive belief that there must be one truth for government and another for the people that government is supposed to serve. Nearly all appeals for greater secrecy, as the Cutler and Moyers statements show, reflect this unstated assumption that the United States cannot effectively govern itself in the open. The world is vast and our enemies are many and powerful, these secretists seem to say. We must make ourselves secure by using the methods of our adversaries. This latter premise has been challenged from time to time outside the government, chiefly on the grounds that we shall come to resemble our adversaries if we behave as they do. But the related premise that secrecy is helpful in a dangerous world rarely is questioned. It is assumed even by advocates of openness that vital military and diplomatic secrets exist which would make the United States vulnerable if they became public. No doubt there are such secrets, but it would be well for those who start with this premise to examine the arguments of Niels Bohr and

Edward Teller on the effect of the principle of secrecy on the development of atomic energy. Near the end of World War II, Bohr suggested that the United States abandon secrecy and return to the free exchange of discoveries and ideas common in scientific work before World War II. Teller, commenting on this idea in 1961, pointed out that "arms-control problems would at once become more manageable" if this principle were adopted. Well aware that the Soviets were not about to share their secrets and believing that it would be unwise for the United States to make a "sudden and sweeping abandonment of secrecy," Teller nonetheless thought that Bohr's suggestion deserved serious consideration. "It strikes at the root of our difficulties," Teller wrote. "It stresses that kind of openness which is natural in free countries and which has been the lifeblood of science." Teller believed that the secrecy which had shrouded the development of the atomic bomb in wartime had produced adverse consequences for the use of atomic energy after the war without conferring the benefits it was supposed to produce:

Secrecy has not prevented our most powerful enemy from developing the most powerful weapons we possess. It is not even obvious that our secrecy measures have slowed down Soviet progress. It is quite obvious, however, that secrecy has impeded our own work. Because of secrecy we have had to limit the number of people who could contribute to the development of our own weapons. Due to secrecy it has become difficult to exchange information with our allies. This led to duplication. It has also led to a less complete realism in the planning of our common defense. Secrecy has also prevented full public discussion of the possibilities of the future development of our weapons. The fact that most of our fellow citizens consider nuclear explosives as weapons of terror rather than of defense may be due to a considerable extent to secrecy. *This is only one face of the more general truth that the democratic process does not function well in an atmosphere of secrecy.*[8]

---

[8] Edward Teller, "The Feasibility of Arms Control and the Principle of

Since Teller wrote these words, the terror which pervades most discussions of nuclear energy has had enormous negative consequences on the development and use of breeder reactors as peacetime energy sources. I don't know enough about breeder reactors to reach a judgment on whether we should be using more of them, and I certainly don't advocate handing over what nuclear secrets we might still possess to other nations. I do believe, however, that advocates of secrecy ought to have the burden of proof in demonstrating that withholding of any material will serve the public good. The opposite premise dominates the government attitude toward secrecy. Tens of thousands of government documents are now routinely stamped "secret" or "classified" by anonymous bureaucrats. Sometimes these classifications reflect the considered judgment of officials who have weighed the conflicting claims of secrecy and openness; more often than not, they are matter-of-fact decisions taken by subordinates who know that they are unlikely to get into trouble for over-classification. One of the most useful antidotes to government secrecy would be passage of a law requiring that all classified documents identify the author of the classification, and President Carter's efforts in this direction seem to me well-founded. If some of the sillier classified material read "stamped secret by order of Assistant Secretary Jones" perhaps we could accomplish through ridicule what we have been unable to do through frontal attack.

Under the present system the few people in government who are on the side of declassification can work for months or years shoveling sand against the tide. In 1970, when working in Washington for Ridder Newspapers, I became interested in the standby plan which had been devised for censorship in the event of a national emergency. One of the provisions of this plan is for a

---

Openness," *Arms Control, Disarmament and National Security,* (New York, 1961), pp. 134-35. The emphasis on the last sentence is mine.

standby censor who would be charged during such an emergency with keeping defense secrets out of print or off the air. When the plan was created during the Truman administration, there was general agreement that the censor should be a newsman of high reputation and that his name should be publicly known. And so it was during the Truman, Eisenhower and Kennedy administrations until President Johnson, without explanation, made the identity of the censor a defense secret. In the early months of the Nixon administration a strenuous effort was made by Samuel J. Archibald, then the Washington representative of the University of Missouri's Freedom of Information center, to declassify the identity of the censor. Herb Klein agreed with the idea but found it was far easier to recommend declassification than to obtain it. These were the pre-Watergate days of the Nixon administration when there were still a few people around — of whom Klein was the most conscientious — who did not regard freedom of information as a plot. But it was slow going for the good guys. At one point Margita E. White, a capable assistant to Klein who now is a member of the Federal Communications Commission, expressed dismay at the red tape involved in declassification. "One wonders if there aren't a lot more classifications like this that we don't even know about," she said. "There's so much work in unclassifying something like this, and it's so easy to put confidential on a piece of paper." Eventually, when it looked as if Klein and White were getting nowhere, I decided to print the name of the censor myself. He was Theodore Koop, a respected CBS executive who was the nation's deputy director of censorship during World War II and the author of a book on censorship, *The Weapon of Silence*. He also was the logical choice for the job, and I heard that his name had been made secret at his own request simply to prevent Koop from embarrassment with his employers if someone identified him as the "secret censor." I was never able to verify this latter point, since Koop declined to respond to telephone calls, and I am not certain to this day how the classification came to be made. In any case I wrote a story identifying Koop as the censor for Ridder newspapers. It was picked up, with my permission, by a freelance news service and distributed around the country, provoking some criticism of me from Nixon administration officials after it appeared in the *Washington Star* on October 25, 1970. As far as I know, Koop's identity was never made public officially, although when I talked to Klein a month after my story he said he was still trying. White called me and said she agreed the censor's identity should be made public but thought it wasn't up to a reporter to decide.

Why is the notion that even a trivial secret must be sacrosanct so deeply rooted in our federal government? Certainly, one of the reasons is that government attitudes in this country, at least until the last few years, have been heavily influenced by the experience of World War II. Most public officials, and most of the editors who suppressed the CIA sub story, either fought in that popularly supported war or grew up during a time when walls of coffee shops and defense plants were festooned with posters cautioning, "A slip of the lip could sink a ship." "Secrets" were what one kept from Nazi Germany and the Japanese; afterward, "secrets" became what was kept from the Soviet Union. It is not surprising that we have been slow in recognizing that secrets really are what are kept from the American people.

Another enduring reason for secrecy in government is its great convenience. Public officials are naturally tempted to paper over a personal embarrassment or a partisan disagreement with a secret classification and say they are acting in the name of national security. Every president since Hoover has been unable to resist this temptation. When Richard Nixon evoked "national security" as a barrier to investigation of his administration's Watergate crimes, he was making the one claim which Americans who otherwise had no use for Nixon were likely to accept. The words "national security" still evoke a popular, patriotic feeling; one of the tragic consequences of the many misuses of this phrase is that it may lead some Americans to believe that the words have no real meaning.

As a whole, the press has performed poorly in making a public case against government secrecy. One reason is that it is reporters and editors, rather than publishers, who have to deal with secrecy and who are most concerned with it. Many of the countinghouse publishers in this country are unwilling to go to court except in defense of commercial interests such as postage rates or antitrust exemptions, and the more sophisticated public officials know it. And publishers are even more likely than editors and reporters to share with public officials the biases born in World War II which equate secrecy with patriotism. Accompanying these problems of commitment is the consistent inability of many persons in the higher reaches of the news business to state the case against secrecy in anything except platitudinous terms involving the people's "right to know." There is no such right, except in the narrow sense that freedom-of-information laws have conferred the right to obtain or peruse particular documents. What there is in the United States instead of a broad "right to know" is a Constitution which forbids the government from controlling the printed press and an obscured legacy of access based on the principle that citizens of a self-governing society must have knowledge about the affairs of a government which exists at their consent. "The role of a free press in a democratic society creates a presumption of a right to access to all governmental proceedings affecting public policy," wrote Irving Brant. The struggle to obtain full access has been a concomitant of the many struggles in English and American society aimed at broadening individual freedoms. Lord Acton, the author of the well-known dictum about the corruptibility of power, also observed that "everything secret degenerates, even the administration of justice." The evolvement of individual rights from Magna Carta progressively limited secret accusation, secret arrest and secret trial, actions which in every case extended individual freedoms and broadened the access of the press. Colonial America's system of non-hereditary public office and electoral accountability depended upon a usually unstated but significant assumption that the participating factions of society would be able to obtain accurate information upon which to make their determinations. No one recognized this better than Thomas Jefferson, whose first draft to the celebrated preamble of the Virginia Statute on Religious Freedom began: "Well aware that the opinions and beliefs of men depend not upon their own will, but follow involuntarily the evidence proposed to their minds . . ." Hamilton recognized a similar unstated principle when he chose a newspaper in which to publish the Federalist papers. But the tradition that representative government flourishes on secrecy also has early antecedents. The Constitution was created in closed session, although the non-innocuous constitutional provision requiring each house of Congress to keep a daily journal was at the time of its inclusion, albeit mistakenly, viewed as a significant guarantee that citizens would be kept aware of the activities of their legislature.

In our time the best statement of the belief that citizens must be adequately informed as a condition of retaining their sovereignty is expressed in the first paragraph of the Ralph M. Brown Act, the 1952 California law which required most meetings of local government bodies in that state to be open to the public.[9] "The people of this state do not yield their sovereignty to agencies which serve them," this law began. "The people, in delegating authority, do not give their public servants the right to decide what is good for the people to know and

---

[9] The spur to this legislation was a series of articles by Michael Harris in the *San Francisco Chronicle* on "Your Secret Government" which detailed the patterns and practices of secrecy among local government agencies.

what is not good for them to know. The people insist on remaining informed so that they may retain control over the instrument they have created."

As any editor who has raised the open meetings issue in a community newspaper knows, there is a popular presumption that a public body which goes into closed session has something to hide. I never worked for a California publisher who was eager to go into court to enforce the Brown Act. In most cases the publisher was not even willing to go into court. Nevertheless, the Brown Act was of tremendous help to me as editor and reporter because the citation of the law's provisions usually would persuade a secretive city council or a board of supervisors to open up a closed meeting. Councilmen often took the view that a closed meeting was a political liability for them if a newspaper chose to make a point of it even though the publisher was unlikely to go to court.

The courts have been less help in this battle for openness than they should have been, partly because of the secretive traditions of the judiciary and partly because most judges do not have to stand for elective office. The last few years have been a period of judicial limitation of freedom of the press, with the emphasis on a deprivation of confidentiality. Though confidentiality is of equal importance to access in preserving a free press, it is by no means as well understood outside the press as the importance of open and public meetings. Sometimes it is not even understood by a newspaper's lawyers. Chalmers M. Roberts, the now-retired diplomatic correspondent of the *Washington Post,* complains that the newspaper's attorneys in the Pentagon Papers case often failed "to understand the nature of the newspaper business they were hired to defend. William R. Glendon, who chiefly handled the case through the Supreme Court, often sounded as though he was defending a traffic violator, so leery was he of accepting the word of reporters and editors on how secret documents in Washington are employed in practice as contrasted to the formal language of the security

regulations." Roberts and other reporters submitted
affidavits (Roberts said the best of them was by Max
Frankel, then Washington bureau chief of the *New York
Times*) intended to make the point that the Nixon administration and its predecessors regularly leaked secret material when it served the government's purposes. "But we
all found that most of our lawyers seemed more influenced by the thought that the papers had been 'stolen'
from the government than by the long history of leaking
classified documents and information by design," Roberts
concluded.[10]

By a 6-3 decision the Supreme Court allowed the
newspapers, which now included the *Boston Globe* and
the *St. Louis Post-Dispatch* as well as the *Times* and the
Post, to resume printing the Pentagon Papers which the
government had temporarily blocked publication of
through court injunction. But it was, as Roberts concludes, "a costly victory." The court did not bar future
prior restraint, merely concluding that the government
had failed to meet the "heavy burden" for its imposition.
One justice in the majority, Byron R. White, even indicated some sympathy for the government's position, if
not for its attempt to secure prior restraint through an
injunction. In his concurring opinion White said that
"terminating the ban on publication of the relatively few
sensitive documents the government now seeks to suppress does not mean that the law either requires or in-
vites newspapers or others to publish them or that they
will be immune from criminal action if they do."

Worrisome as the court's decision might seem in regard to future questions of access, it is the lost case of
Earl Caldwell that has posed immediate problems on the
issue of confidentiality. Caldwell is the *New York Times*
reporter who properly refused to disclose his sources in
the Black Panthers or even to appear before a grand jury
to discuss them. Anyone who is familiar with the Pan-

<hr>

[10] Chalmers M. Roberts, *First Rough Draft,* (New York, 1973), pp. 323-324.

thers can hardly help being aware that any other course by Caldwell would have jeopardized his sources. Nevertheless, ever since Caldwell, reporters have been going to jail in increasing numbers for failing to reveal their sources in response to subpoenas. These subpoenas have involved all three television networks and such prominent papers as the *New York Times,* the *New York Daily News, Newsday,* the *St. Louis Globe-Democrat,* and the *Washington Star.* But subpoenas also have been issued to reporters on the *Everett (Wash.) Herald,* the *Keene (N.H.) Sentinel,* the *Dayton Journal* and the *Lowell Sun.* Two reporters and two editors of the *Fresno Bee* were sent to jail for contempt because they refused to reveal their sources in a criminal case and cited California's shield law which states that an editor or reporter "cannot be adjudged in contempt by a judicial, legislative, administrative body, or any other body having power to issue subpoenas." The judge, Denver C. Peckinpah, took the view that the shield law interfered with his judicial powers.

Judicial assaults on freedom of press such as this one invariably will lead to additional suppression of the news. Reporters who attempt to do more than print handouts must rely on confidential sources, often people who are far down in the system of government. These sources depend on confidentiality for their job, their reputation and their peace of mind. Reporters and editors have demonstrated a commendable willingness to go to jail to protect their confidential sources, but this is an insufficient protection both for the sources and for society. "Even if every reporter in the country were willing to go to jail, it would not solve the confidentiality problem," wrote A. M. Rosenthal, managing editor of the *New York Times.*[11] "There is the impact on the sources to be considered." Rosenthal observes that some sources who previously came forward now may be reluctant to do so and

---

[11] Rosenthal, "The Press Needs a Slogan."

adds: "We will never know what this loss of confidentiality of sources will cost because we will never know what we might have known. It seems entirely plain that the destruction of confidentiality of news sources will have an impact on how much the public knows about every aspect of public affairs. There will simply be fewer and fewer people in government and out of government willing to take the risk that the press will be able to protect them. It will not all happen tomorrow but it will happen as long as this country is ready to say that the price of dissidence is exposure." The inevitable consequence of the destruction of confidentiality will be the dominance of the official version of reality wherever government touches upon American society. "This is not a matter of special privilege for newspapermen but for the First Amendment," Rosenthal wrote. "You can't tell a carpenter he is free to practice his trade as long as he uses no tools. You can't tell a newspaperman that he has a free press as long as he does not use his tools and among them the essential tool is confidentiality of sources."

Not everyone in the news business has demonstrated a similar zeal in behalf of the First Amendment. And even those publishers and editors who have been zealous sometimes are quite willing to engage in news suppression themselves. On most newspapers there are "sacred cows" that receive a special standard of treatment. Sometimes the sacred cow is a personal friend of the publisher or a community interest that is important to him. Sometimes it is a powerful business interest or a public official. Occasionally, although more rarely, it is a political party. On the *San Jose Mercury* publisher Joseph B. Ridder was reluctant to print even the slightest criticism of Republican politicians whom he favored. In 1969 the newspaper's then-political editor, Harry Farrell, and I spent several weeks investigating the activities of a powerful Republican state senator, Richard J. Dolwig of neighboring San Mateo County, who at the time was chairman of one of the legislature's most important committees. We found, among other things, that Dolwig:

—While serving as chairman of a legislative committee studying measures that would have made drastic changes in state condemnation laws was the attorney for clients involving highway-right-of-way and settlement claims against the state.

—Had authored legislation enabling a development firm to fill San Francisco Bay with 28 million cubic yards of sand in the process of "reclaiming" an island for a subdivision development. Copies of checks and a telegram we had obtained showed that Dolwig had received at least $25,000 for this service and was seeking at least $10,000 more.

—Had met with a notorious gambler who had since been convicted of racketeering, conspiracy and interstate transportation of property obtained by fraud and income tax evasion in an effort to obtain a reduced sentence for an associate of the gambler convicted of telephone tampering. Dolwig had testified in court that he could not remember the name of the judge whom he asked to lighten the sentence, but contradicted this claim in a statement to an FBI agent.

There was plenty more, all adding up to apparent conflicts of interests for a state senator who then chaired a committee which was the traffic cop, or bottleneck, for many of the bills considered by the California Legislature. Farrell and I put together a draft of a series on "The Secret Life of Richard Dolwig" and then called the senator several times in an effort to get a response to the accusations. Dolwig did not return our calls. He did, however, call the publisher, who told Farrell he was killing the series. At no time did Ridder or any editor of the newspaper dispute any of our findings nor object to my decision to publish the material elsewhere. Ridder just said he wasn't running anything critical of Dolwig, who told intimates shortly after he learned of our prospective series that he would not seek another term in the Legislature. Five years after this suppressed series, Dolwig

and six other men were indicted by a federal grand jury
for allegedly defrauding a group of real estate investors.
Dolwig and five of the men (one was acquitted) were convicted of conspiracy and of involvement with racketeer-
influenced and corrupt organizations. Dolwig, by now
sixty-seven, also was convicted of two counts of mail
fraud, three counts of travel to defraud and one count of
transporting money obtained by fraud. Farrell sent me
the banner story in the Mercury about Dolwig's conviction with the written notation: "Poor Dick — if our story
had run, he'd be out by now!"

Some newspapers still suppress stories for commercial
reasons. Far more widespread, however, is a custodial
philosophy that discourages reporters from doing stories
"harmful to the community" or that might cause trouble
of any sort. The New England Newspaper Survey found
that a "don't-rock-the-boat" attitude existed on many of
the dailies, an attitude which took these three forms:

> First, some reporters are hired in part on the basis of
> their willingness to accept the status quo. Lawrence
> Smith, managing editor of the Laconia (N.H.) Evening
> Citizen, says, "We're looking for someone, number one,
> who can jell in the community."
>
> Second, the news department is encouraged to think of
> enterprise reporting as coming second (or last), even
> when the paper has the resources to go beyond routine
> local coverage.
>
> Third, the paper's owner sees the paper as a custodian,
> not a crusader. Charles A. Fuller, publisher of the
> Brockton (Mass.) Enterprise, says, "We don't dig under
> the carpet to any particular extent. We don't go looking
> for trouble . . . I take my living out of this city and I figure
> it's my job to do everything I can for it."[12]

Sometimes "don't-rock-the-boat" can be quite explicit.
David Rohn of the Indianapolis News tells of a proposal
made by him and a college intern at the paper to do a

[12] "Evaluating the Press: The New England Daily Newspaper Survey,"
edited by Loren Ghiglione, (Southbridge, Mass., 1973), p. 4.

price comparison story. "But the editor said we shouldn't offend the advertisers and we couldn't use the name of the store," Rohn says. "You can't do a price comparison story without naming the stores." The Indianapolis papers, part of the Pulliam group, follow a vigorous policy of suppression on some newspaper stories, particularly with political figures whom they dislike for one reason or another. Former Senator Eugene McCarthy says in *The Year of the People,* a book about his 1968 presidential campaign, that the *Indianapolis Star,* the sister paper to the *News,* "practically ignored me in its 'news' coverage when I campaigned in Indianapolis and other parts of Indiana."[13] He contrasts this to the performance of another "arch-conservative" newspaper, the *Manchester (N.H.) Union Leader,* which denounced him editorially and once or twice called him a "skunk" but which was "very fair in its news coverage of what I said and what I did in the state of New Hampshire." McCarthy adds: "This, I think, is the important test of the integrity of a newspaper." I know something about how the Indianapolis papers can operate against a political figure who has incurred their wrath. In June 1975 I did a long story for the *Washington Post* on the attempts of the Indiana Republican Party to come back from an election which cost the state five GOP incumbent Congressmen. One of the sources quoted in the story was L. Keith Bulen, the longtime Republican national committeeman who is considered one of the outstanding national organizers in the GOP. Writing about Indiana Republican politics without mentioning Bulen would be as unthinkable as writing about Democratic politics in Connecticut without mentioning John Bailey or Republican politics in Mississippi without referring to Clarke Reed. My story was sent over the Los Angeles Times-Washington Post wire service and the *Indianapolis News* played it on page one and used more than three columns of the story. How-

---

[13] Eugene J. McCarthy, *The Year of the People,* (New York, 1969), p. 78.

ever, the newspaper skillfully deleted all references to
Bulen, especially a paragraph which said: "The party's
leading professional, the flamboyant and capable L.
Keith Bulen, resigned his national committee post late
last year after a campaign against him in the *Indianapolis Star* and vague allegations that he used his
political influence to help obtain liquor licenses. Bulen
has not been indicted, and it is the belief in GOP circles
that he never will be, but his valuable services have been
lost to the state party." Bulen, still unindicted, often has
said that the Indianapolis papers have prohibited use of
his name in any story unless the reference is a critical
one. After this experience I believe him.

Such suppression does more to damage newspaper
credibility than a hundred attacks on the press by
Richard Nixon or Spiro Agnew or by what Rosenthal
calls "the anti-Establishment establishment." If the
claim of the press to public access rests on the notion that
it is representing the people, how can this claim be made
in good conscience by publishers who suppress important
information for partisan or personal reasons? Defense of
the First Amendment has a hollow ring from such men,
and it is unconvincing to their readers. The people are
not fools. Usually they know far more than either publishers or politicians give them credit for, and they are
likely to be especially sensitive about hypocrisy in those
who purport to speak for them. Information important to
public governance is being suppressed in this country,
and the press should fight for access to it while maintaining the confidentiality of its sources. If the press expects
to win, it had better come to the battle with clean hands.

CHAPTER FOURTEEN

Beyond the Watergate Legacy

*Investigative reporting now colors everything
we try to do. Many of the stories which are being
pursued today have been exposed over and over
again in the past decade. What is the purpose of
it? What are we trying to do? Much of it is
mindlessness that has no meaning.*
—Haynes Johnson

William W. Broom came to Washington in 1956 as a
regional reporter for the three Ridder newspapers in
California. Though he concentrated on Congress, as most
regional reporters do, he hung around the National Press
Club and came to know other reporters and Washington
personalities. But he did not know many people from the
executive branch of government. One day, in the early
1960s, Broom and Walter Pincus were invited over to the
White House to attend a private briefing by Walt Whit-
man Rostow. As Broom remembers it, both he and Pincus
were "surrogates" at the briefing, he for Walter T. Ridder
and Pincus for columnist Charles Bartlett. Rostow filled
them full of stuff about Vietnam. He told them that the
United States and South Vietnam were going to win the
war. The subject of the briefing was the new gadgets that
Rostow said would help win it, among them a new snake
repellant and an instant water purifier and a device that
would help soldiers see in the dark. Rostow said that the
United States would spend $100 million on these
gadgets. "A lot of it happened," Broom says. "They spent
the $100 million on this crap and it didn't help. I was so
green I didn't ask about the hearts and minds."

Unlike most reporters who make it to the nation's capital, Broom didn't stay in Washington. In 1965 he became
editor of the Long Beach, Calif., newspapers published

then by the late Hank Ridder. When Ridder asked him in 1966 for advice on the paper's Vietnam position, Broom told him that "we had to stick with Lyndon on the war." Ridder did. Broom changed his mind a year later, and he remembers bitter arguments with prominent people who still supported the war. He has thought many times about that Rostow briefing. "The reason we were so wrong on Vietnam," Broom now believes, "was that almost everyone in Washington when it started had been in service in World War II. We were caught up in the 'can do' mindset, in the belief that we could do anything. Few people asked about the Vietnamese. People weren't interested in Vietnamese politics. American newspapers were covering the war like it was World War II with tank battles in central France. It was just as much our fault as the damn government's fault. I believed as they did. I hadn't thought about it that much."

Broom came back to Washington in 1971 as bureau chief of the Ridder Publications. One of the first things he noticed was the "mean and skeptical" questioning at White House briefings. The World War II attitude toward government had changed. "It was largely because of Vietnam," says Broom. "Both the White House press and the Pentagon press felt they had been had." That feeling was prevalent in the Washington press corps when Richard Nixon was elected president. Indeed, it was partly because this feeling was prevalent in the country that Nixon was elected. But the Nixon people did not realize this when they, too, were greeted with "mean and skeptical" questions. "Ziegler was too dense and too inexperienced to understand what was going on," believes Broom. "He and the Nixon crowd felt that the press was taking after them because of hatred of Nixon. That wasn't the reason for most of them. The press acted the way it did because reporters felt they had been fooled and didn't want to be fooled again. Nevertheless, they were fooled, which shows you how great is the power of government. Basically, we're dependent on what they say.

Basically, we're restricted to what they put out."

These are harsh truths from a capable journalist. What happened to the press in Washington, in the decade of our Vietnam involvement and of Watergate, was a reconditioning of many reporters in their view of government. An attitude of basic trust that was tinged with skepticism was replaced with an attitude of suspicion in which trust occasionally intervened. Through a process akin to journalistic radioactivity, this same process slowly took place throughout the country. The basic premise that a public official was telling the truth was replaced by the premise that he is lying unless it can be proven otherwise.

I have argued elsewhere in this book and will do so again shortly that government, particularly the White House, holds the high cards in its relationships with the press and usually succeeds in conveying its chosen message to the world. What I am talking about here is something else — an attitudinal change which profoundly affects the nature of the adversary relationship between government and the press. Good reporters always have been properly skeptical of what public officials told them, and good public officials usually have been aware of George Christian's admonition that "reporters bite." But these reporters and the public officials also shared an assumption about the desirability of their political system and a related assumption that the proper functioning of government and of press were necessary to make that system work. Many years ago a normally skeptical reporter, with a few drinks in him, told me that all of us — in politics, in government, and in the press — were more like each other than we were like anyone else. What he meant was that the relatively small number of people who thought about government and who cared and worried about it possess a common purpose. That bond was shattered by the overlapping legacies of Vietnam and Watergate, and replaced by a tenuous link of disbelief in any assertion of the government. On June 8,

1975, the lead story in both the *Washington Post* and the *Los Angeles Times* was a dispatch with a Hong Kong dateline written by George McArthur of the *Times* staff which reported that "American warplanes conducted heavy bombing raids in Southern Vietnam on the day of the American evacuation from Saigon." The story, based on "authoritative sources," was denied before it ran by the White House and the Defense Department. White House Press Secretary Ron Nessen wrote *Post* editor Ben Bradlee a letter contending that the story should not have run at all, and *Post* ombudsman Charles Seib weighed in with an editorial page criticism that chided both papers for failing to follow up on the unproven story. Three days after this article appeared, Bradlee replied in a "Dear Ron" letter in which he associated himself with the Seib criticism. "Maybe this is one of the rottenest legacies of Watergate," Bradlee concluded. "We ran a great many flat denials, with the most specific attribution, of stories with anonymous attribution. And the stories were right, the denials were bullshit. I do appreciate your thoughtful letter, and I reiterate that I associate myself with Mr. Seib's piece."[1]

The conviction that government is either lying or withholding information *is* a rotten legacy of both Watergate and Vietnam. But it can be a useful legacy, also, if it teaches us to be less dependent upon official sources, particularly in Washington. In a 1973 analysis of where the *Washington Post* and the *New York Times* get their news, Leon V. Sigal found that 58.2 per cent of all information in both papers came from routine sources such as press conferences (which provided a quarter of all

---

[1] The denials in this case were correct. After several weeks of silence and investigation the *Times* on July 25, retracted the story on page one and sent the retraction over the *Times-Post* wire service. The next day the *Post* retracted the story. Seib thought the correction a bit grudging but praised both papers because they did not try "to escape with a two-paragraph correction put among the truss ads or tacked on to a news story. They put it on page one for all the world to see."

information), official proceedings and press releases.[2] Another 15.7 per cent came from informal channels, such as background briefings and leaks. And 25.8 per cent came from a category which Sigal listed as "enterprise," mostly interviews which in many cases also served official purposes. This means that the two newspapers usually considered most skeptical, independent and critical of government wound up printing pretty much what the executive branch of government gave out. "Imbedded in the word news medium," wrote Sigal, "is a connotation that aptly defines the function of the press: it mediates between the officialdom and the citizenry of the United States. Like a pipeline carrying water from a reservoir to a city, it has some effect on what arrives at the end of the line. Not all droplets that enter the pipeline end up in the same destination; some are routed elsewhere, others evaporate en route. Yet the effects of the pipeline are minor compared to the source of the water — the reservoir. Similarly, newsmen, by adhering to routine channels of news gathering, leave much of the task of selection of news to the sources." Or, as Tom Wicker put it in a 1972 speech, reliance on official sources for news is "the gravest professional and intellectual weakness of American journalism."

For all the disbelief in what government tells us, I see no evidence that the Vietnam-Watergate legacy has diminished this reliance. The forms of journalism conspire against it. Radio news uses mostly official dispatches, as processed by the wire services.[3] On television, where

---

[2] Leon V. Sigal, *Reporters and Officials, The Organization and Politics of Newsmaking,* (Lexington, Mass., 1973).

[3] This account, and this book, has not given radio, particularly "all news radio" the attention it deserves. Its function has been summed up well by Arthur W. Arundel, president of Arundel Communications (WAVA) in Arlington, Va., and a pioneer of news radio: "We are by necessity skimpy and superficial. It would take thirty hours to read the Sunday *New York Times* on the air. What we have done is raise the consciousness of people about the news."

thirty seconds is a long time, most narratives of necessity include the official version of the story. Sometimes that is all they can convey. And most newspapers still are crowded with "day stories," based on formal hearings and announced events. What Watergate has done is remind us that the official version of these events is not necessarily the real one. Watergate reminded us, too, that the old journalistic value of shoeleather can prevail in an electronic age. "Reporting is more than an intellectual exercise," says Harry Rosenfeld, the *Washington Post* editor who was in charge of the metro staff during Watergate. "The best reporters, usually, are those who work their way up through the police beat. They develop an instinct for hard work and limited trust of experts. It wasn't an accident that the metro staff got the Watergate story." "The reason," says *New York Times* investigative reporter Nicholas Gage, "the other papers missed out on Watergate, in my opinion, is that they tried to cover it like any other story — on the phone — whereas Woodward and Bernstein were out there ringing doorbells."[4]

Watergate also is credited with renewing a widespread interest in investigative reporting, a phrase which is in some sense redundant. Any good reporter on any story seeks to perform an investigative function. In any case, the interest is nothing new. It was once called "crusading reporting" or simply "projects." Whatever we call it, I question whether there is much more of it than there was before. What there certainly is more of is use of the term "investigative reporting" to describe stories which are not investigative at all. A good example of stories in this category are the leaked accounts from congressional committee staff members about decades-old transgressions of the Central Intelligence Agency, the Federal Bureau of Investigation and the Internal Revenue Service. It is Haynes Johnson's view that the press failed the

---

[4] Quoted by Robert Daley in "Super-Reporter: The Missing American Hero Turns Out To Be . . . Clark Kent" in *New York,* November 12, 1973.

American people when it treated the material leaking out about these agencies as revelations without pointing out that the abuses of which Congress complained were widely known to Congress in the past. "There's nothing new about the CIA abuses of its charter; they've been documented for at least 12 years in this country, over and over again and by many people in the news business," says Johnson. "There's no secret that the FBI was leaking material and that it had files on congressmen. We wrote in our book[5] how Johnson sat up in bed reading J. Edgar Hoover's FBI reports. We forget there's a larger meaning to this, and a larger problem. And I think if we only look for the one-day wonders, the sensational exposé and a kind of feeling that everybody's a bad guy, without an appreciation for the problems and the complexities of the issues that they must deal with, then we're doing a disservice."

One of the difficulties with real investigative reporting is that it can be a high-risk, low-yield proposition which diverts a significant section of the news budget. Even publishers who are willing to risk it and editors who value it often want a quick payoff on their investment. This is a prescription, more often than not, for shoddy journalism. "Watergate has made more editors believe in investigative reporting and has given reporters a freer hand," says reporter Mary Neiswender of the *Long Beach Independent-Press Telegram*. "However, editors expect too much too soon and the follow-up on investigative reporting is frequently bad. This ties the story — like an albatross — to the reporter for a long, long time." The need for a quick payoff restricts investigative reporting on television, which is limited in any case by the unfairness of the Fairness Doctrine. Robert Pierpoint of CBS, who was well ahead of the print journalists in investigating Nixon intimate Bebe Rebozo, believes there are two

---

[5] Richard Harwood and Haynes Johnson, *Lyndon*, (New York, 1973), p. 129

reasons why there is not a great deal of investigative reporting on television. "The first reason has to do with the very real problem of getting a picture of a story that is complex and mainly intellectual, or mainly requires private talking on the telephone with people who don't want to be seen and don't want to be quoted," Pierpoint says. "You have to do a great deal of digging and getting little bits and pieces of the story here and there. And it doesn't suit itself very often to television coverage. Television, after all, is a visual medium. Sometimes you can be lucky and can with imagination, as we did with the Rebozo story, illustrate some of it. Once in a while when you get a story where there is conflict between personalities, as there was in that one, you can get the personalities to answer or to talk to you on camera. But if you take a story like the great example of Woodward and Bernstein on Watergate where you're going down and meeting a guy in a garage at three in the morning, it's not very easy to show that on camera. And if you came out day after day with stories that were fascinating and possibly true but you couldn't illustrate them, I think it might have almost a bad effect on the public. They would begin to question your credibility. But that's really not the most important reason, in my view, why you don't see much investigative reporting on broadcast journalism. The real reason, I think, is that this is show business. And the name of the game in show business is to get your picture on the tube. And you don't get your picture on the tube very often when you're spending hour after hour making phone calls and piecing together the little bits and pieces of a story that you finally manage to get on the air, maybe after weeks or months of work."

What is needed, I submit, is a far broader definition of investigative reporting for both print and broadcast journalists. Reporters, if they are to be true to their calling, must deal in essences, not accidents. They must seek to help their readers and their viewers form what Lippmann called a reliable picture of the world. It was

Lippmann's contention in *Public Opinion,* published in 1922, that the primary defect of representative government, and of the press, was "the failure of self-governing people to transcend their casual experience and their prejudice by inventing, creating and organizing a machinery of knowledge." The consequences of that failure lie all around us now as we struggle to comprehend the economic, environmental and social changes that are taking place in our lives. "The real task of journalism," says Bill Moyers, "is to create a new form to tell the dull, dry important stories in a way that people will understand." This means an attempt to explain the processes of government and of industry and an attempt to report coherently about food production, water tables, energy sources, climatic cycles, medical research, health care, government reorganization, revenue sharing, regional planning, transportation, weapons systems and a thousand other subjects. "One of the reasons people keep talking about the lessons of Watergate," Dick Harwood wrote in a Jan. 18, 1972, memo to the national staff of the *Washington Post,* "is that events of the past year have shown us how much we have to learn. Above all, we have been taught that our knowledge and understanding of the universe with which we deal is very limited. 'National affairs' is a bottomless pit that we have neither charted nor explored except in a superficial way. Somehow we have got to comprehend it and probe it more effectively. We must read more, think more, talk more to one another about ideas ... There are resources within the newsroom that are untapped, and all over this city and country. We need, in short, more intellectual ferment. We need more creativity in our definitions of news."

It seems to me that we also need more creativity in defining the role of newspapers in a society which increasingly takes its news from television. Freed from the necessity of dispensing bulletin news, newspapers have lost the vital bond of immediacy they once shared with their readers. Newspapers have more options now, but the reader, too, has the option of not bothering with a newspaper that is uninteresting, unresponsive or seemingly irrelevant to his daily life. Americans no longer crave newspapers, and their addiction will continue to diminish unless newspapers fill a need that is beyond the scope of broadcast journalism.

And what of reporters in this process? As they pass beyond the boundaries of workaday journalism and seek to explain essences instead of accidents, will they lose the earthiness and practicality long common to the trade? After all those years of receiving psychic rewards instead of money, will they now become so well-paid that they cease to understand the economic problems of those who live less comfortably? What of a reporter's independence and professionalism? In a society of one-newspaper towns, does not the reporter owe a duty to the reader that transcends loyalty to a particular employer? How does he exercise this duty and keep his job? And what about a reporter's own ethical standards? Do they meet the exacting code he expects of others? Does the reporter deal honestly with his own biases and his only conflicts of interest?

These are unresolved questions that will be answered differently by different reporters. Even to the degree they can be answered by a generality, I don't have the answers. But I am encouraged by the self-awareness, insight and reflectiveness of many of the young men and women who are coming into journalism. My oldest son is one of these reporters, and it seems to me that he and his colleagues grapple more effectively with the contradictions and perplexities of the news business than we did at a similar age. I wish these new reporters well. We have left many tasks to our children.

Bibliography

BOOKS

Adler, Ruth, (editor). *The Working Press.* New York: G.P. Putnam's Sons, 1949.

Advisory Committee on Intergovernmental Relations. *Federal-State-Local Finances: Significant Features of Fiscal Federalism.* Washington, D.C., 1974.

Alsop, Joseph, and Alsop, Stewart. *The Reporter's Trade.* New York: Reynal, 1958.

Alsop, Stewart. *The Center.* New York: Harper & Row, 1968.

Anderson, Patrick. *The Presidents' Men.* New York: Doubleday, 1969.

Argyris, Chris. *Behind the Front Page.* San Francisco: Jossey - Bass, 1974.

Aspen Institute Program on Communications and Society. *Television As A Social Force: New Approaches to Criticism.* Palo Alto, Calif., 1975.

Bagdikian, Ben H. *The Effete Conspiracy.* New York: Harper & Row, 1972.

_____. *The Information Machines,* New York: Harper & Row, 1971.

Bell, Jack. *The Splendid Misery.* New York: Doubleday, 1960.

Bernstein, Carl, and Woodward, Bob. *All the President's Men.* New York: Simon & Schuster, 1974.

Boyarsky, Bill and Nancy. *Backroom Politics.* Los Angeles: J.P. Tarcher, Inc., 1974.

Brennan, Donald G., (editor), American Academy of Arts and Sciences. *Arms Control, Disarmament and National Security.* New York: George Braziller, 1961.

Broder, David S. *The Party's Over.* New York: Harper & Row, 1972.

Buchanan, Patrick J. *The New Majority.* Philadelphia: Girard Bank, 1973.

Cannon, Lou. *Ronnie and Jesse: A Political Odyssey.* New York: Doubleday, 1969.

Cater, Douglass. *The Fourth Branch of Government.* Boston: Houghton Mifflin Co., 1941.

Christian, George. *The President Steps Down.* New York: The Macmillan Co., 1970.

The Citizens Conference on State Legislatures. *The Sometime Governments: A Critical Study of the 50 American Legislatures.* Kansas City, Mo.: Bantam Books, 1971.

Cohen, Bernard C. *The Press and Foreign Policy.* Princeton, N.J.: Princeton University Press, 1963.

Cohen, Richard M., and Witcover, Jules. *A Heartbeat Away.* New York: The Viking Press, 1974.

Emery, Edwin. *The Story of America As Reported In Its Newspapers From 1690 to 1965.* New York: Simon & Schuster, 1965.

Epstein, Edward Jay. *News From Nowhere,* New York: Vintage Books, 1974.

Fowler, Gene. *A Solo in Tom-Toms.* New York: The Viking Press, 1946.

Friendly, Fred W. *Due to Circumstances Beyond Our Control.* New York: Random House, 1967.

Frost, David. *The Presidential Debate, 1968.* New York: Stein & Day, 1968.

——————. *The Presidential Transcripts.* New York: Dell, 1974.

Ghiglione, Loren, (editor). *Evaluating the Press: The New England Daily Newspaper Survey.* Southbridge, Mass: Ghiglione, 1973.

Gramling, Oliver. *AP, The Story of News.* New York: Farrar & Rinehart, Inc., 1940.

Harwood, Richard, and Johnson, Haynes. *Lyndon* (A Washington Post book). New York: Praeger Publishers, 1973.

Hecht, Ben, and MacArthur, Charles. *The Front Page.* 1928.

Hess, Stephen. *The Presidential Campaign: The Leadership Selection Process After Watergate.* Washington, D.C.: The Brookings Institution, 1974.

Hess, Stephen, and Broder, David S. *The Republican Establishment.* New York: Harper & Row, 1967.

Hiebert, Ray Eldon, (editor). *The Press in Washington,* New York: Dodd, Mead & Co., 1966.

Kalb, Marvin and Bernard. *Kissinger.* New York: Dell, 1974.

Kornitzer, Bela. *The Real Nixon.* Chicago: Rand McNally & Co., 1960.

Laski, Harold J. *The American Presidency.* New York: Harper & Bros., 1940.

Lee, James Melvin. *History of American Journalism.* New York: The Garden City Publishing Co., Inc., 1917.

Lefever, Ernest W. *TV and National Defense.* Boston, Va.: Institute for American Strategy Press, 1974.

Lippmann, Walter. *Public Opinion.* New York: The Macmillan Co., 1965, 1921.

MacNeil, Robert. *The People Machine: The Influence of Television on American Politics*. New York: Harper & Row, 1968.

McCarthy, Eugene J. *The Year of the People*. New York: Doubleday & Co., Inc., 1969.

Mencken, H.L. *Prejudices: A Selection*. New York: Vintage Books, 1955.

Nixon, Richard M. *Six Crises*. New York: Doubleday, 1962.

Packard, Reynolds. *The Kansas City Milkman*. New York: E.P. Dutton, 1950.

Perry, James M. *Us & Them*. New York: Clarkson N. Potter, Inc., 1973.

Pollard, James E. *The Presidents and the Press*. New York: The Macmillan Company, 1947.

_____. *The Presidents and the Press: Truman to Johnson*. Washington, D.C.: Public Affairs Press, 1964.

Prouty, L. Fletcher. *The Secret Team*. Englewood Cliffs, N.J.: Prentice Hall, 1973.

Reston, James. *The Artillery of the Press*. New York: Harper & Row, 1966.

_____. *Sketches in the Sand*. New York: Alfred A. Knopf, 1967.

Rivers, William L. and Rubin, David M. *A Region's Press: Anatomy of Newspapers in the San Francisco Bay Area*. Berkeley: University of California Press, 1971.

Rivers, William, and Schramm, Wilbur. *Responsibility in Mass Communication*. New York: Harper & Row, 1957.

Seldes, George. *Freedom of the Press*. Indianapolis: Bobbs-Merrill Co., 1935.

Sheean, Vincent. *Personal History*. New York: Doubleday, Doran & Co., 1934.

Siebert, Fred S., Petersen, Theodore and Schramm, Wilbur, (editors). *Four Theories of the Press*. Urbana, Ill.: University of Illinois Press, 1963.

Sigal, Leon V. *Reporters and Officials: The Organization and Politics of News Making*. Lexington, Mass.: D.C. Heath and Co., 1973.

Sussman, Barry. *The Great Cover-up: Nixon and the Scandal of Watergate*. New York: The New American Library, Inc., 1974.

Swanberg, W.A. *Citizen Hearst*. New York: Charles Scribner's Sons, 1961.

Toland, John. *The Rising Sun*. New York: Random House, 1970.

Wasington Post, Staff of the. *The Fall of a President*. New York: Delacorte Press, 1974.

_____. *Of the Press, By the Press, For the Press (And Others, Too)*. Washington, D.C.: 1974.

White, Theodore H., *The Making of the President 1960*. New York: Atheneum, 1964.

Wills, Garry. *Nixon Agonistes*. New York: The Houghton Mifflin Co., 1969.

Witcover, Jules. *The Resurrection of Richard Nixon*. New York: G.P. Putnam's Sons, 1970.

ARTICLES

Arnold, Martin. "Newspaper Trend: Stress Local News, Cut National and Foreign Coverage," *New York Times,* July 8, 1975.

Bagdikian, Ben H. "Congress and the Media: Partners in Propaganda" *Columbia Journalism Review,* January-February 1974.

Barnes, Peter. "Farewell, Free Enterprise," *The New Republic,* October 17, 1970.

Bernstein, Carl. "Watergate: Tracking It Down," *The Quill,* June 1973.

Bingham, Worth, and Just, Ward S. "The President and the Press," *The Reporter,* April 12, 1962.

Boyarsky, Bill. "Politics: How TV, Press Determine What Is News," *Los Angeles Times,* October 10, 1974.

_____. "Three Papers Withheld Story About Sub," *Los Angeles Times,* May 20, 1975.

Bradlee, Benjamin C. "Backgrounders: A Conspiracy in Restraint of Truth," *Washington Post,* January 2, 1972.

Broder, David S. "Political Reporters in Presidential Politics," *The Washington Monthly,* February 1969.

Cannon, Lou. "The Reagan Years," *California Journal,* November 1974.

_____. "Ron Nessen's Briefings: The Missing Questions and Answers," *Columbia Journalism Review,* May-June 1975.

Cater, Douglass. "News and the Nation's Security," *The Reporter,* July 6, 1961.

_____, and Bartlett, Charles L. "Is All the News Fit To Print?" *The Reporter,* May 11, 1961.

Clayton, James E. "Interpreting the Court," *Columbia Journalism Review,* Summer 1968.

Daley, Robert. "Super-Reporter: The Missing American Hero Turns Out to Be . . . Clark Kent," *New York,* November 12, 1973.

Darnton, Robert. "Writing News and Telling Stories," *Daedalus,* Spring 1975.

Dennis, Everette E. "Another Look At Press Coverage of the Supreme

Court," *Villanova Law Review,* Spring 1975.

Diamond, Edwin. "Boston: The Agony of Responsibility," *Columbia Journalism Review,* January-February 1975.

Friendly, Fred W. "What's Fair on the Air," *The New York Times Magazine,* March 30, 1975.

Gerbner, George. "Newsmen and Schoolmen: The State and Problems of Education Reporting," *Journalism Quarterly,* Summer 1967.

Gershen, Martin. "Covering New York's School War," *The Quill,* November 1969.

Green, Michael. "Nobody Covers The House," *Washington Monthly,* June 1970.

Harwood, Richard. "Putting People Into Pigeonholes," *Washington Post,* March 18, 1971.

Hess, Stephen. "Is The Press Fair?" *The Brookings Bulletin,* Summer-fall issue 1974.

Hester, Al. "The Journalistic Stepchild," a paper for the Citizens Conference on State Legislatures, 1975.

Holmes, Henry Allen. "Ethics in Journalism: A Growing Awareness," Department of State, 1974-75.

Keppel, Bruce. "New Look in the Capitol Press Corps," *California Journal,* July 1975.

Kerrick, Jean S., Anderson, Thomas E., and Swales, Luita B. "Balance and the Writer's Attitude in News Stories and Editorials," *Journalism Quarterly,* 1964.

Kristol, Irving. "Is the Press Misusing Its Growing Power?" *(More),* January 1975.

Lardner, George E., Jr. "Two Views of Objective Reporting: An Analysis," a master's thesis at Marquette University, 1962.

Lemert, James B., "Craft Attitudes, the Craft of Journalism and Spiro Agnew," University of Oregon, 1970.

Littlewood, Thomas B. "What's Wrong With Statehouse Coverage," *Columbia Journalism Review,* March-April 1972.

_____. "The Trials of Statehouse Journalism," *Saturday Review,* December 10, 1966.

MacKenzie, John P. "The Warren Court and the Press," *Michigan Law Review,* December 1968.

McCarron, John, and Stark, John. "What We Think About Everything," *Chicago Journalism Review,* September-October 1973.

Mintz, Morton. "Comparative Journalism," *Columbia Journalism Review,* May-June 1975.

Morris, Roger. "Henry Kissinger and the Media: A Separate Peace," *Columbia Journalism Review,* May-June 1974.

Newsweek. "Salvaging the Sub Story," March 31, 1975.

Nayman, Oguz B. "Professional Orientations of Journalists: An Introduction to Communicatory Analysis Studies," *Gazette,* Winter 1973.

Otten, Alan L. "The Press and the '72 Campaign," *Harvard Political Review,* Winter 1974.

Reston, James. "The Issues of Life Are Plain No Longer," *The Quill,* May 1975.

Rivers, William L. "Summing Up the Challenges to Journalism," *The Quill,* March 1971.

Rosenthal, A.M. "The Press Needs A Slogan: Save the First Amendment!" *New York Times Magazine,* February 11, 1973.

Salzman, Ed. "A Personal Perspective: All the News That Fits," *California Journal,* November 1974.

————. "TV Hacks Ax Sacra-Antics," *New West,* February 14, 1977.

Seltzer, Louis B. "The Knowledge Explosion — What It Means To Journalism," *The Quill,* August 1967.

Sheldon, Courtney. "A Vote of No Confidence for Background Briefings," *APME News,* June 1972.

Simon, Paul. "Improving Statehouse Coverage," *Columbia Journalism Review,* September-October 1973.

Tannenbaum, Percy H. "Communication of Science Information," *Science,* May 10, 1963.

Tracy, Phil. "Canned Goods From Capitol Hill," *(More),* September 1975.

von Hoffman, Nicholas. "Covering Politics: The Economic Connection," *Columbia Journalism Review,* January-February 1975.

Welles, Chris. "The Bleak Wasteland of Financial Journalism," *Columbia Journalism Review,* July-August 1973.

Wilkins, Roger. "From Silence to Silence," *(More),* July 1975.

Wills, Garry. "What's Wrong Wtih This Magazine?" *(More),* June 1975.

Wilson, James Q. "Abolish 'Reform,' " *The Alternative: An American Spectator,* May 1975.

Witt, William. "The Environmental Reporter on U.S. Daily Newspapers," *Journalism Quarterly,* Winter 1974.

Wolfe, Tom. "Why They Aren't Writing the Great American Novel Anymore," *Esquire,* December 1972.

————. "The Birth of the New Journalism," *New York,* February 14, 1972.

Wolfson, Lewis. "The Press Covers Government: the Nixon Years from 1969 to Watergate," A study by the American University Department of Communication for the National Press Club.

Index